The Seal

A Priest's Story

Timothy J. Mockaitis

Foreword by Francis Cardinal George
Archbishop of Chicago

To order additional copies of this book, contact:
Xlibris Corporation
1-888-795-4274
www.Xlibris.com
Orders@Xlibris.com
53719

CONTENTS

"*The Seal* serves as a sharp reminder that we cannot take religious freedom for granted or stand aside when it is under duress, if this freedom is to continue to be a valued dimension of the life of our country." (Francis Cardinal George—Archbishop of Chicago)

"This revelation of a brazen attempt to violate the sacred privacy of the confessional and the constitutional rights of a vulnerable suspect should alert all of us. What happened in Oregon is a warning. I highly recommend this book." (Sr. Helen Prejean, Author: *Dead Man Walking* and *The Death of Innocents*)

"This case has more twists and turns than an Agatha Christy novel." (Sean Hannity—Fox News Network.)

"This is the ultimate nightmare between Church Law and Constitutional Law." (Roger Cossack of CNN on *Burden of Proof.*)

"This is unprecedented in American history . . . a Nazi tactic . . . the relationship between a priest and a penitent is sacred and cannot be violated . . ." (William Donohue—*Catholic League for Religious and Civil Rights*).

"This is naked facism, truly the end of the line . . . it yanks at the very pillars of separation between church and state . . ." (William F. Buckley).

"Out of no where, as it must have seemed . . . , the performance of a rite . . . enshrined in secrecy became a matter for the media, for the courts, for the public at large . . ." (Judge John Noonan—9th Circuit Court of Appeals).

"It is difficult to imagine any more blatant and bald-faced an affront to the basic tenets of a religion, short of intentionally committing acts of sacrilege as a matter of state policy." (Amicus Brief—9th Circuit Court of Appeals).

This book is dedicated to:

Father Jean-Baptiste-Marie Vianney

The saintly Cure of Ars

11

FOREWORD

In *The Seal*, Father Timothy Mockaitis describes clearly and directly a bizarre incident and its sequel, in which his priestly ministry involved him in 1996. It happened before, during and after the brief time that I was Archbishop of Portland. It engaged the attention and concern of that archdiocese, of the United States Conference of Catholic Bishops, of the Holy See and of many other religious groups in the United States.

In its implications for liberty of religious practice in the United States, it was ominous. In its finally unresolved outcome, it remains as a warning of the fragility of religious liberty in this land which, in some ways, pioneered the constitutional theory and practice of that liberty. The early tendency in the United States history "to make politics almost the object of religious aspiration" (P. Hamburger: Separation of Church and State) has evolved in a secular culture into an active threat to the freedom of religion.

This book's case in point is, in large part, the outcome of a failure of the instruments of government and those immediately responsible for them to remember and understand history. The separation of church and state is an institutional arrangement that has taken on the force of dogma. Yet there is evidence aplenty of the Founders' belief that government can aid religion and religiously motivated activities and even favor religion in general over the unbelief of a secular culture which itself has taken on many of the claims of religious obligation.

In fact, the intention of the Founders was to protect all religion by forbidding the establishment of any one church. They were proposing on the part of the state to safeguard religious freedom in a regime of denominational and cultural pluralism; they were not asserting an indifference to religion nor the equivalent of state religious neutrality. John Adams could declare: "Our Constitution was written for a moral and religious people."

Because these facts are either deliberately not acknowledged or forgotten, the way has been left open for secularist ideologies to make religious faith appear as an enemy of the State and of personal freedom. In a growing number of instances, this is the experience of the Catholic Church in the United States today.

Father Mockaitis, in his recounting of the Portland incident, shows how, in Oregon, this attitude manifested itself in the actions of some responsible for the administration of justice and the penal system. With a cynical disregard for priestly ministry, they consulted only their own immediate pragmatic purposes. This book serves as a sharp reminder that we cannot take religious freedom for granted or stand aside when it is under duress, if this freedom is to continue to be a valued dimension of the life of our country.

Francis Cardinal George, O.M.I.
Archbishop of Chicago

13

ACKNOWLEDGMENTS

This story began in silence but has cried out for recognition. In the long process of writing a tale that is true to the real issues at hand, I owe my deepest gratitude to those who have accompanied me on this journey. To Nan Phifer, for her trust in me when the writing began, for her wisdom, support, encouragement and faith. Thanks to you Nan! To Veronica Yates, for her expertise in the beauty of the written word, for her humor, friendship, and her constant availability. To my friends and family who patiently offered me time and honesty. To the many others over the years of developing this narrative who offered their insights, comments and questions. To the good people of St. Paul Catholic Church in Eugene, Oregon who supported me throughout this event not only as their pastor but I hope also as their friend. To Peter Boulay for his interest and research.

PROLOGUE

The wind was brisk, an early Fall, as I walked from my car towards the Oregon State maximum security prison. The old weathered stone building which reached its long, thick arms out far to the left and right seemed to rise before me. As I hurried up the steps to the main reception area, troubling memories of past events returned as I opened the door. They rushed and stared at me as if suddenly awakened after a restless sleep. I sighed deeply, walked over to Allen, a fellow member of the clergy and regular pastor at the prison, waiting at the main desk. We shook hands, then turned to the busy female police officer whose attention to our need was little more than routine. I took note of this day, September 11, 2006.

After all the necessary security procedures, with the protection of two guards, Deacon Allen and I made our way through corridors within the prison walls where we stopped and stood behind the guards as lines of prisoners passed quickly by us. Many were engaged in rowdy conversation, a few addressed the guards who seemed to respond like old buddies, but most just kept on moving by out to the main courtyard on this sunny afternoon. Although I stood there in clerical black with white collar, none took particular notice.

Ever since the spring of 1996 the memory of the unprecedented violation had never left me. Not long after I first met Conan Wayne Hale, now on death row, I found myself faced with what seemed like intractable odds under very different conditions than I faced today. The state of affairs which linked the two of us together more than ten years ago had been extraordinary and had forever marked my priestly life; something I could not nor should forget.

Since his verdict in 1998, I often wondered whether right justice had actually been accomplished. It had been eight years since his trial so I knew the time had come to see this inmate again—to see for myself the transformation I was told this young man, with a very troubled past, had made. Many mockingly say, "Everyone find's Jesus in prison." I was told he had found more than Jesus.

As we began our walk I noted the facility held over 2,000 prisoners and many were out that afternoon. They played baseball; shirtless men lifted weights in a large caged area at the center of the courtyard, or ran in the sunshine as we walked on the sidewalk that surrounded an expansive, grassy field. Prison guard escorts were mandatory for our protection in the event a fight should break out. There was no indication of impending disagreements. It seemed a strange day in the park.

At the far end of the courtyard, stood death row—a solid, two-storied, gray, nearly windowless building which could be taken for a warehouse. Could the judgment which placed Hale on that row reserved only for the most heinous crimes and, as the public often assumes, the most toughened criminals, be considered humane treatment? We entered through the security doors, passing by more guards, and then we proceeded down the hall to a visitor's area dissimilar from any other I had seen. Three jail cells lined one wall. My eyes darted around the sea of grayness in this sparsely furnished room with only two chairs and a small square wooden table in front of the cells. I then heard voices from the corridor. Conan Hale entered, escorted by two guards. He wore a plain tan shirt with dark blue pants, his ankles were chained together and his wrists as well.

The guards appeared to jostle him as he glanced at me and smiled. "Hey!" he said as he tried to lift his secured hand. He appeared to be joking with the guards as if they were friends. The guards swiftly placed him in the middle jail cell, took off the handcuffs, and locked the cell door. He seemed a bit heavier than I'd remembered, but his eyes seemed more alive and he looked far less tired. His face was clean shaven and his hair was cut short. Then, with a smile, he sat down on a bench where we would talk with the bars between us—he, like a caged animal, and I disturbed to see him this way. Yet, he seemed strangely light of spirit. Deacon Allen and the guards left the room for what would be our time assigned alone—about fifteen minutes.

I pulled my chair up close to the bars and with a somewhat awkward feeling, I said, "It's been a long time, Conan." He reached through the bars, shook my hand and said, "Thanks, brother. You've lost weight."

I said I didn't think so. "You can write about this in your book if you want to," he said. I had written to him not long before about the story I was researching. I said, "I probably will.

"Much has happened in both of our lives Conan" I reflected. "I've moved around to a different assignment and was caught in other responsibilities. I never followed up after the trial but I had a lot of things on my plate."

Hale then said, "Yeah, I was pretty angry for a while. I felt betrayed and forgotten like no one cared; neither the church or you. I remember when I first met you. I needed to talk to someone, to say I was sorry. But that's in the past."

"I know," I said, momentarily taken aback by his remembrance, "I was in a tough position at the time. It's not that I didn't care. I wasn't sure what the next move would be then it all came to an end and you found yourself here." I changed the subject to the real reason for my visit. "Deacon Allen told me how impressed he was with you."

"Really?" he said. "He's been a big help. When Fr. Jim was here we talked about a lot of things in my life but God was often the major topic. I asked to learn more so we talked about the Church, the Rosary and Mother Mary. I started to read a book he gave me but it wasn't easy to understand, then I learned to pray the Rosary every day and now I pray it with my friend, Jeff, another guy down from my cell. Fr. Jim helped both of us understand the faith. When he left last year, I felt really bad, and then Deacon Allen came."

As he spoke, he gestured with his hands, occasionally in the form of hands at prayer as he mentioned how regularly he prayed the Rosary. I was taken aback at the near casual spirit of Conan Hale considering the heavy weight of his charges. I wasn't sure what to expect from him but I was glad to see he held up well. More than once he mentioned "Mother Mary" and I began to sense that his faith was a life-line for him; a road to sanity in the midst of a dark, unnatural environment.

I was eager to show my pleasure and wanted to be supportive. I wanted to reach out and give him a pat on the shoulder but the bars prevented that. His enthusiasm was contagious and I couldn't help but believe him.

Sounding a little more downcast, he said: "I've seen a lot of ugly things here. I know that some of that was in me. I've done some bad things. My friend, Jeff played a big part in my conversion. He prayed for me and taught me more about what he learned about the Church. One time he felt so bad that he held up a crucifix and pointed it at me." He offered a smile at these words. "But, you know, it made a difference—the prayer and all. I have a long way to go but I cried tears of sorrow the more I learned about the faith from him. I still have a lot to deal with but I think, I *know*, I've changed."

I agreed. "I imagine you have changed, Conan."

He continued, his voice enthusiastic, "I feel different. I'm really excited about being a Catholic. I heard about an order of Sisters in Africa who pray for inmates. Deacon Allen gave me their address. I sent them my name and they wrote back saying they were praying for me. I'd like to do something to support their work with children. I thought about selling some of my artwork, then sending them the money."

"Well," I remembered, "You're drawings are well done."

"Thanks," he said with an almost wistful smile. "Maybe I can do something with that."

"Use what God has given you, Conan." I added.

"I will," he said emphatically.

"Prayer is very powerful," I said.

"Deacon Allen brings communion to Jeff and me each week. He's been a big help."

"Well," I added, "Allen asked if I would say a Mass while I was here; just the three of us. I could then offer you communion during that Mass."

"That would be great," he said. "After we're done, I have a drawing for you. Unfortunately, it's not here so I'll send it to you. I can get your address."

I was struck by his religious zeal, which he expressed in simple, almost playful, childlike ways. Though I sat before a thirty-two-year-old man, who faced the most grievous of charges, he felt more like an impressionable teen-ager, and I wondered if he fully comprehended the verdict laid upon him. I knew that he had been through a long series of appeals but I never broached the subject nor did we say anything specific about what initially brought us together. I thought, another time.

Still, I realized that my visit—any visit—would be an important time for anyone condemned to death. I could sense from his animated speech that he was glad I came and I thought, almost sought my approval like a child seeking to impress his father.

As we conversed, it wasn't long before, the grace of forgiveness was given to this man again and I could not help but see this as a kind of beautiful symmetry.

Afterwards, I went out to the hall and called Allen back in. We prepared the plain wooden table in the room with a few basic items I had brought for this Mass: bread, wine, a book of prayer, and a simple chalice. I stood behind the table, placed a white stole across the back of my neck and looked at Conan who sat and watched behind the bars with a smile of anticipation. Deacon Allen sat to my left and we began together in this stark setting: priest and prisoner reunited.

As it came time for communion, I approached Conan who knelt on the floor, feet shackled, hands folded with bowed head. He looked up and raised his hands, one over the other, palms up to receive this sacred bread as I extended my hand through the bars.

Before long, the Mass concluded and it was time to leave. Our time ended with a handshake, and then he signaled a last farewell—a youthful

"Thumbs Up" sign from behind the bars of the middle cell. "Thanks, brother," he said as he stood behind the bars, "I'll send you the drawing as soon as I can get some money for stamps." I told him there was no hurry but I would look forward to seeing it.

Then he added, "Write to me or better, come visit again."

I told him I would.

As Deacon Allen and I walked down the corridor my spirit, earlier tense, was now grateful. However, Conan and I never talked about what his future might be. No date was pending for execution. I wasn't sure how to broach that subject since the enthusiasm for his faith was so tangible yet, I knew that additional appeals were still ahead for him and the outcome was uncertain.

As I returned to the parking lot and entered my car, I reflected on this amazing moment of re-connection. Ten years before matters were very different as the interests of state and church found themselves in an unprecedented battle for our Constitutional rights. Serious suspicions were held against this inmate when he, along with the Catholic sacrament of penance itself, would stand trial throughout a series of proceedings which would erupt in headlines of outrage across this nation and beyond. This is the true story of that conflict and my involvement as a key player, although unwillingly.

However, I have often wondered how much priests should articulate their own struggles, confusions, doubts, and fears. The people we serve and the church have high expectations about who we are and how we should present ourselves. But this event became a challenge to those expectations so I carry my voice in this narrative with honesty. Although I offer this account as my true story, it belongs to all of us as citizens in this free nation since our Constitution is meant to endure.

It began in the spring of 1996 when I made a benign pastoral visit to a county jail. I didn't know the events of that seemingly routine day of service would spiral into one of shattered trust.

CHAPTER 1

Shattered Trust

Monday, April 22, 1996 was a sunny spring day and the morning cool was refreshing with a fresh breeze and a hint of new, expanding life in the air. The call for me had come not long after Easter when I arrived at the Lane County Jail in Eugene, Oregon dressed in the recognizable black clothes and white collar of a priest. After a quick glance, I noted the sharp contrast of the massive, gray jail—a windowless, two-story concrete building, then began my climb up the stairs to the main reception area. I knew nothing of why this young man had been jailed but I presumed things would go as smoothly as they had in the past. Yet, I knew I could not linger. There had been a death in my parish, and I was due for a graveside service later in the morning.

I owed this visit to Roger, a volunteer lay minister at the jail who had informed the authorities well in advance that I would be coming. The inmate had filed a "kite"—a request to see a Catholic priest to celebrate the sacrament of penance. I had been here before but it was my first visit to this man.

Behind a small reception desk, just beyond the entrance, I encountered a familiar woman in a dark blue uniform. "You're a few minutes late," she said, her voice raised in authority. She struck me as a single-minded woman determined to enforce jail policy. Months before, this same jail receptionist asked that I remain in the visitor's area. "We know who you are as a Catholic priest," she said, "but we are sometimes unsure what religious congregation is represented by others. So, this is our way of regulating those clergy visits in a fair manner." Apparently, all clergy visits were to take place only in the visitor's area. At the time, I didn't feel it would be right for me to object to jail policy but I wanted to challenge her odd reasoning.

I signed in and confirmed the inmate's name, Conan Wayne Hale, as I took note of a familiar sign—nearly three-feet-high—which listed rules for visitors such as: "No defacing of walls and windows" and among other expectations, in large bold type, **"No recording equipment allowed."** By now I was familiar with these regulations and always felt I could speak freely. Though I stood before a familiar steel door, no matter how many times I'd come, the walk through a metal detector and the piercing buzz of the lock still unsettled me.

I showed myself into the visitors' area. Metal clanged against metal behind me as the door banged shut. The fresh scent of spring outside became a faint memory—the expanse of open sky lost, forgotten in this narrow windowless room to be inhabited only by the inmate and myself. Six low stools, parallel to the walls, faced a glass partition that extended to the ceiling, preventing any physical contact between visitor and inmate. Telephone receivers, one for the inmate, the other for the visitor, were prominent in each booth as all seemed in secure order.

The sound of footsteps echoed in the hallway, the inmate entered from behind the glass partition, took a seat and the accompanying officer closed the door behind him, leaving the inmate and I in the barren visitors' area in full view of one another. He was a young man of average build, with short, dark blond hair, and what at first appeared to be a relaxed smile. I guessed him to be in his early twenties; he was the most youthful of the inmates I had seen. We were alone.

We picked up our receivers and offered our introductions. I smiled, and began with the usual small talk, asking about his morning. His voice was even in tone and fairly relaxed, but his smile changed to somewhere between nervous and friendly, and his pale eyes weary beyond his years. As we conversed, he became unsettled as he moved about, back and forth in his seat yet overall, he spoke freely. I assumed this first time meeting was a bit intimidating but I had confidence of his truthfulness. I felt sad that such a young man would be incarcerated. As I sat face to face with this inmate, I could not help but remember that God is not bound by walls or human imperfection.

I reached into the pocket of my coat and pulled out a stole, a narrow piece of cloth draped over the back of the neck and down the front on both sides of the chest, which is the traditional sign of a priest's sacramental authority worn during the celebration of Catholic sacraments. It was purple in color, the shade of penitence. I hesitated for a moment as I glanced behind and around me for reassurance of privacy. I then turned, faced the young man and began with the move of my hand in the sign of a cross, "In the name of the Father, and of the Son and of the Holy Spirit . . ."

This deeply personal sacramental relationship offers the penitent the hope of conversion and the restoration of new life. That sacrament is an encounter between an individual and a merciful God with the priest acting as an intermediary—a human face and voice with which to seek counsel and pray for forgiveness. As the Church believes, in that guarantee of privacy, one human speaks freely to another in the conviction of faith with Christ himself present wherever two or three are gathered in his name.

In spite of this less than ideal setting, where privacy is a limited expectation, it is assumed that priest and penitent can converse securely. It is never my concern to act as judge or jury; but we ministers of the sacrament, who also need to confess, are often humbled by the sincerity and honesty of a penitent here confined in this most vulnerable of circumstances. This particular relationship, under the privacy of the Sacrament of Reconciliation, or confession as a more familiar name, would remain forever sealed. But, that privacy had been challenged before.

Civil law which governs the affairs of this country has granted autonomy to religious bodies and has shown historical respect for this particular religious ritual. Early on in our history, American civil law gave deference to church rules in matters decided as long ago as the early 1800's. Courts in this land have recognized that our Constitution protects religious practices. A case in 1813 known as *People v. Phillips* was called upon to decide whether a Catholic priest to whom an oral confession had been made could be ordered by a civil court to reveal what the penitent said in confession. The court ultimately held that the priest's interest in the free exercise of his religion was particularly worthy of constitutional protection: "It is essential to the free exercise of a religion that its ceremonies as well as its essentials should be protected. The sacraments of a religion are its most important elements . . ." (People v. Philips)

In 1973, in Doe v. Bolton, the high court stated that: "The right to privacy has no more conspicuous place than in the physician-patient relationship, unless it be in the priest-penitent relationship." The establishment clause of the First Amendment was written in order to protect the church from the state and not the other way around.

Religion is entitled to benevolent treatment respectful of the special place religion has in the lives of our citizens and in our constitution. Certain relationships are essential to both the individual and the common good and so they have been granted certain privileges: attorney-client, doctors and patients, husbands and wives, clergy and penitents are viewed as sacrosanct. They encourage trust and the moral and physical well-being of citizens so all fifty States have adopted statutes providing that at least some of these communications are privileged. I sat confident of this historical precedent.

As this young inmate and I leaned forward, telephone receivers in hand, separated by the window pane partition, his words flowed through me to a forgiving God. Here we ended our encounter in the same way it began: " . . . In the name of the Father, and of the Son and of the Holy Spirit . . ."

The confession concluded, I checked the clock, noting I barely had enough time to prepare for the graveside service at a local cemetery on the outskirts of Eugene. In the moment I felt no urgency, only the need to say goodbye to this young man as I trusted in God's patience. But, it was time to leave so I stood up and pressed the button on the wall, signaling the officer at the desk that our visit had ended. Once let out from the visitors' area, things changed rapidly. I checked the time again, waved goodbye to the receptionist, and hurried down the stairs.

Outside, the sun was brighter than I'd remembered; the low hum of city traffic, a comfort to me. I wondered if the inmates left inside could hear the sounds of life rushing by. I brushed these thoughts away, inhaling deeply of the fresh spring air. My attention now diverted to the grieving family waiting at the graveside. I presumed today's confession—as the hundreds of confessions I had heard over the years—would remain forever between the penitent and the God who created him. I would be wrong about this. What I assumed was the end of the story would be only the beginning.

*   *   *

About ten days later, on my day off, I dropped by my parish office at St. Paul Catholic Church. The day was cool so I wore a light, tan-colored spring jacket, sport shirt and casual pants. I'd simply planned on checking some paperwork left the day before when I spotted a small, yellow message note in my office mailbox. Janet, our receptionist, had written a one-line request to return a call to a reporter from *The Register—Guard,* the local Eugene newspaper. It read: "Re: Response to D.A. using recording of confession in Court." I had no idea what this was about so I asked Janet. She didn't know, but explained that the reporter, one I had never met, a Bill Bishop, definitely wanted to be called back. Janet's voice convinced me the call couldn't wait until the next day.

I rushed to my office and phoned, but received his voice mail so I left a message, and decided to wait for his return call while I went through more of the morning's mail. It wasn't long before he called back.

"Fr. Mockaitis, this is Bill Bishop with *The Register-Guard.*"

I responded with hesitation, "Yes, Mr. Bishop, I got your message. I'm confused."

"Father, I was wondering if you saw a Conan Wayne Hale at the Lane County Jail about ten days ago," Bishop said, his voice flat, matter-of-fact.

Startled as to how he would know and why he would be asking this I glanced at my personal calendar from the previous week and answered with a question, "Why do you ask?" I leaned forward at my desk, elbows and arms resting on the desktop, anxious to hear what this man had to tell me.

"Well, Father, it seems someone authorized by the district attorney tape—recorded the conversation you had with Mr. Hale and is considering using it in court. I was going through public records at the courthouse this morning looking for anything that might be newsworthy, and ran across a copy of a search warrant that permitted the sheriff to listen to the contents of that tape. Your name and that of Mr. Hale are written on the search warrant. What can you tell me about this?"

Taken aback at hearing my name and the inmate's in the same context as "search warrant" and "tape-recording," in what Bishop called "the conversation," I was puzzled as to how to respond. Bishop's words left no doubt that the inviolable seal of confession had been broken. I composed myself enough to ask, "What are you saying, Mr. Bishop," as I searched for a fitting response, leaving it to him to explain further the full purpose of his call.

"Father, I have a copy of the warrant here and it appears entirely clear. I can read you the warrant if you like," he said, with a raised and more eager tone. Frankly, I wasn't sure what to say to that, but he began reading before I had the chance to reply. Bishop read the warrant: "Information on oath having this day been laid before me the contents of an audio tape cassette recording of the confession made by Conan Wayne Hale to Father Mockaitis located at the Lane County District Attorney's Office you are therefore hereby commanded to search the above described audio cassette tape for evidence.'"

"Judge Bryan Hodges signed it on April 23, apparently the day after you visited with Hale," he concluded, now expecting my reply.

"They can't do that! This cannot be used in court," I said, outraged at what he'd read, and feeling backed into a corner. My response seemed totally simplistic, and I seriously worried about what he planned to do with the information.

Sounding even more unbelieving than I, the reporter then came back, "You mean you didn't know they taped this?"

"No," I said, my voice strong in affirmation, my tone a bit recovered. "Why would I allow such a thing?" This reporter had somehow assumed I'd had foreknowledge of the taping. I was amazed. It seemed bizarre to imagine this conversation with Bishop was taking place at all since no one had ever heard of such a secret taping. He found my astonishment, and hence, the secret nature of this action, to be his "lead," the focus—the essential core of his story. He said would publish the story for the Saturday morning edition of *The Register-Guard.*

Caught off guard, I knew this would demand a straightforward response that needed to be confronted quickly. There was nothing I could do to stop him since the story was ready for press and he had a copy of the search warrant in hand. On some defensive level, I found myself minimizing this sudden, bewildering conversation. He went on to describe the main contents of the article he would prepare for the next morning's edition. It would contain my response to his phone call, which was minimal, and some general background information on Hale. My mind went to a troubled place, consumed with profound implications, heartrending for any penitent who places trust in the sacred encounter of a religious ritual respected throughout America and ones dangerous to religious freedom at-large. That my conversation with this perceived informer was relatively brief did nothing to minimize the far-reaching threat to constitutional and individual liberties. I felt certain Bishop knew this incident was extraordinary, and the dread of what he might write beset me.

When I hung up, I could sense anger in myself as the reality of this unprecedented violation sank in. I sat in my chair and stared at the wall; my hands clenched, folded. Was I unconsciously praying for an answer? It was a helpless feeling. I needed some time to decide what the first move should be, but I did know something had to be done and done rapidly. I tried to calm myself with the thought that the reporter's story would be lost on the back page. He won't be writing much, I told myself. What's there to say?

Despite the overwhelming seriousness of the matter, I still wasn't getting it. I didn't want to "get it." I wanted to avoid it, dismiss the whole affair as far less than the grave violation it really was. I prayed for some direction as if I stood on a high wire seeking to catch my balance. I tried to convince myself this was not what the reporter imagined it to be. I only had his word and his own perception to go on. Moreover, what information was given to the judge that moved him to sign that warrant? Making every effort I could muster to minimize the importance of the phone call, my own questions haunted me most. Though unsettled I was able to stand up, grab my jacket and left the office with the decision that a higher authority than myself needed to be informed as soon as possible.

As I returned to the main reception area I met our parish business manager, Maurice. Maurice was a soft-spoken, intelligent, sixty-year old with a catchy, dry wit. He was known for his ability to understate the seriousness of a matter in order to make a point.

Maurice greeted me with a pleasant smile and good-natured curiosity in his voice, but was surprised to see me on my day off. "Father, what are you here for today?"

"Maurice," I said flatly, "you'll never believe the phone call I just got."

After working in the parish for a number of years, Maurice knew well enough that we receive all sorts of requests and phone calls, most expected some peculiar. He grinned in understanding, and rolled his eyes.

"What sort of phone call is it now?" He could tell from the sound of my voice that I had just heard something far beyond the ordinary.

I told him about the message from the reporter as best I could relay the conversation. Maurice knew I was an occasional visitor to the jail and recognized this as an important ministry. As a life-long Catholic, he was well aware of the gravity of the confessional seal and familiar with the purpose of the clergy-penitent relationship.

Within a few seconds, his face grew stern. He glanced down and shook his head slowly. There was a darkness and heaviness in his tone, "You're not kidding." He paused for a moment. Then he looked back at me and said, "This is no joke. This is a very serious offense."

"Maurice, right now I'm shaken from the news," I said. My now edgy speech grew anxious as I confronted something so unfamiliar.

"Are you all right?" he asked.

"I'm fine, Maurice," I said, "But, I need to get on this right away. This Bill Bishop told me that he found a copy of a search warrant signed by a judge to listen to this recording. I'm not sure what else he might have found with it. He said he was going to do a story for tomorrow's paper and he implied the D.A. might want to use the tape in court."

"A search warrant for a confession? That's absurd." Maurice blurted this out with probably more force than he'd intended, as he raised his arms, commenting on the sacramental nature of the conversation, then emphatically added, "Are you sure?" his hands on his hips, "They can't play this in court." Now he was just as agitated as I was. His shock revealed itself by the sound of his raised voice. Maurice stood up straight and arched his shoulders back in disgust.

I then expressed my own irritation, "Maurice, all I know is what the reporter told me."

"Well, let's see what they say in the paper," he said. His tone implied that what might be published in the morning edition most likely would be different from the conversation I had relayed. I suspected he was a bit suspicious of the degree of accuracy one could expect from the media. But more than that, he was angry and portrayed what I myself felt about this strange turn-of-events.

"I'd begin making some calls very soon to your bishop," Maurice stated, "Who did this?"

"I don't know who did this," I said, "but apparently the district attorney authorized it, according to the reporter who called."

"Its' pretty outrageous is all I can say," said Maurice with an air of contempt. "Let me know if I can help,"

"Thanks. I'll let you know what happens. I imagine you'll read about it anyway." I responded.

Jolted into reality by this sensible man, though I agreed with him, I still hoped against the odds that it was less momentous than we imagined. In spite of being a Catholic since childhood and a priest of the Church for almost twenty years, I never dreamed of hearing, much less being part of, this sort of news. I was not prepared for this but knew I should not carry this alone. I thanked Maurice for his advice and made sure he understood that I shared his shock and outrage.

On the way out, I noticed Janet was away from her desk, preparing to close up for the day. I wanted to leave as quickly as possible so I didn't bother to seek her out to say goodbye. She may have overheard our conversation since we were not shy about our voices. I headed home to the parish's two-story townhouse across the street and entered through the dark brown front door. Among the countless thoughts in my head, I knew that members of the Catholic faith would likely understand the magnitude of this breach but I wasn't sure how the general public would respond. Right now there was nothing I could do about that and hoped whatever fall-out was coming, we'd be able to hold back the water.

I laid my papers on the dining room table, fell into my chair, and grabbed the remote control for the television, searching the local stations for the evening news. Nothing was mentioned so I breathed a sigh of relief. Then I remembered, with thanks, that I had been invited to a parishioner's home for dinner. I didn't think I'd reach the bishop on a Friday evening, and there was no public news on this, so I concluded this would need to wait. I put the matter aside for the time being, said nothing to my friends, and briefly prayed for some understanding. How long my emotional confusion between victim and hero would last, I had no idea.

That night my sleep was restless, but adequate. While it isn't the healthiest trait, I've learned over the years to somehow disconnect from bad news if necessary, as a means to cope, and sometimes as a way of providing the sort of objective support often needed for others in times of crisis. In this matter, however, I still hoped I was making more of the reporter's call than necessary. My wishful thinking was short lived; it lasted only until dawn, when the morning edition arrived on my front door step.

*   *   *

I woke early. Still in bathrobe and slippers, I opened the door with apprehension and found the newspaper rolled up in the usual spot. I picked it up, unrolled it, and there it was on the front page: **Suspect's Exchange with Priest Recorded**. Below the headline was a color photo of Hale, the inmate whose confession I'd administered. Serious suspicions of murder had been brought against this young man.

The victims of a triple-homicide were discovered on a cold, star-studded night in late December 1995. The bodies of three teenagers were found on a logging road: a boy and girl, both fifteen, and a younger boy of thirteen. All three were shot with a .38 caliber pistol. The two older teenagers' nude bodies were arranged in a sexually suggestive position, while the second boy was clothed in a girl's dress. Hale and an accomplice were considered the prime suspects.

Now, in May of 1996, *The Register-Guard* published the article which read, in part: "Prosecutors have acquired a tape recording of a conversation between Conan Wayne Hale and a Catholic priest that was made during a sacrament of reconciliation at the Lane County Jail. The contents of the tape aren't revealed in a search warrant affidavit, written by Jeffery Carley, a Lane County sheriff's detective. A court order late last month allowed investigators to listen to the recording . . .

"Prosecutors have named Hale as a suspect in the Dec. 21 murders. Hale, 20, hasn't been charged in the triple homicide case. He remains in the Lane County Jail in lieu of $180,000 security. To be released, he would have to post $18,000 in cash. Mockaitis said Friday he wasn't informed that a tape recording of the jail conversation had been made or that it was to be turned over to prosecutors.

"'Certainly, as far as the church is concerned, that is privileged information and should not be used in a court of law,' Mockaitis said. "'Inmates at the Lane County Jail are notified that their telephone conversation may be recorded. However, they are not informed that conversations in the jail visiting area might be recorded,' sheriff's Lt. Dan Heuvel said. 'Recording conversations in the visitors' area, where visitors and inmates are separated by a windowpane and talk to each other over telephones, 'is not a routine procedure by any stretch of the imagination,' Heuvel said.

"District Attorney Doug Harcleroad said Friday that he expects a legal fight over the admissibility of the taped conversation if prosecutors try to use it. He said the Hale case is the first time in his memory that prosecutors have tried to obtain information from the jail regarding conversations between clergy and inmates."

If the reporter had asked me anything about the contents of the tape recording, I would have neither confirmed nor denied any information. He never did. Yet, because he quoted my name on the search warrant, I could not deny I saw this young man.

From this first news report, a chasm between investigators and the Church seemed inevitable, and the legal fight District Attorney Doug Harcleroad predicted would be just the tip of the iceberg. Something had to be done quickly. I didn't turn on the television to catch a morning reference to the article.

I could waste no more time. I needed to call a higher authority ASAP. I dressed, ate some breakfast, and waited till about 10 a.m. when I placed a call to our Auxiliary Bishop Kenneth Steiner. We were awaiting the appointment of a new archbishop, but since that position was still vacant, Bishop Steiner was serving as Administrator of the Archdiocese until the new archbishop was appointed. He had served as our auxiliary bishop for eighteen years and was serving as pastor of a large parish in the university town of Corvallis, Oregon. I was fairly certain he hadn't heard about or seen the Eugene news article. I was to become an informer to this Bishop as the reporter, a very different Bishop, had called me.

When Bishop Steiner wasn't occupied with other duties, he was a man who loved to play golf. On a day as cool and gray as this, I wondered if he might be out on the course. The bishop's answering service let me know he would be out until later that afternoon. I stressed I'd appreciate a call back as soon as possible because this was "very important."

Grabbing the front page of the paper again, I didn't know whether I wanted to pray, get angry, take a walk to calm down, or just wait for the fallout. I was thankful no wedding was scheduled in our parish on this Saturday in May. I returned to the office. Fortunately, I was able to concentrate on some homily notes in preparation for weekend services. The scriptures related a joyful resurrection story. Around me everywhere were signs of new life. Not long ago, we had concluded the dramatic and joyful celebrations of Holy Week and Easter Sunday. As a parish, we welcomed the newly baptized now fully initiated into the Catholic community. The Church was filled with fresh azaleas and Easter lilies and the blessed baptismal water. The tall, gold and white Easter candle, symbolizing the light of the risen Christ, had stood prominently before the pulpit.

Next weekend would be Mother's Day. While it is not a religious holiday, the Church would be filled with mothers, grandmothers, and their families. We had every cause for rejoicing, but now I felt I'd been handed a cross in the midst of it. Still, I found a resolve to not let this cross crush me with its weight. Larger issues were at stake than just my own.

In addition, I was uncertain about Hale himself. What did he know about this if anything? When last I saw him, he appeared generally calm and thankful, and at the time I was reminded of the very essence of Jesus' message of forgiveness: Everyone is given a chance for conversion. I wondered if Hale's sense of betrayal, as a penitent, was now as tangible as mine. Had he forfeited all his rights as a prisoner? I knew that the free exercise of a prisoner's religious practice was not prohibited despite their restricted movement and obvious security concerns. Considering the suspicions against Hale, and this appalling attempt to gain evidence, what sort of treatment was accorded to him? Afflicted with these thoughts, I returned home to wait for the Bishop's call. Then, around three o'clock that afternoon I heard a familiar voice.

"Tim, Bishop Steiner. I got your phone message. What's going on?"

"Bishop, you'll never believe the call I got yesterday." I spoke with the same words I'd used when I had spoken with Maurice the day before. I filled him in with my best summary of the events as I referred to the article in the morning *Register—Guard* and waited for his response.

"What? You're kidding. Are you sure of this?" he said. I found his response frustrating, but familiar, as it was the same as Maurice's when first I'd told him about the reporter's phone call. Considering what mine had been, I certainly was not about to judge his first reaction to the news.

"Bishop, I'm holding the paper in my hand and I'm looking at the article. I'm very sure," I said.

"Well, I don't have a copy of the Eugene paper here so I'll try to find one later today. I'm scheduled to have a Mass at the Mission Church this evening, so I'll pick up the paper on my way out there or on the way home. Let me take a look and I'll call you back this evening around nine."

"That sounds fine. I appreciate this, Bishop," I said. I felt as if I'd just dropped a bomb on this good man, although I also knew I'd done the right thing. Right now, I just needed to find a way to carry on.

I approached the Saturday evening schedule at the parish with apprehension. Considering the events of the past two days and the article in the morning paper, I knew parishioners would express their opinions. I didn't know if blame would be sent my way. Customarily, people come to share in the Sacrament of Reconciliation on a Saturday afternoon; then an evening Mass is offered for any parishioners who may want to attend. I knew I had friends among parishioners but I was in the dark about what to expect in the face of such an event. What emerged was panoply of emotion. Most parishioners were shocked, angry, disbelieving, but all expressed genuine support for me

In various forms I heard, "We're praying for you, Father," as a common response from the people. Whether they understood the extensive implications at this early point or not, it felt as if every Catholic shared a collective outrage. This intrusion was beyond what people imagined possible. The confessional is among the few truly protected and sanctified human relationships that is absolutely guaranteed to be confidential under all circumstances, perhaps even more privileged than lawyer-client due to the added protection of Church Law. Catholic or not, most people instinctively know you don't "bug" a confessional or whatever place may serve for that purpose. To describe this as shameless would be an understatement.

As Saturday evening Mass began, I made an effort to keep the focus of the liturgy on the season of Easter. The beauty of the surroundings in Church, the spirit of new life in the resurrection of Christ, the upbeat tone of the scriptures and music helped to disconnect from the stress of the last two days. Yet, I found it impossible to avoid commenting on the news report. I let the people know I had notified Bishop Steiner and was waiting for his return call. After Mass, however, I could tell from parishioners' initial comments that this would be the main topic of conversation for an indefinite period of time.

I shared a meal with an older couple in the parish, and then returned home around 8:30 p.m. to wait for the bishop's call. By 9 p.m., the promised call came in.

"Tim, I have a copy of the Eugene paper and I see the story. We have to do something. This is very bad." Bishop Steiner said.

I broke into an uncomfortable smile as I lowered my head and leaned forward in my chair, the phone receiver cradled against my ear, "Exactly. What do you suggest?"

"Well, let me get hold of Fr. Mike Maslowsky to begin with," he said. "With his law background I think he could advise us on where to begin. We'll probably get hold of Tom Dulcich as well. He's an attorney that we have often called upon. I will give Mike a call this evening and then I imagine we'll be giving you a call sometime tomorrow. I don't think we can waste any time on a response."

"I agree, Bishop, that's at least a beginning," I said, relieved action would be taken, though now concerned as to how the matter may escalate on all sides.

Fr. Maslowsky was someone who gave me confidence that this issue would be confronted with resolve. He was articulate with a sharp legal mind so I felt he was an obvious choice to take the lead in this initial brainstorm session. Originally, his career choice was law. He attended Northwestern Law School in Portland, Oregon and became an attorney with a prestigious law firm in Portland. After three years, he left the practice of law and then attended the Pontifical Gregorian University in Rome in study for the priesthood. Ordained a priest in 1987 for the Portland, Oregon Archdiocese, he returned to Rome in 1989 and entered further studies where he eventually received a doctorate in Sacred Theology from the Gregorian University. The choice of Fr. Mike was wise.

While I suspected legal issues must be involved, the Bishop's suggestions—while totally reasonable—made me feel this was definitely not going to die easily and that a focused and balanced response would need to be given. As I hung up the phone, I realized a growing sense of irrational guilt was rising in me, as if this whole thing were my fault. The 11 o'clock news did nothing to bring comfort.

It was the first televised reference to the story in *The Register-Guard*. The emphasis and rising tone of the reporter's voice stressed how this was considered a serious matter by the secular press. No mention was made of any word from Douglas Harcleroad, the district attorney. Yet, my underlying sense was the reporters were siding with the district attorney and pointed out the increasing evidence against the suspected inmate was a justification for this secret taping. I thought, was I exaggerating the gravity of this event once again? I was well aware there were grieving families as a result of these murders but this particular intrusion of a religious ritual also bore some weight. It was a precarious position for both church and state. On Sunday I knew I would encounter the majority of the parish at the Masses. But for now, I needed to get some rest. Prayer, yes, but I found it hard to form words.

*   *   *

The breaking news of the previous day clearly tempered the joy of the Easter season on that mid-spring morning. As expected, as parishioners arrived for services, over and over again they expressed outrage and disbelief about what by now had become a Sunday morning headline. Many were direct in their criticism, others quite specific in their disgust.

Parishioner's shared my confusion as they entered the Church near where I stood on the front steps that Sunday morning: "What was that district attorney thinking?" "Father, are you all right?" "Outrageous!" "Disgraceful!" Most tried to find suitable words to describe what happened, but since there was no such previous violation, that effort became elusive. I could not have agreed more with their confusion, so I appreciated their support. While I could allow myself to take on a victim role and seek pity from my supporters, I knew that would defeat any hope for success in our future efforts. This was already bigger than myself.

Shortly after the final Sunday Mass concluded, I retuned home around 2 p.m. I was anxious to receive the promised phone call from Fr. Mike and whoever else had been contacted by Bishop Steiner. The phone rang. It was Fr. Mike Maslowsky.

His voice was friendly and supportive. He had arranged a conference call between himself, Bishop Steiner, and Tom Dulcich, one of the principal Archdiocesan attorneys. I patiently waited for everyone to check in before we began. This was new territory for me, as I was unfamiliar with the details of such legal maneuvering but was eager to hear of their strategy.

I summarized the visit to the jail, the phone call, the story in the Saturday morning paper. Most of this conversation told the story of the events as I experienced them. I reassured these men it happened exactly as reported. From the tone of the conversation, it was obvious we were all treading on new ground. Not only were there legal issues and obvious religious freedom violations, but the very integrity of the sacrament and all we presumed about respect for religious ritual was at stake. And, I could sense this was significant beyond our Catholic self-interests. As the conversation continued, I felt encouraged I would not be kept in the dark about these matters, but any sense of personal control over this passed from me.

"This could create quite a mess," Fr. Mike said, "But I feel we can stand firm on Constitutional grounds. My gut tells me that a First Amendment violation is pretty likely. We need to meet with this district attorney and see what he has to say. I intend to call him tomorrow and we'll let you know, Tim, as quickly as I can on what the arrangement will be. That should be the first step in our strategy. One thing is not negotiable—that tape has to be destroyed. We'll handle the details of setting this up and keep you informed. Tim, be careful about what you say to whom. The sacramental seal remains in place."

"I'm well aware of that, Mike," I said, for I was very familiar with the confidential nature of a confession. I knew of the grave consequences the Church placed on a priest who would deliberately break the sacramental seal: automatic excommunication was the penalty. While I was grateful for his support, the suggestion to remain quiet, aside from the sacramental seal, would become more frustrating than I imagined.

Tom Dulcich agreed with Fr. Mike's suggestion: "Yes, it's best to begin with the D.A. himself. This will need to be handled carefully. I'm not sure what's been created here so we'll need to deal with things as they come up. It'll be interesting to hear what Mr. Harcleroad has to say. This is pretty remarkable. I don't know of any lawyer who's ever litigated such a situation but it's clear that privacy and religious freedom issues are involved. This Wayne Hale hasn't been charged with anything has he?"

"No, I think that's clear from the news report," I answered. "But, they seem pretty anxious to slap charges on him."

"Well," said Tom, "this isn't the way to do it." His voice was emphatic.

Fr. Mike mentioned he would need to relate this information to the Papal Nuncio, the Pope's representative to the United States, in Washington, D. C. His statement struck me with its broad implications. The Vatican would likely be next.

"Thanks. I feel more settled for the time being. At least there's some sort of plan to tackle this," I added.

"I don't know how successful we'll be with the district attorney," said Fr. Mike, "but right now, it's worth our time. That tape has to go."

We all agreed and Bishop Steiner gave his blessing to move forward.

We ended our conversation. I sensed no time would be wasted but I found myself unsettled by the prospect of this.

I walked over to the front window of my home where I caught the bright sun and noticed green grass spread out below—fresh, new foliage growing on the trees—all of it so beautifully serene. I reflected on the dizzying speed with which matters were now moving, just two days after the phone call from the reporter. I prayed to God that our action plan would go well and, as had become an integral part of my prayers, I prayed for the inmate Hale.

Yet, I wondered why I blamed myself for being the cause of so much trouble. The idea of a search warrant issued to uncover the content of a sacramental confession was deeply offensive, regardless of a penitent's status or condition. This was an aggressive tactic on the part of law enforcement agents that called for my need to rise above self-defeating emotions. I knew I could do that despite the fact I had been made an unwilling victim. Still, I was energized by the commitment of these men to move this forward and I hoped I could be a part of the solution.

The need for the Church to speak with one voice was understandable but I too wanted to be heard and understood; to tell my story. I was conflicted with my desire to be obedient but also to have my day in court. I felt this was being taken away from me and that I would be forgotten in the mix.

The days ahead brought an increased amount of reporting—what some might consider media frenzy—throughout the state of Oregon. With these escalating reports, I began to save everything. Maybe I was unconsciously attempting to have some control over the uncontrollable. I recorded television news reports, cut out newspaper articles—collected anything that expressed growing outrage for I felt this would need to be told and a primary source is the most reliable measure of truth.

Probably the most upsetting at the start of this affair was a faxed copy of the affidavit given to the judge requesting the search warrant. The affidavit was that of the lead investigator in Hale's case, Detective James Carley at the Lane County jail. This affidavit spurred the warrant the reporter discovered when he called me on the previous Friday. On that document Carley mentioned, "I learned from Sgt. Bud Spencer, supervisor at the Lane County Adult Corrections Facility, that on or before April 18, 1996 Conan Wayne Hale made arrangements to have a Catholic priest visit him on April 22, 1996, for the purpose of making a confession."

I assumed they speculated Hale would be truthful in speaking to a priest. Then, an even deeper sense of the scheme behind this whole affair came to light. The detective who had requested the warrant stated, "I know from my experience and training that the Catholic confession is an integral part of Catholicism. It is a sacrament. The basic tenet of confession is that a person is absolved of his or her wrongdoing upon making a full and complete acknowledgement of what that wrongdoing is. After a person gives the acknowledgement of what he or she has done wrong, the priest prescribes a penance. Upon performance of that penance a person is absolved of his or her sins." A chill overcame me. They had recorded this *because* it was a sacrament.

I read and reread these papers, remembering the search warrant. It was a rough way to begin the week. The most alarming words made reference to the day and the time I was scheduled to visit Hale and that " . . . the conversation was recorded on an audio cassette tape, then retrieved from the recording machine." This legal document affirmed that the real reason for the taping was to snoop for so-called evidence in the investigation against Hale. They knew exactly why I came to the jail, when I would be there, and they had taped covertly. Could they really have plotted to use the voice and words of a penitent to convict himself?

*   *   *

Shortly after the news broke in the press, a local television station announced a lead story for the 11 o'clock evening news. It urged viewers to tune in and catch a statement from the district attorney, Mr. Doug Harcleroad, to hear his rationale for the secret taping. I was prepared to hear him speak so with video recorder on, I was ready to tape this newscast. I wanted to hear the D.A. explain his reasons but the description given by reporters and the district attorney himself went beyond what I expected.

It opened with a proclamation by the female reporter: "Jailhouse conversations between a priest and a suspect are not confidential. Surprised? The priest was. Conan Hale's conversation was recorded and prosecutors have listened to the tape as part of their investigation. The priest had no idea he was being taped and other clergy are outraged by what they call a breach of confidence."

Fr. Vincent Lopez, Principal of the local Catholic High School, was seen walking outside on the grounds of the school, accompanied by a reporter. There he stated how "outrageous" this whole affair was. How "I've never heard of such a thing before" and how "there would be much explaining to do" on the part of government authorities. "When a person goes to confession, they know the absolute promise of confidentiality. If that were not true, no one would ever go."

Then, the report moved to the district attorney who had been interviewed in his office. Mr. Harcleroad stated, "The law allows for the recording of conversations in jails in Oregon. The only exception for that is the attorney/client privilege."

Referring to the district attorney, the reporter added her voice-over, "Harcleroad stated it makes perfect sense that priests be recorded in jails just like everyone else."

Then the district attorney, looking at the reporter, added: "Who knows what sort of things might get planned by individuals coming in to a jail with suspects, including priests or ministers. There have been priests and ministers who have committed criminal acts." It felt as if a bomb had dropped.

I sat in disbelief by what the television reportage implied. While I understood the jail's need for security, I was no stranger to the visitors' area. What sort of security risk was I to the jail? What sort of criminal act was I plotting in coming to hear the sacramental confession of this inmate? Planning for what? No, the Church is not above the law, but this act was beyond the pale. It sounded to me more like a cover up for what seemed to me self-seeking absolution for the surreptitious act of taping they'd committed.

Mr. Harcleroad's statements further raised the question: "Was their reason to suspect some sort of secret relationship, some plotting between priest and this particular inmate, who was a suspect of the sheriff's office? What sort of characterization was now out in the public as to who I was? There must have been something more to this that I, in my initial shock, was not yet ready to see.

What followed next bordered on the ludicrous. The news station had conducted a call-in phone poll and broadcasted the poll results to the question: "Should conversations between a priest and a suspect in jail remain confidential?" 65%—Yes; 35%—No. Apparently Catholic theology was being determined by a television ballot

Anger surged inside me as I closed my eyes, leaned forward and sighed in frustration. I hit the remote power button off with a vengeance and stood up as I threw the remote control back on the chair. This had turned into a nightmare. Now I had an inkling of what we were all up against. This ancient private relationship, about which there are still some fundamental questions today, was now fair game. I wanted to fight, and fight this all the way.

CHAPTER 2

Confrontation: Church vs. State

* * *

"For Christianity is a fighting religion. It thinks God made the world—But it also thinks that a great many things have gone wrong with the world that God made and that God insists, and insists very loudly, on our putting them right again." (C.S. Lewis—*Mere Christianity*)

* * *

Confrontation: Church vs. State

Ongoing coverage of the secret taping stretched like a wild fire growing far beyond Oregon. The "jailhouse taping," as *The Register-Guard* had tabbed its story, was being picked up by out-of-state newspapers, television, radio, and even used by some as fodder for national columnists. In the midst of the media swell, I was also troubled about the health of my father, who suffered from a returning cancer, and the welfare of my mother who obviously bore the most personal burden of his condition. My father's prognosis was not hopeful and my family and I prepared ourselves for what appeared to be his final months or weeks. Even so, the fight was on; we all had to move forward. By now the initial shock of the reporter's phone call had solidified into a desire for right justice.

The first step came on a Tuesday morning—about five days after the first story had run in the local newspaper—when I found another yellow message note in my mailbox. This time it was welcome: "Please call Fr. Mike-ASAP." The anticipated call finally had arrived, and with it came the promise of what our next move would be. I hurried to my office, placed the call, and Fr. Mike's secretary put me right through. I was anxious to hear Fr. Mike's voice as I stood by my desk.

"Tim, how are you doing?" Fr. Mike said, his voice pleasant and even.

"Well, I'm fine," I said. "I assume you're calling about a meeting with the district attorney. I'm ready to get on with this."

"I'm glad to hear that, Tim," Fr. Mike said. "Tom Dulcich and I have arranged a meeting with Mr. Harcleroad for this Thursday morning in Eugene. He gave us an 8 a.m. appointment and we definitely want you there. I don't imagine this will be lengthy, but it will give us a chance to share our concerns and hear his response. Can you make it?"

"Of course, I'll be there," I said firmly as I sat near my desk.

"That's great." Fr. Mike said,

"We'll keep you informed if there are more developments in that regard between now and then. Tom and I will meet with you in the courthouse a little before eight. I'm not sure where his office is, but I'm sure you can find it."

I added, "I need to ask, Mike, is this legal in Oregon? The district attorney claims it is."

"Well," Fr. Mike responded, "the clergy-penitent privilege is not specifically stated in the Oregon Constitution but there is certainly protection against government interference in religious worship. There is an Oregon statute that prohibits the obtaining of information by telecommunication devices without the permission of the one being recorded. Then, there is a statute which grants a clergy-penitent privilege. However, in Oregon, the clergy-penitent privilege protects the penitent more than the clergy."

Surprised, I asked, "So what does 'protects the penitent' mean?"

"That means only Hale can give you permission to say what's on the tape." Fr. Mike added.

Startled, I said as I leaned on the desk before me, "Well, that doesn't work. I can't say anything about that tape no matter what the penitent allows me to do."

Fr. Mike agreed. "You're right, Tim. You can't. That's what makes this whole thing so thorny. When you come to a jail, there is little expectation of privacy yet this action went beyond what is customarily respected as a privilege both for religion and for privacy. I really find this whole thing unbelievable. Even in jail, and maybe especially there, this relationship must be protected. Our feeling is that this was not legal based upon principles of the free exercise of religion. I doubt this has ever happened before, at least not in this country. The Oregon Evidence Code may be of help as well. We'll take a more detailed look at these statutes and codes but we first need to go directly to this district attorney and hear what he has to say."

"What if he refuses to budge?" I questioned, my voice raised in concern.

"I guess we'll cross that bridge if we need to but we have no intention of compromising on the issue of the tape. He may have backed himself into a corner here." Fr. Mike assured me with a confident tone.

"I'm with you both on that," I said.

"Until then let us handle this right now," Fr. Mike added. "I'll direct the conversation with Mr. Harcleroad. Tom will be present as our legal counsel. You don't need to say anything."

"Thanks, Mike," I said, my curiosity now satisfied. "Sounds like a good plan. I'll see you there."

Yet, again I felt that frustration in which staying quiet would be tough. Maybe it would be possible to end this tragedy with our visit to the D.A. I hung up the phone and sat down to reflect quietly on what was ahead of us.

Fr. Mike had already turned to a much higher Church authority: the Vatican. The Penitentiary, more formally known as *The Tribunal of the Apostolic Penitentiary*, is chiefly a tribunal of mercy, responsible for issues relating to the forgiveness of sins in the Roman Catholic Church. It remains an office in service to the Church throughout the world to monitor and resolve issues concerning the sacrament of penance.

Officials of the *Penitentiary* were incredulous at the news. They needed convincing that such an unheard of violation of the sacrament had actually transpired. Was there a confessional in the jail, and if there was, why was it not used? The representatives of the *Penitentiary* were informed there was no confessional in the Lane County jail, and likely none anywhere in Oregon's jails or prisons.

The Holy See (the Vatican) was appalled not only that such a violation took place but that such an egregious violation was carried out by United States government officials, whose responsibility it is to uphold the rights of privacy and religious freedom. The Vatican supported the Archdiocese: *The tape must be destroyed immediately.* Church officials feared this abuse was an ominous sign. So did I.

I imagined news of the sacramental violation had spread rapidly at the Vatican and, at some point, Pope John Paul II himself had likely been informed. In this country, Fr. Mike, reported to the Papal Nuncio at that time, Archbishop Renato Martino, the Pope's liaison with the Catholic Church and the United States, located in Washington, D.C. Communiqués later became monthly updates as the Archdiocese agreed to keep the Holy See appraised on the progress of the litigation. As always, we are never far from Rome in this universal community of the Catholic Church, which likewise had an interest in the eventual outcome.

At issue in this case, appeared a series of Oregon statutes. Their detailed explanations would be too lengthy to quote here but one, in particular, seemed especially disturbing in light of the taping.

O.R.S. 133.724 concerns conditions under which communications could be intercepted. They explain that, "A statement demonstrating that there is probable cause to believe that an individual is committing, has committed or is about to commit, a particular felony of murder, kidnapping, arson, robbery, bribery, extortion or other crime dangerous to life . . . ." This statute in particular could be used as a reason for the tape's legality based on suspicions the investigators may have had. As Mr. Harcleroad stated in his early television interview, "You never know what sort of planning is going on . . ." This unusual justification seemed to beg an answer to my earlier question, "What did the D.A. suspect about my coming to the jail?" It felt like a twisted rationalization in light of the purpose for my visit. Or, perhaps, a stretch for the situation?

On the other hand, the Clergy-Penitent privilege, under "confidential communication," states: "Confidential communication means a communication made privately and not intended for further disclosure except to other persons present in furtherance of the purpose of the communication." The only "other person" who should have been present was Hale. At issue, at this early stage, was the now tense, delicate communication "not intended for further disclosure" between priest and penitent and the state's effort to carry on their investigation without respectful boundaries. Regardless of civil law, the clash had formed between civil and church interpretation.

The meeting with the district attorney would be an opportunity to terminate this exploitation. But could we do it?

I was still aghast at the implication drawn by Mr. Harcleroad that the taping was done out of some fear of illegal acts being planned during my visit. And now, I was going to face this man who said it made perfect sense to him to record priests just like anyone else. I wondered what our chances were of moving a man like this whose own words, in my estimation, showed at best to neither understand nor to respect the sacrament or at worst, to disregard religious freedom or the Fourth Amendment. I found myself resisting the temptation to find truth at the extremes rather than in the middle ground. Our meeting with the district attorney was an opportunity to set this thing to rest, or to begin a process to make that happen. Could we do it?

*   *   *

The morning of May 7 began earlier than usual. I wanted to be fresh and fully awake for our meeting with the district attorney so I rose early enough to prepare. Nevertheless, my thoughts were full of the impending confrontation—an unpleasant way to shake off the night. After the usual morning rituals, and that necessary first cup of coffee, I had a quick breakfast of wheat toast and cereal, dressed in my black suit with white clerical collar and left at 7:15 a.m. My prayer before God that morning was for fortitude. I was being asked to walk where I had never been.

It was an easy drive from the parish to the courthouse in downtown Eugene, a short fifteen minutes away in the light early morning traffic. As I approached my destination, I noticed that the main street divided the two county buildings. Uncertain in which building I would find my companions, I parked between the two buildings, fed the parking meter, and began searching for the district attorney's office.

Both three-story buildings were gray concrete; they looked secure for official government business, but I was feeling anything but secure as I picked up my pace. Unable to locate a directory or receptionist at the first building and with only about twenty minutes to spare before our meeting, I was feeling the pressure of time. I crossed the street to the second. Little activity was going on at this early hour, but a great deal was going on in my head; thoughts raced between this meeting, parish appointments, and an appointment with the dentist scheduled for later in the day. Relieved this encounter with the district attorney would finally take place, yet time was short.

Near the main reception area, I was greeted by a stern-faced security guard who stood at the bottom of the stairs. I inquired about the location of Mr. Harcelroad's office, and was startled by the guard's short, dismissive response. He pointed his index finger upward and stated coolly: "At the top of the stairs."

I brushed off his flippant tone, climbed the stairs and found Fr. Mike and Tom Dulcich waiting at the top. I felt out of place with these two key players. Fr. Mike, dressed in a black suit and clerical collar, was tall, wiry and articulate. He had the appearance of a disciplined runner and was no stranger to the legal process. As a former lawyer he understood the force of law and the responsibility of those who claim to defend it. Attorney Tom Dulcich, known as a skillful litigator, had been chosen to represent the Archdiocese in this matter. He was a friendly, calm man, a bit shorter than Fr. Mike, but of a similar frame. In his light gray business suit with a dark blue tie, he provided the professional complement. I, on the other hand, had no formal legal background, but did know that an historically respected privilege in this country and our protected religious liberty, had suffered a serious breach. I hoped this private time with the district attorney alone—where no media had been informed—would be our opportunity to offer an olive branch and give Mr. Harcleroad a respectable way to save face, and ultimately to relinquish the tape. We exchanged brief neutral comments as we waited for the district attorney to appear.

Within a few minutes, we spotted Mr. Harcleroad striding calmly down the hall in our direction. He was middle-aged, with a receding hairline—a familiar figure to Lane County residents where he had served as district attorney for eleven years. A lawyer since 1973, President of the local Rotary Club, and other public service made him well known in many parts of the community. Surely, I thought, he has done much good but what was at the bottom of this outlandish attempt—desperation?

He smiled politely, greeted each of us as Fr. Mike lead the introductions, and then extended his arm toward an open door, where he escorted us into a cramped conference room where we took our seats at a rectangular table. We arranged ourselves in positions more defensive than confrontational. Mr. Harcleroad sat on one side of the table. Behind him were bookshelves, floor to ceiling. The three of us took our seats across from the district attorney.

We were about to begin, when the door to our left suddenly opened and in walked another man, unplanned, who was dressed more casually in dark slacks, a long sleeved white shirt rolled up from the wrists, open at the collar with a dark tie loosened at the neck. He appeared older than Mr. Harcleroad.

"Gentlemen," Mr. Harcleroad broke in, "I'd like you to meet the assistant district attorney, Joe Kosydar."

He closed the door behind him then turned, smiled, reached for our hands and shook them one by one as he made his way over to my end of the table. I was mystified by his arrival since we expected no one except Mr. Harcleroad at this private meeting. Yet, it was reasonable the district attorney would want another witness.

Mr. Kosydar, remained standing with hands in his pockets, leaned against the wall and looked down at us as he began small talk about his early family life in Portland. He told us which parish and Catholic school he'd attended, how he'd served as an altar boy, and he then went on to name a few priests he'd known in his younger years, asking us if we knew if these particular priests were still around.

Since he spoke only about the past, his current status with the Church was not clear. I surmised from his childhood stories that he no longer practiced his Catholic faith but that was not an issue that was relevant at this time. We were unclear as to why Mr. Kosydar thought this information was meaningful to our purpose; it felt more like an attempt to impress us, strike a common bond, or to simply let us know he had a Catholic background before we began our discussions. I felt offended by his attempt to minimize the seriousness of our meeting with the district attorney. We were not there for casual chat. Mr. Harcleroad remained silent during Mr. Kosydar's exchange. He occasionally glanced at him but for the most part appeared to take a neutral stance.

I recalled that the wording on the detective's affidavit indicated it was known that my conversation with Hale was "a sacrament of the Church." Had Mr. Kosydar composed those revealing words, knowing, as a Catholic, the purpose and nature of the sacrament? I pondered this scenario but kept these thoughts to myself.

When the assistant district attorney finished with his personal life story, he promptly turned his attention to Fr. Mike and sat in the chair next to me. I turned away from him. His choice to sit by my side raised my level of resentment. Mr. Harcleroad, seated on his high-backed, leather chair, leaned back with his elbows resting on the arms of the chair. He looked directly at Fr. Mike but said nothing, apparently waiting for him to start the conversation. Fr. Mike, a little older than the district attorney, spoke in a low key and friendly tone, beginning with a brief explanation of our position.

"Mr. Harcleroad, we appreciate your taking time for us this morning," Fr. Mike began. "We are here to see what sort of arrangement may be possible in regards to this unfortunate, perhaps misunderstanding, about the recent events involving Fr. Mockaitis and the inmate Wayne Hale at the Lane County jail. I feel it's necessary to express our concern and that of this Archdiocese about the issue of the tape recording of a conversation between Mr. Hale and Fr. Mockaitis in the Lane County Jail last month. We are very disturbed by the existence of the tape and have made it clear this was not an ordinary conversation but one that transpired between Mr. Hale as the penitent and Fr. Mockaitis as priest-confessor. As Catholics, we consider this to be one among our seven sacraments; a core and fundamental element of our sacred worship. To Catholic people here in Eugene and throughout the Church, this particular sacrament is most sacred and deeply personal."

The district attorney's face was expressionless—unreadable.

Fr. Mike continued, "We understand you are not of the Catholic faith so it might be helpful to summarize our belief. For Catholic people the opportunity offered in this sacrament is to seek healing and forgiveness for one's transgressions. We believe Christ offers this Sacrament of Reconciliation as the opportunity for sinners to recover grace and return to friendship with God and neighbor. As one who represents Christ in this sacrament, the priest has the absolute duty to protect confidentiality. We have always viewed this priest and penitent relationship as private and absolutely confidential. So, the issue revolves around the *reason* for Fr. Mockaitis' visit and the facts that were met during his visit with Mr. Hale for the sacrament to be valid, as he described them to us earlier. The actual tape recording of this conversation between priest and penitent is most likely unprecedented in this country and we view it as a direct violation of religious freedom and a serious breach of confidentiality which is protected by our First Amendment."

Fr. Mike began to quicken his pace and strengthen his voice for emphasis but avoided any tone of confrontation. He was not one to back down easily.

"He is forbidden as a Catholic priest to reveal any of what Mr. Hale or any penitent may have said to him. That obligation applies in all cases. For a priest who knowingly reveals the contents of a confession of sins, the penalty is automatic excommunication from the Church. In short, Mr. Harcleroad, our central concern is about the existence of this tape, and the search warrant signed by a local judge, which effectively broke the seal of the sacrament. The very existence of the tape is deeply offensive. Mr. Dulcich, our attorney is here since we feel there could be civil rights issues involved around privacy that may need to be explored."

All the while, Tom sat listening, taking notes. I did the same. The district attorney appeared unmoved by the excommunication penalty. Mr. Harcleroad leaned forward and offered a response as he gazed directly at Fr. Mike:

"The monitoring of conversations in the jail is not unusual. Officers at the jail monitor on an inmate by inmate basis, the intercom conversations of inmates. It is a known fact that privacy in a jail setting is not guaranteed. The jail had monitored Hale's conversation with about 90% of his visitors. Hale was aware that his communications with visitors were being screened. Oregon is a one—party—consent state. This means that a conversation may be recorded as long as one person involved in the conversation consents."

Fr. Mike questioned, "Is there a record of monitoring his visits with clergy from other denominations? You state that 90% of his conversations were monitored, not all of them. Would he have allowed conversations with other clergy to be taped? Mr. Hale is a suspect and has not been charged with the crime you are investigating."

Mr. Harcleroad responded more firmly than I expected, "We are trying to solve a triple homicide and we will use all legal means to do it. I don't know about other clergy visits. I believe we were in our legal rights to tape that encounter based upon our reading of Oregon law. I do feel that jailhouse conversations between inmates and visitors, including clergy, are not an exception. It makes perfect sense to monitor such conversations. The only exception for privacy in the jail is that between an attorney and their client as I explained recently in a news report."

Did the D.A. know he'd touched a raw nerve? I had no reason to believe that Hale knew our conversation would be recorded. We did learn that his other clergy visits were respected then shifted uncomfortably in our chairs as he continued and said, as he glanced directly at me, "I wouldn't be surprised if this has not happened before." He sat back and resumed silence.

Taken aback by his words, I presumed his comment referred to my previous visits, and I wondered if other confessions were monitored or recorded, and how did jail policy play into this? The whole thing felt like a set up and I was struck with fear and anger; near hostility.

Fr. Mike glanced in my direction then gratefully jumped in, "Fr. Mockaitis, on previous visits, had administered the sacrament of penance to other inmates at the jail. To his knowledge, none of those communications were intercepted or recorded. In Oregon there is a statute that supports the clergy-penitent privilege. I have a copy of the statute here."

Fr. Mike turned to Tom who, after shuffling through some papers in his brief case, lifted some papers and closed the brief case on his lap. Fr. Mike took the paper and read: "It's statute OR 40.260(2) and reads: 'A member of the clergy shall not, without the consent of the person making the communication, be examined as to any confidential communication made to the member of the clergy in the member's professional character.' I don't think that Hale has given his consent to Fr. Mockaitis to speak. This recording, in essence, forces Fr. Mockaitis to break the seal of the sacrament as the tape is listened to. Our church forbids this explicitly.

"But, even if he did, the problem here is that no matter what Mr. Hale may say, he cannot release Fr. Mockaitis from his obligation to maintain what we define as the seal of the sacrament. We feel that this method used to gain evidence during the priest-penitent conversation entangles a government agency in the free expression of religious faith."

The district attorney stated, "Well I don't think we are interested in what Fr. Mockaitis may have said. However, I believe there is a written transcript of the tape as well," he added in an unapologetic tone.

Although his unemotional expression seemed to soften, I was hard pressed to read any hint of embarrassment or remorse. I sensed the presence of evil, not in these men, but in the nature of the violation itself. My thoughts went to an uncomfortable place, dark and sinister.

Fr. Mike returned, his tone strong, making our position more explicit, "Our concern is that we view the very existence of the tape—and now you tell us of a written transcript—as a living violation of the sacrament. What was expected to be a sealed conversation, surrounded by the belief of divine forgiveness, has been unsealed by the act of recording and the issuing of that search warrant. Fr. Mike spoke with resolve, leaving no question as to what we expected to accomplish.

"We are here to offer an olive branch—a way to bring this to a peaceful conclusion by requesting the tape and transcript both be destroyed immediately. Its existence raises both legal and constitutional questions as a violation of first amendment rights. We also request any additional copies of the tape or transcripts be destroyed as they should never have been made in the first place, and an order be given to all those who have heard the contents of the tape to remain silent. Finally, that an absolute and binding promise be given to never do this again,"

Mr. Harcleroad sat straight up in his chair, clenched his hands, lowered his head for a moment, then turned to all of us and said:

"Gentlemen," He leaned forward and gazed at the three of us. "I appreciate your explanation but I must remind you, this tape is now an item of potential evidence in the investigation of Mr. Hale. I will take your requests under consideration but I cannot destroy evidence and I'm sure you would agree that evidence gathered in the face of a serious crime is essential to bringing charges against a suspect. This is our duty as law enforcement officers. Three children were brutally murdered in cold blood. Let's consider the bigger picture here.

"It is not within your control to require the destruction of evidence in a capital case. What you are requesting would be considered detrimental to a state-court criminal proceeding."

Looking more intently at Mr. Harcleroad, Fr. Mike said, "Well, that is precisely my point. We are not here to interfere in the sheriff's investigation but from our understanding and the universal understanding of this relationship between penitent and priest, the contents of this tape have nothing to do with the investigation of Mr. Hale. This is a sacrament of the Catholic Church protected as a privileged relationship. We are here to speak to this one issue alone. I believe a way can be found that would save you further public embarrassment. This could be over and done with quickly and we'd be on our way,"

The district attorney offered an alternative, "Perhaps the next time Fr. Mockaitis visits the jail we can offer him an attorney/client room if he is more comfortable there. That's something I can't guarantee at this time, however. I'll talk with the Lane County Sheriff's Office," he said.

I could no longer remain silent. "Mr. Harcleroad," I said clearly, "When I was given permission to enter the jail, I was told I was not permitted to visit with inmates anywhere except in the visitors' area. After I was cleared for visits to the jail, I was told by the female officer at the front desk that this was an important way to maintain some control on clergy whose denomination was not as recognizable as the Catholic Church."

"Well, I can take that up with the sheriff's office," he said.

Returning to the jail was farthest from my mind. I could only think that there would never be another time. How could there be? Any sense of security or trust had been shattered.

Then Mr. Kosydar spoke, "Considering the potential charges against Mr. Hale and the ongoing investigation, I don't think destruction of the tape is possible. As lead investigator in this case I can tell you that only those concerned with the case directly have listened to the tape. I don't believe Hale's court appointed attorney has heard the tape but I've already listened to it." A shock shot through me with these words like a quick surge of electricity and I found myself momentarily fixed in my chair. I was apprehensive of the danger in what might yet be uncovered

I flashed back to a conversation I had with two parishioners which was now made ominous. A police officer named Pete, who shared my disgust over the whole event told me, "Father, everyone knows what's on that tape. It's the talk of the force." Shortly after the police officer's comment, Judge Thomas Coffin, a man I greatly respected in the parish, in reference to my visit to the jail, said: "They [state officials] continued to create the illusion of confidentiality in order that you would keep going there." At the time, this observation felt more like speculation. But now, hearing the district attorney say that he wouldn't be surprised if taping had occurred before made it sound far from impossible. We needed to resolve this issue quickly before it spun out of control even further.

What was coming next? District Attorney Harcleroad confirmed Mr. Kosydar's statement, "I agree with Mr. Kosydar. Destruction of the tape is not in our best interest at this time."

By now we had reached a clear impasse. The mood in the room had turned from polite cordiality to Kosydar's unsolicited Catholic autobiography, followed by a tense, thirty-minute debate. There was no point in continuing the conversation. The destruction of the tape recording(s) and its transcript(s) would not be granted, which was unacceptable and non-negotiable as far as the Church was concerned. The best we could hope for was an order to cease playing the tape and perhaps some effort to silence those who may have heard it. Mr. Harcleroad was informed that any further dissemination of the contents of that tape would be considered an additional breach of trust. Though the demands of the church may have seemed self-serving to some in light of the serious accusations against Conan Hale, the church was only demanding its rights.

The district attorney finally said, "I'll see what I can do to limit the information."

Apparently, circumstances at the jail that April morning created an opportunity too convenient for investigators to resist. Jail authorities knew about the issuance of a kite (a written request by an inmate to see a particular attorney, family member, or clergy)—from Hale to have the sacrament of penance administered and that there was no warning either posted or told to me that my conversation with Hale would be monitored. In fact, plans had obviously been made to do so well in advance, since it was known ahead of time why and when I was coming. Those details seemed evident from the reading of the investigator's affidavit and during our meeting with the district attorney.

As Tom and I began to close our folders, Fr. Mike added with a raised tone and quickened pace, "How that will be done is a matter for debate. Our intention is not to make your job more difficult Mr. Harcleroad or to interfere in any criminal proceeding. But, the Church does not intend to let this matter die. We are determined to take whatever measures are necessary before the courts to have this tape sealed and destroyed. If we loose in one court we will continue to appeal our case." There was now far more than Oregon law and the Catholic Church at play here.

While some may question whether I had an obligation to actively assure myself that confidentiality would be respected in the jail, I considered the following: No such action had ever taken place before and I was given no other option to visit with inmates except in the visitor's area; the priest-penitent privilege protects communications between a person and a clergy member; I assumed the state would abide by that law as the universal tradition of respect for this relationship between priest and penitent was no secret; there was no way of knowing whether a priest-penitent conversation had ever been taped before so why would I assume otherwise? The fact that the state formed a conscious plan to secretly tape record, made the offense all the more egregious.

Ethics and morality were replaced by the desire to prosecute at that golden moment. The state's right to investigate and the church's obligation to defend religious liberty and the integrity of the sacrament were in conflict. How could the content of a Catholic sacrament, in the proper forum, with no harm or intrusion done to the inmate and presenting no security threat to the jail, be considered evidence in any courtroom? On one level the answer to that question appeared obvious. Yet, this visit to the district attorney's office was not a trial, and we were not sitting there as judge and jury. Jesus teaches us what to do when offense is committed, "If your brother sins against you, go and tell him his fault in private . . ." (Mt 18:15). We did this. Now it was time to go.

We stood up and offered our polite goodbyes in the face of this now futile effort.

"Thank you for your time, Mr. Harcleroad." Fr. Mike said. "We will take this matter under further advisement."

Mr. Kosydar stood along with the D.A. We shook hands with less than an enthusiastic response and said simply, "Thank you," then walked out of the conference room.

As we descended the stairs to the main floor in silence, we glanced at each other, hurried out the front doors into a welcome blast of cool, fresh smelling spring air. My thoughts were fiery. Tom suggested we stop for a cup of coffee to review this experience. I wasn't sure if we needed a shot of nerve-jolting caffeine right then, but I didn't care.

Small coffee shops abound in this university town, and we found one about two blocks from the courthouse. Outside the café were round tables, surrounded by white wicker chairs. Only a few patrons sat inside at this mid-morning hour. We found a corner table where a young woman, probably a college student from the University of Oregon, approached to take our order. She returned with three coffees, none of them de-caf, and we said nothing about the morning's experience until she was out of earshot. Anger and resentment raced through me and I wondered if I was alone in my confusion.

Tom finally broke the silence, "Fr. Mike, your thoughts?" Tom sat back, with one leg crossed over the other, and took a sip of coffee. He was a gregarious man who was not easily fooled. The smile on his face told me he had his own perspective to share.

I broke in, "Mike, you did a superb job."

Fr. Mike joked, "I think we need a SWAT team to bust in and get that tape!" We laughed uncomfortably, but fully appreciated his dark humor. "I think it's time we put on the boxing gloves," he added.

"I agree," said Tom. "Their attempt to justify this plan to nose around for evidence is a case of the end justifying the means. I don't think they got it."

I added sarcastically, "Oh, I think they got it all right. This entire thing feels like a setup. Mike, you mentioned the Oregon statute again which seems to have limited protection for the priest. That's what we potentially have here isn't it?"

"Yes" Fr. Mike said as he took a sip of his coffee. "While Church law forbids that, civil law and the clergy-penitent privilege is not consistent; it's not a clone state to state. Historically, there are stories about priest's submitting to arrest rather than break the sacramental seal. Maybe under torture during Communist occupation or under Hitler I imagine we have other tales about priests going to their death rather than reveal the contents of the sacrament. Communist authorities in Poland even bugged Pope John Paul's confessional when he was a Bishop, in order to find some reason to bring him down due to secret information they feared he may be passing on. They never did. But, every state has some form of this privilege on the books."

"Well, I'm not sure I'm attracted to the prospect of martyrdom right now, nor that this equals a Hitler or Communist police" I mused.

Fr. Mike added: "Well, the very fact that this taping was done is outrageous" he said. I think the District Attorney and the investigators are far more concerned about what Hale said on the tape than what the priest said to the penitent. And that is where we need to concentrate our efforts."

"What about that assistant district attorney?" I added, "What role do you think he played in this?"

Tom answered, "I don't think we're looking to go there right now. Who did what is less important to us right now since we'd like to keep this thing out of the courts if we can. But, that may change. Correct me if I'm wrong, Fr. Mike, I don't' think the church is seeking retribution."

"No, not at all," Fr. Mike agreed, "We need to get to the bottom of this but it remains a very precarious balance. That church and state line is never solid."

Neither Fr. Mike nor Tom wanted to speculate on Mr. Kosydar's role and the Church wanted to keep this away from personalities and center on the core issues at hand. However, I could not deny my feelings and I found myself struggling not to pass judgment. I was just venting my frustration as I wondered about the wording on the search warrant. I thought about the phone call from *The Register-Guard* reporter a week earlier. If he hadn't called, who knows how or in what later setting I would have heard about the taping?

The three of us had spent close to an hour in a fruitless attempt to negotiate a process acceptable to everyone. From a strict legal perspective, the district attorney's position was justifiable. Any information related to this investigation would be considered "evidence" of some sort but I wondered if he had indeed backed himself into an unintentional corner. Yet, I believe his seemingly dismissive understanding about how deeply people hold their religious beliefs, and the long tradition of this country in respecting this privilege, was astonishing. He was not an evil man but this was an evil act. He and the investigators were blinded by their desire to file charges.

If the district attorney had agreed to work with us, that could have been the end of this story. Was this just an overly zealous investigation to bring swift justice? Some knee-jerk reaction to a once in a lifetime opportunity no one involved took time to think through? Law authorities seemed determined to do all they could to bring charges against Hale, who had not yet been charged with the murders but remained a suspect, but this was obviously an investigation without boundaries.

Nonetheless, this appalling incident was fast becoming a hot topic of conversation around the parish. I could sense that parishioners shared my sense of personal violation. So, Fr. Mike suggested that he visit St. Paul parish the coming weekend. Parishioners needed reassurance that the Church had acted on this matter swiftly and his presence also would offer a public sign of support for me.

"You'd be most welcome, Mike," I said. "I appreciate your support here. I don't know where this thing is going right now."

"Well, neither do we but I think we can stay on top of it," Fr. Mike said. Tom agreed. The local media would be notified about Fr. Mike's visit to the parish, which would give the church an opportunity to speak directly to this issue in the proper setting. At this time, the church's main concern was to protect the integrity of the sacrament and to uphold the constitutional right to religious liberty. Tom felt our position was firm under the Constitution.

*   *   *

In addition, the detective's affidavit and the search warrant were evidence of the jailers' intent to maintain the secret nature of this unconventional method. The more we learned about the facts of this case in the first days, the more I felt investigators had taken "wide latitude" in their effort to search for potential evidence. Despite Mr. Harcleroad's disconnect from our interests, I think the three of us could sense that privacy and civil rights concerns loomed on the horizon.

The Fourth Amendment limits our government's powers in the criminal process. Prohibiting the police from searching a person's belongings without a warrant is designed to prevent invasive police behavior because people have a basic right to personal privacy.

Fr. Mike's comment about "putting on the boxing gloves" spoke from a lawyer's perspective. I sensed that his upcoming visit to the parish would begin a process far beyond our discussion with the district attorney. He touched a chord in my own perception as a Catholic, a priest, and an American citizen.

CHAPTER 3

A Gathering Storm

*   *   *

"If you do not take the distinction between good and bad very seriously, then it is easy to say that anything you find in this world is a part of God. But if you think some things really bad, and God really good, then . . . You must believe that God is separate from the world and that some of the things we see in it are contrary to His will." (C.S. Lewis—*Mere Christianity*)

*   *   *

The confrontation in the district attorney's office exposed the vast chasm between ourselves and investigators—those so eager to file charges against Conan Wayne Hale. After our debriefing over coffee that morning, I returned to St. Paul Parish, troubled by the morning's events, where I found the entire staff waiting to hear the results of our peacemaking efforts. As soon as I opened the door of the office, I was peppered with questions: "Well, how did it go?" "What did the district attorney say?" "Did he give you the tape?"

I felt sad I could share only our first failed efforts but I knew we had just begun our endeavors to thwart this attempt to obtain so-called evidence in the investigation. It felt to me that the District Attorney's strategy had blurred the lines between right, wrong, ethical, moral and immoral with a rampant relativism, justifying the taping based on the jail environment and the suspicions against Hale. The fault did not lie in the essential responsibility the district attorney had to investigate this crime but the method used to obtain evidence and now what seemed the cynical interpretation of the clergy-penitent privilege, rather than the sharp distinction of respect for the privilege itself. I was not accustomed to such disrespect. Was this outright animosity for things religious, an arrogant resistance to admit responsibility, or truly a clueless revelation for the deep religious sense of so many people? These thoughts ran through my mind. While our team was attending to the legal issues before us, I had the luxury to process the real motives and beliefs behind this appalling behavior. It was the only way I could begin to make sense of it all, if that was possible, and find a stable center in the growing confusion of these early days. One thing was certain: the matter now would reverberate far beyond the walls of the Lane County jail.

Reports and analyses in both broadcast and print news were piling up. The speed at which the news spread and the consistent themes of disgust, outrage, and astonishment, struck by all the reports was amazing.

That Friday, May 10, 1996, Oregon's Catholic newspaper, *The Catholic Sentinel*, published a story with the headline: **Church Presses for Tape's Destruction**. In part, it read: " . . . the issue has become a cause of concern for the Vatican . . . The Church will go to court if necessary, to ensure that the tape never gets played again . . . the taping of the sacrament by prosecutors is a transgression that is without precedent in this State or the United States."

The Church was committed to persist, and insist very loudly, on putting things right again. Fr. Mike's upcoming visit to St. Paul's would be the first of many steps in defense of the church's position. Whether this taped confession—this so-called evidence—was legally admissible or not in Hale's future trial was yet to be determined. We had no way of knowing if the interests of the Church would be taken seriously by secular legal institutions.

*   *   *

In preparation for Fr. Mike's visit on the weekend of May 12, officials of the Archdiocese had notified television stations and the Eugene newspaper. Fr. Mike's purpose in coming to the Sunday Mass at St. Paul would be to offer support for me, and to reassure parishioners by explaining where things stood and what our continued efforts would be. It was also a golden opportunity to speak to the public for the first time about this strange event. I wondered how long state officials would remain silent. However, as that Sunday event approached, the local press was anything but quiet. Meanwhile, my heart was growing increasingly confused as I felt myself lost in the uproar of a growing discussion on rights and privileges. I would learn, however, that this uncertainty could become strength.

Far beyond the religious press, the secular media was equally verbose and anticipated the obvious controversy created by the taping. Words printed in the Saturday, May 11th edition of *The Register-Guard* were telling: "The actions are an attempt to address what Catholic leaders say are widespread shock and outrage . . . 'This whole incident presents a very serious challenge to our people because it calls into question the secrecy and confidentiality of their own confessions,' said the Rev. Michael Maslowsky . . . 'Emotions and feelings are very raw at this moment . . .'

"'If it turns out that the taped (conversation) was unlawfully obtained, then the prosecution is in serious trouble . . . If they knew this was a sacramental conference and taped it anyway, that's just flabbergasting . . .' said David Schuman, a legal expert in criminal procedure . . .

I could think the big picture was essential here, as the district attorney had reminded us in our failed meeting with him. But, as tragic as the death of three teen-agers had been, in this case, the big picture was freedom of religion in America. As we gathered for this Sunday service we were about to exercise that freedom. But my desire to be heard on this topic became an ever present force. The struggle between my wanting to be heard and the necessity to remain focused with one voice of the church remained a personal trial for me—a raw emotion that provided surprising determination.

Most of the secular press seemed eager to hear from Church authorities who brought their case to the court of public opinion quickly in these early days. The state and in particular the district attorney remained hidden but more news was heard that weekend as Hale's counsel expressed her opinion. The Sunday morning *Register-Guard,* carried a front-page article entitled: **Attorney Wants Tape Preserved**. No doubt reporters would be seeking our reactions to this, as well as other questions they had already planned on asking.

The story stated that Conan Hale's court appointed attorney Terri Wood claimed she had not listened to the recording, but requested that: " . . . the tape not be destroyed until a court can review the way it was obtained and its potential admissibility as evidence . . ."

Whether to preserve the tape, order it destroyed, play it for those who had not yet heard it, or simply lock it up were the choices offered by both sides. It seemed more and more this effort would be tried in the court of public opinion as well as under the law of the land while the church would need to be cautious yet anything but passive. I was stretched far beyond any comfort zone and took refuge in the present moment. Despite the confusion, it was time to move forward. Damage had already been done.

Our parish normally had three weekend Masses; Fr. Mike had planned on being present for the 10 a.m. Mass—the largest of the Sunday Masses.

By 9:30 that morning, the church began to fill with troubled parishioners. Most were well aware of Fr. Mike's visit and they wanted more information about the status of this conflict. It seemed our collective attention was attuned to the unprecedented invasion of privacy. I remained preoccupied by the usual preparations.

Though St. Paul Church was built to seat five hundred people, extra chairs were brought in for the overflow crowd. Besides this being a Sunday in the Easter season, it was also Mother's Day, so attendance soared with a noticeable increase in extended family members. In addition, reporters hungry for information already had assembled on the front steps of the Church. Members of our parish staff had requested that they respect our worship and not disrupt the service.

*   *   *

Parishioners streamed into the church. I stood in my usual spot at the front door—just below the top steps—greeting them, shaking hands, and wishing them "Happy Mother's Day." However, it all felt strange; almost play acting, as I tried in vain to ignore the swarm of reporters poised with their cameras, notepads, and questions just opposite me on the lower steps. As he stood there, surrounded by mostly well-behaved media, Fr. Mike found himself the target of questions at the start.

I then noticed two women, who had slipped out from the circle of reporters, heading my way. It appeared they'd escaped unnoticed to grab an interview with the priest who heard Hale's confession. At first, I was surprised by their boldness, but they politely identified themselves as reporters from the British Broadcasting Corporation, the BBC. One had flown up from Los Angeles, and the other had just arrived from London on another assignment and this was added to her schedule. Accompanied by a cameraman, they asked if I would grant them a brief interview. I agreed because I felt that for the first time, I could speak my peace in some sort of public forum.

Parishioners weaved around us, negotiating the short steps, as we moved over to the far side to clear the entryway. In what seemed an instant, the cameraman thrust his camera between the reporters and me and I instinctively stepped back for a moment. They held a more personal empathy for the serious nature of this violation than I had observed from some earlier news reports. The young woman from London seemed especially stunned by the event. Both asked questions about the scene at the jail and how I was feeling about this affair. In their own words, they described it as "terrible" and "shocking." However brief that moment was, I was relieved I could speak out and I appreciated their supportive comments.

I grew awkwardly flattered by the attention and felt conflicted between sudden celebrity and the duty to remain in the background. We'd been trained that the priesthood is not about status but about service. Still, in that moment, the universal implications of this sacrilege struck me.

I glanced quickly at my watch and noted we had about ten minutes before the liturgy was scheduled to begin. I caught Fr. Mike's eye, as we both acknowledged the choir reviewing several songs with the congregation—our cue to end our greetings and interviews. We rushed up the steps into church, and went directly to the sacristy to vest for Mass. Close behind, reporters dragged in cables, positioning themselves as discretely as possible along the back wall of the church.

As Fr. Mike and I vested in the sacristy, I knew whatever words he spoke to the assembled community would be clear, precise, and carefully chosen. We left the sacristy and lined up at the entry of the nave to join acolytes and the lector. As main celebrant and pastor, I was clothed in a white and gold vestment with an image of hope: the risen Christ embroidered on the front of the large and draping outer garment. Fr. Mike stood by my side, his taller frame covered in the traditional white alb. Over his neck and down both sides of his chest to knee level he wore a white and gold stole with a representation symbolizing Easter joy. Priests wear the stole as a sign of their authority to celebrate the sacraments of the Church.

I glanced to the front of the Church and gave the usual wave of the hand to the choir director, indicating we were ready to begin. In this fight for control between church and state, I couldn't help but wonder who was really in charge. I swallowed hard as we began and took refuge in the familiar ritual of the liturgy.

The congregation stood as we processed toward the main sanctuary—all joined in singing the opening hymn of joyful "Alleluias." Despite the extraordinary presence of the media, who stood along the back walls of the church with cameras poised, the gathering took on a festive air. The fragrance of floral perfume permeated the atmosphere amid varied colorful corsages and outfits worn by honored women on this Mother's Day.

The music continued while we bowed in reverence to the main altar, and then entered the sanctuary. Banners hung overhead and the warm glow of candles echoed the flame of the tall Easter candle. I inhaled the pungent fragrance of lilies. When the expectant crowd sang "Amen," I welcomed everyone, wished the women a "Happy Mother's Day," and then introduced Fr. Mike. I informed the congregation that Fr. Mike Maslowsky has graciously volunteered to visit St. Paul parish this weekend as a representative of Bishop Steiner and as the designated voice of the Church in this incident.

With a mix of tension and hope, I began the Mass by moving my hand in the shape of a cross as I invited all to begin, "In the name of the Father, and of the Son, and of the Holy Spirit." With arms extended, my palms extended toward the people, I greeted the standing congregation in the ancient words of St. Paul, "The grace and peace of God our Father, the love of Christ, and the fellowship of the Holy Spirit be with you." And the people enthusiastically responded, "And also with you." Then I continued with the Introductory Rites—the acknowledgement of human weakness and sins in the celebration of God's mercy, the *Lord, have mercy,* followed by the sung *Gloria,* which ended by all singing, " . . . *in the glory of God the Father, Amen."*

With raised hands, I opened with, "Let us pray. Father in heaven, author of all truth, a people once in darkness has listened to your Word and followed your Son as he rose from the tomb. Hear the prayer of this newborn people and strengthen your Church to answer your call. May we rise and come forth into the light of day to stand in your presence until eternity dawns. We ask this through Christ our Lord." The community responded, "Amen!" The congregation then settled in their seats to hear the lector, a parishioner, who read the first two Scripture passages filled with messages of Easter hope.

Following the reading, Fr. Mike rose to proclaim the Gospel—a joyful story of the appearance of the risen Lord to his Apostles by the Sea of Gallilee. At the conclusion, I sensed more than mild tension as we all turned our attention toward Fr. Mike in a different way. We were waiting for another message. He put on his reading glasses, and unfolded the letter from Bishop Steiner, an official letter, which had been sent to all pastors in Catholic pulpits across western Oregon that weekend. With his voice raised near the tone of a tenor, articulate and clear, Fr. Mike read slowly, with poignant emphasis.

The Bishop's explicit words left no doubt of the position of the church as what felt like a standoff aligned itself for a showdown:

" . . . I bring to your attention a most serious situation that occurred in Eugene, Oregon, regarding the Sacrament of Reconciliation . . . Absolute confidentiality is intrinsic to the sacrament. It cannot be compromised . . . These events chronicle a blatant violation of the sacrament and a direct threat to the practice of our religion.

"Throughout history, Catholic priests, by reason of their priestly ministry, have been obliged to make the sacrament available to Catholic penitents . . . the Church resolutely defends the inviolability of the priest-penitent relationship. In the situation in question, it was the Lane County authorities, not Fr. Mockaitis, who violated the sacrament. In response to the civil authorities' shocking disregard of our religious practice, I have asked the Lane County district attorney to destroy the tape and to guarantee the future integrity of the sacrament of penance for the incarcerated.

"I ask for your support and prayers as we seek a swift and proper resolution of this situation."

Fr. Mike removed his glasses, folded up the letter and laid it aside before he went on with something even more personal. I was struck by his serious demeanor and was fixed on his voice.

"I am here first of all to express solidarity and support with Fr. Mockaitis," he said. Then he blasted the action committed by the jail authorities and laid out the issues of concern. "No government agency in this nation or in the free world has ever adopted as policy the clandestine recording of confession. This is the kind of practice one would expect under a totalitarian government. It's not the kind of policy one would expect to be implemented by an agency of the state that is dedicated to upholding the Constitution.

"This is an issue that goes well beyond the Catholic Church and touches the very foundation of religious freedom. If they can do this, what else can they do? There's real apprehension about what an action like this means in terms of practicing one's faith, no matter what the religion. To my knowledge this is unprecedented not only in Oregon but is unprecedented in the United States. I would hazard to guess that it's unprecedented in the free world. If Fr. Mockaitis had any idea he might have been recorded, he never would have heard that confession. He did not break the sacramental seal or betray his priestly responsibility."

Fr. Mike further expressed the Church's responsibility to "Guarantee the integrity of the sacrament both for the penitent and the sacredness of the sacrament. The seal of the sacrament is privileged, it is confidential and it is inviolable and it cannot under any circumstances be open to anyone."

To make clear the position of the Church was entirely justified in asking for the immediate destruction of the secret tape, he reaffirmed the Church's intention to continue its fight as far as possible, " . . . for as long as it takes to return the right balance between church and state." His tone rose with passion, "When you have an action that is so blatant and so flagrant, it quite frankly boggles the imagination. It makes people wonder if this happens elsewhere or are confessionals being bugged? How sacred and secure is the sacramental seal? As early as the fifth century we hear about private confessions being under the seal of this sacrament."

In the course of this passionate speech, I remembered his comment about bringing out "the boxing gloves." I took note of the congregation; the people rapt in attention. Their silence startled me but I was filled with the presence of righteousness. Fr. Mike had struck a chord in our collective conscience.

His passion laid bare the widening chasm where the sacramental seal hung in the balance. His words left no doubt what the front line issues were and where the standoff lay: it was between Caesar and God.

Fr. Mike closed his remarks with words I found humbling and comforting. He referred to me as "a fine pastor, a good man who faithfully serves his Church." He then quoted from the second reading: "For it is better to suffer for doing good, if that be the will of God, than for doing evil." (1 Peter 3:17) He turned to me and commented, "You are suffering for a good deed." To the congregation, he added, "I now ask you to hear the voice of every priest and the voice of people throughout this Archdiocese, to now join your voice in showing your deep affection and appreciation to Fr. Mockaitis." He then turned around, faced me, and raised his hands.

The congregation rose and filled the Church with overwhelming, unremitting applause. I lowered my head and did the best I could to maintain some composure with this unforeseen response as I felt I never deserved this reaction. My emotions were rarely so torn between embarrassment and public recognition. We priest's are trained to avoid the limelight and I well knew that I was not the only one whose rights were trampled here. Still, the words of the second reading, which Fr. Mike had quoted (1 Peter 3:17) about "suffering for a good deed" was a sign to me that in God's vast plan the words were neither separate from the violation nor coincidental. I found myself deeply moved for the outpouring of support. This spontaneous sign of affirmation was an answer to prayer as I found myself burdened with a sense of personal responsibility for this entire mess.

After the applause subsided, I took a moment to gather myself, stood up, and with a deep breath I smiled and waved at the people in appreciation as the Mass then continued. I knew this would not be easy but I knew I could not let it overcome me. We priests give and give to our people, sometimes feel taken for granted, but now it was my time to receive from them.

Despite the conspicuous but respectful presence of the media, we proclaimed our Creed, and the Mass continued as usual. As I distributed Holy Communion, many who approached smiled, and a few of them placed their hands on my arm in a show of support. After the final blessing and dismissal we processed out of the church. Behind us, reporters scurried to get ahead of the crowd.

As is customary, I shook hands with parishioners as they left, then one man approached me, placed his hand on my back and said, "Father, that's the longest applause I've ever heard." I could only bring myself to smile and say, "Me too." Another parishioner commented, "Father, how does it feel to be the only priest in the world this has ever happened to?" While his comment was meant to be an observation, I wondered about its truth. Such a case had never been tried in a court of law, but the "only one in the world" was a bit much to digest at the time. Yet, I was the only priest I knew of who had been singled out in a thus far unprecedented event. I was, however, reassured to hear the public acknowledge that not only were the priest's rights trampled but also those of the inmate. My continued concern for what Hale might be thinking was an ever-present reminder of the sacramental violation. What was this scandal doing to him? There was no way for me to find out without jeopardizing everyone involved and the ongoing litigation. None of us was free to speak with Hale, or go beyond the news of public record about this case. Parishioners, however, had greater latitude.

Zealous news media began to seek them out. As reporters searched the crowd outside, one parishioner, Jim, said, "It's unfortunate that our local government can take my freedom of religion, whether I'm Catholic, Jewish or whatever, and violate those rights with no regard as to what has been taken from me."

Peggy, a mother of six, felt the actions of the sheriff's office and district attorney had undermined the basis of the sacrament which is, to seek forgiveness from God. "To have that forgiveness taken away from anybody is terrible," she said. "His [Hale's] right and his forgiveness have been taken away."

Fr. Mike, standing on the front steps of the church, found himself surrounded by cameras once again. In response to a reporter's questions about the front page story in that morning's *Register Guard*, he stated, "Hale's attorney's request to preserve the tape doesn't' change the Church's request to destroy it." He said the broader issue of constitutional protections overrides Hale's criminal prosecution. "Our [the church's] concern with him is as an individual who has sought reconciliation with God."

Distance between true and false, moral and immoral, church and state, freedom and intrusion, privacy and civil rights grew wider. It became a quagmire of complex proportions. For the near future, it would be a matter for research and conversation among attorneys. Neither side would retreat at this point nor was I ready to concede. This was only beginning.

*   *   *

The phone at St. Paul Church rang unremittingly with calls from morning broadcast news shows and the print media for the next two weeks. The district attorney and I easily could have made the talk show circuit. *The Today Show, Good Morning America, CBS Morning News, Nightline,* the *BBC, Dateline, Geraldo Rivera,* and the *Washington Post* were among the most prominent news sources who reported on this affair. I had read that even the Italian daily newspaper *La Stampa* commented on the case: "Not even Franco would have done such a thing!" As one caught up in the eye of this storm I found my emotions to be raw and my spiritual life grew increasingly troubled. Although I never felt it would become a personal crisis of faith, I found God to be silent through prayer but speaking through an inner sense of resolve to carry this through. Much of what I had preached to others had become a sermon for me.

Our parish secretary Barbara often greeted me with a message from some news source that wanted to talk with me. She would chuckle, "I know what you're going to tell them." Officials with the Archdiocese never forbade me to speak but they did emphasize the importance of speaking with one voice. While I understood the concerns of the church, I was feeling lost in the mix as if carried along on the tide of litigation, supported by the church's key players but personally isolated in my experience. I had not heard much from my brother priests, with the exception of a few, in the way of personal support and concluded no one really understood what this was for me. Besides, even if I was asked, I wasn't sure I could articulate what I was feeling. This wasn't weakness but it was a grand confusion. It was a frustrating exercise in self control and I resisted the temptation to blame. Yet the flurry of media reporting continued. First it began with the newsprint, both local and national, then moved on to the national media personalities.

Local newsprint became more descriptive on the extent to which the televised media was attempting to seek interviews with the primary players. *The Register-Guard* wrote on May 17: " . . . The BBC is on the line, wishing to speak with Mr. F. Douglass Harcleroad . . . So are *Nightline, Dateline, 60 Minutes, Newsweek* magazine and a host of TV stations, newspapers and radio talk shows—not to mention an army of media stringers, producers, researchers and free-lancers. In other words, this is a very big deal . . ."

Quoting an editorial opinion in Oregon's other large newspaper, *The Oregonian*, it stated: "Other prosecutors haven't made their cases by trampling the privileged communication between clergy and confessor . . ." In the end, the district attorney took no phone calls in regard to this matter nor commented publically.

The controversial *New York Times* was added to the broad scope of reporting as it twice wrote comprehensively. The Rutherford Institute, a center based in Virginia that defends religious liberties, was getting ready to fight a legal battle to keep the tape from being used in court and Dave Fidanque, executive director of the Oregon chapter of the American Civil Liberties Union spoke out . . . "Is there no zone of privacy that we as citizens have from the government?' . . ." Further words were blunt in their assessment.

"William Donohue, President of the *Catholic League for Religious and Civil Rights*, 'described the taping as a 'Nazi tactic' . . ."

In a follow-up article on May 26, 1996, the *Times* added that the Vatican signaled its concern about the violation of the secrecy of the confessional anywhere that religious rights are threatened. A Vatican spokesman, Dr. Joaquin Navarro-Valls, said that it was the duty of the church to "safeguard the rights of Catholic faithful to profess their faith . . . ."

The flurry of reporting was tiresome for its redundancy but was impressive both for its global perspective and the speed at which the news spread. Yet, it made the day to day duties that were still my responsibility as pastor colored by what became a mantra of conscious thought. I found I could go no where to hide from the news. It walked with me.

At one point I was told Mr. Harcleroad had received hate mail from the public—an action certainly not justified under any circumstances. This was not about character assassination but about bringing things back into right order. However, I soon realized the media were more interested in hearing my version of the story. If only they could get an interview with "the priest" they would have scored well. But, the last thing the Church wanted was more media blitz. Also, the issues before us were far too comprehensive and as yet not clearly formed. Noted national media personalities such as NBC News anchor Tom Brokaw and well known reporters from both CNN and the FOX news network, then began to speak and the tone became passionate. More than just reporting, however, the legal implications of the case found an audience.

One afternoon a parishioner contacted me by phone and said, "Father, you might want to watch CNN tonight. There's going to be a discussion of your case." I thanked him for the tip. That evening I sat before the television, unsettled as I faced for the first time the giant news story this had become, video recorder on, my hand on the remote control. I found myself anxious but eager to hear their take on the now famous case and wondered what new perspective might be added that was not already said. CNN's *Burden of Proof* show carried a thirty-minute debate segment. The legal implications of the case were spelled out as the participants volleyed back and forth.

Reporters, Greta Van Sustern and Roger Cossack, seated on chairs side-by-side hosted the *Burden of Proof* segment and lead a panel discussion with Fr. Mike, by teleconference, as spokesman for the Church. A group of constitutional lawyers and a member of the American Civil Liberties Union, were all seated casually on a two level tier in the spacious studio in which cameras and ceiling lights were prominent, surrounding the participants. However, there was no representation for the district attorney or anyone associated with the taping. I imagine they had been contacted.

Ms. Sustern opened the segment, looking directly at the camera, with an eager and clear voice, she began: "You'll never believe this next situation." Mr. Cossack labeled the event, the "ultimate nightmare" as the law of the Church was pitted against Constitutional law.

Looking at the large screen to his left, Mr. Cossack addressed Fr. Mike: "Tell us what happened, Father." Fr. Mike retold the details about Hale's request, my visit, and the discovery of the taping then briefly summarized the long history of this sacrament:

"Since the fifth century we have recognized a history of private encounters between a priest and penitent. By the twelfth century the Church applied the sacramental seal universally with the penalty of excommunication upon a priest who knowingly breaks the seal of the sacrament. That same penalty remains today." He then ended, "The Church has a responsibility to protect the integrity of the sacrament."

One of the panel added, "The state has the responsibility to protect the public safety. To prosecute individuals who have committed serious offenses and to protect the public from those who pose a danger to society."

Mr. Cossack then posed a thorny scenario: "Father, what if an individual confesses to a priest, in the context of this sacrament, a heinous murder or his plans to carry out such an action? Doesn't the priest have an obligation to reveal this information for the sake of public safety?"

Fr. Mike said, "The priest remains bound by the sacramental seal. However, he does have an obligation to judge the sincerity of the penitent. To determine whether his sorrow for sin is legitimate with the intention to repent or whether he is making a mockery of the sacrament. In such a case he may withhold absolution for sin but the sacramental seal remains."

The question of Fourth Amendment violations was raised. It seemed, in the case of the secret taping, "The right of the people to be secure in their persons, houses, papers, and effects, against unreasonable searches and seizures . . ." was a probable offense. As Fr. Mike said, "The protection offered by the Fourth Amendment extends to private conversations."

However, in reference to this case, "Those against the First Amendment are ambiguous," noted Terry Reed, a criminal defense attorney.

Mr. Reed then expanded the issue of admissibility. "Considering the grievous nature of this case, a triple homicide, the tape may be judged admissible. We have families in shock over this. It is not clear whether a privilege is attached to the priest who may have heard statements uttered in a surrounding that is highly monitored."

Art Spetzer, a representative for the ACLU joined in, "Mr. Hale is a suspect. He is innocent and has not been charged with this crime. Does he lose his right to the free exercise of his religion? The judge should determine this tape inadmissible."

Fr. Mike added, "Any incarcerated individual who is charged with or suspected of such a crime, has a constitutional right to religious liberty. He is faced with the dilemma; the loss of his soul or the loss of his liberty."

While most news anchors expressed shock and dismay, some were sympathetic to the position of the district attorney. I was told controversial talk show host Rush Limbaugh had offered his boisterous opinion of my expectation of privacy.

A line was drawn in the sand in this legal nightmare as I sat with mixed emotions between gratitude and suspicion. It wasn't long before another twenty-four hour news program took up the issue. This time, a representative from the State of Oregon was present on the *Fox Network* and added a somewhat more personal point of view. *Fox* added Sean Hannity and Alan Colmes to its list of reporters. A youthful looking, dark haired Mr. Hannity opened the segment with an eager voice, "This case has more twists and turns than an Agatha Christie novel." The report proceeded to raise similar issues as seen earlier on *CNN*.

*   *   *

As I listened to both of these reports, I flashed back to our conversation over coffee following our futile meeting with the district attorney as Tom Dulcich's prophetic comment on this being a case of "the end justifying the means" was fulfilled in my mind. Yet, which end outweighs the other and what means are justified?

From the local, to national, then to the international stage the story jumped with amazing speed. The world appeared very small but with a collectively large voice.

At a United Nations committee of the U.N. General Assembly the Papal Nuncio at the time, Archbishop Renato Martino, reviewed the issue of religious intolerance: " . . . such incidents occur even at the hands of officials whose countries' constitutions recognize the right to religious liberty and to freedom of conscience."

Further news from Rome was received from a seminary student from Oregon who was studying at the North American College in Rome and read about this affair in *The International Herald Tribune*. The student then, now priest, John Cihak, faxed me a copy of the Rome news report, along with a supportive letter for prayers.

"Dear Fr. Tim," John wrote . . . "Let me just say I applaud your efforts at preserving the integrity of the Sacrament of Penance, and in doing so, protecting the human conscience . . . be assured of my prayers."

Then, the issue became fodder for caricatures. *The Catholic Star Herald* in Camden, New Jersey, carried an editorial cartoon of a priest attired in black suit and clerical collar, overshadowed by a scowling police officer. The officer says, "I will not advise a person in the confessional of his Miranda rights!"

In another opinion cartoon, a priest sits in a confessional, and on the other side of the wall an inmate kneels. He is dressed in jail stripes, his eyes closed, hands folded. The inmate says, "Bless me Father for I have sinned big time . . ." The priest leans back with eyes wide open in shock at the angry-faced police officer who looms above and behind him. With a tape recorder in hand, the officer barks, "We'll handle this one, Padre!"

By now, even the legendary *60 Minutes* had contacted me from its CBS studios in New York. The late Ed Bradley had called to ask if I would go on the air to discuss the event. I learned of the details from Mr. Bradley's secretary, but grudgingly shared my disappointment and begged off due to the position of the Church. Although disappointed, she said, "We understand, but if matters change, we would be willing to speak to you again."

I knew I couldn't remain static in my reactions to all that was being said in print and in the public media but needed to move beyond, to rise above them, and to attend to the matter at hand with a focus beyond my self. Duties of parish life became at times a welcome distraction, a place to hide from this unsolicited course in the legal justice system.

While the mantra of outrage from the print and televised media was gratifying, one nationally respected journalist and author, the late William F. Buckley, added a distinguished perspective as he threw his hat in the ring. He called the taping a direct challenge of a supra-national right and evidence of "naked fascism." On May 14, less than two weeks after news of this offense broke in the press, the founder of the *National Review* vehemently challenged the position of the State in an opinion piece entitled, *Stop or I'll Shoot.*

Mr. Buckley wrote in his characteristic irony:

"Except that one has to believe nowadays that everything is possible, we'd have called flatly impossible the situation in Eugene, Oregon . . . a suspect in jail asks to see a priest. Fr. Mockaitis appears in prison and is led to one of those cubicles with plastic partitions through which prisoners speak to lawyers, family—and clergy. The prisoner tells the priest he wishes to make a confession. The priest recites the introductory rites, hears the man's confession . . . and leaves.

"Now hear this. During the entire business, the prosecutor has taped the exchange. And now the district attorney . . . announces that he intends to present the tape to a grand jury.

"At their battle stations, the Archdiocese cited an Oregon statute that holds that all exchanges between priests and their consultants are confidential. The Attorney General fired back with another statue that holds that all conversations except those between lawyers and their clients, can be recorded, even if surreptitiously. The prosecutor points out that the exchange is no longer truly private, inasmuch as the technician who recorded it is privy to its contents, as also the typist who put it on paper. But that is nothing more than an attempted distraction. If a secret is to be guarded, it matters that as few as necessary should be told it. There is a difference between what has been done, and what it is proposed the State of Oregon do.

"Now this is naked fascism, truly the end of the line. The relationship between a priest and a penitent is sacredly inviolate. A historian some time ago paused to reflect that in recorded history there is no instance of a priest violating his confessional oath, except presumably under torture . . .

"What is now proposed in Oregon is a direct challenge of a supra-national right. The ancient and venerable distinction is between what we owe to Caesar and what we owe to God. Sometimes the line is evasive. Sometimes it is as clear as the sun at noon. The idea that the state should intercept a communication between a penitent and his confessor yanks at the very pillars of separation between church and state. It is reassuring that the American Civil Liberties Union is intervening in Oregon to try to stay the hand of a district attorney who is perfectly prepared to acknowledge the sanctity of proceedings between prisoners and their lawyers, but prepared secretly to record and subsequently to publicize exchanges with a priest who serves, in the Christian understanding, in place of God himself.

"This is an absolutely clear-cut case justifying civil disobedience. If the state tells a citizen he may not pray to his own God, the state is by that very act a tyrant, meriting disobedience even with the use of force, if necessary to prevent the usurpation.

"A movement should instantly be organized in Oregon to impeach and disbar the district attorney. It is inconceivable that movement would fail to get the backing of thoughtful people of every faith. Direct appeals should be made to everyone in the chain of command. To judges, jurors, bailiffs, stenographers, janitors: Refuse to cooperate with the proceeding in any way. Any intervention by police should be resisted as confidently as one would have refused a Gestapo agent attempting to interrupt proceedings in a synagogue.

"Nothing less than the discharge of the district attorney will serve as a sign of contrition by the government of Oregon, this act of contrition to be done with the music and noise and fireworks that properly mark a celebration over tyrannical initiative." (Used with permission).

One might wonder about the reaction of the district attorney to Buckley's editorial. *The Register-Guard* reported: "Harcleroad is not amused . . . 'I haven't talked with Mr. Buckley. I don't know if he knows Oregon law or not," said Mr. Harcleroad.

At the same time, a member of *The American Civil Liberties Union* in Eugene added further to the mix: "All of us Americans like to think, at least we used to like to think, that we have a zone of privilege around us that the government cannot penetrate . . . that has always been extended to the person who is in prison . . ."

* * *

Despite this widespread protest and the support of parishioners, I found myself experiencing an odd suspicion of visitors to the parish who might be asking "too many questions" about how things were going. This irrational suspicion of people had formed a strange twist of my mind. Not surprisingly, my questions showed up in my dreams—the kind you wake from and wonder if it really happened but so vivid there's no chance that you'll forget it. One night, I found this to be true:

In my dream state, Hale and I sit together in a jail cell. We have both been arrested for some unknown reason. I hold in my hand a key that will unlock the cell and release the two of us. I give that key to Hale; he opens the cell and we escape together. The police rapidly begin their pursuit. I'm filled with great fear that I will be captured as the one who planned this daring escape. We approach a bridge, not knowing whether to jump or run, but then I woke up—startled, confused, and disturbed.

Later and throughout the morning, I wondered about the meaning of that dream. I believe the "key" was the sacrament we had celebrated. With the forgiving love of Christ, I had the ability to offer this man freedom. Without taking away the need for responsibility or restitution for sin, I could offer the "key" of forgiveness that opens the door to healing. And now, my dream told me, I feared that I would be held responsible and punished for exercising my ministry. It was undoubtedly the strangest penitent experience I had ever known.

In spite of this, I knew that life could not stop. So I carried on with my daily pastoral duties, but I remained preoccupied in my thoughts about the case as the entire affair stood unresolved with no clear direction in sight. The kindness of parishioners and friends and my own desire to see this through to the end had given me strength in spirit that I attributed to the power of prayer. I stood grateful for what seemed to keep me above the battle.

As the story continued to catch the attention of commentators, a much broader picture emerged. If the Church remained quiet, the implications would challenge our entire understanding of law and its limits in this country. As had been stated in numerous ways, the fear of certain protections being gradually chiseled away stood front and center in this struggle, and the mere existence of the tape had become a symbol of that fear. We were all treading delicately on new, untried ground. Someone other than myself needed to embrace responsibility. The Archdiocese fervently tried to stay ahead of the situation, to prevent the taped sacrilege from being played again and to ultimately see that tape destroyed. In the end, it was also a matter of corrective justice through some admission of responsibility for the covert taping. That was about to come my way in varied forms.

CHAPTER 4

Olive Branches Extended

* * *

* "When we forgive evil we do not excuse it, we do not tolerate it,
we do not smother it. We look the evil full in the face, call it what
it is, let its horror shock and stun and enrage us, and only then do
we forgive it . . . You will know that forgiveness has begun when
you recall those who hurt you and feel the power to wish them
well." (C.S. Lewis—*The Joyful Christian*)

* * *

As events unfolded, I found myself confronted by the need to forgive
what I felt was unforgivable. Apologies from the district attorney, Roger,
my contact at the jail, Conan Hale, and the Judge who signed the search
warrant to listen to the tape, became a strange mix of motives and reactions.
These key players, who reached for olive branches, stretched me to go
beyond myself and begin a process of personal healing which emboldened
me to rise above a self-centered naval gazing, to feel sorry for myself, and
begin to see this as a way to apply the honorable value of reconciliation.
This entire event felt to me like a profound violation of the sacred right
to forgiveness. As a member of the clergy, I found this especially offensive.
Both Hale and myself, and by association the church, every person of faith,
and tangentially every citizen of this country, was wronged by the events
at the county jail.

None of these regrets were solicited which made them all the more
startling. Some came in words, others in actions, but not all were equal in
nature. I share them in the way I responded for it became a curious study

in human nature, especially my own. Saying "I'm sorry" is not easy, but to forgive the offense, though necessary, can be daunting. One of the most controversial apologies came from the district attorney himself.

Fr. Mike told me that the district attorney had been urged to offer me an apology. Mr. Harcleroad had been pressed to do so by the *Catholic League for Religious and Civil Rights*, among other organizations. No specific promise or timeline had been proposed for the apology by the D.A. until one month after the offense and just after Mr. Harcleroad had been reelected for another term. Although he ran unopposed, in light of the outrage and accusations in the press over the last month, I was distressed at this man's reelection. It was business as usual. I recalled William Buckley's demand for the district attorney to resign. Apparently the public majority wasn't convinced—more likely unaware—of Buckley's challenge for civil disobedience and peaceful protest. I was frustrated that his apology now needed to be *arranged*.

Mr. Harcleroad proposed that Fr. Mike and I come to his chambers downtown, in the same room where we had first met. Television cameras would be allowed, and no doubt newspaper photographers and reporters would be invited as well. Under glaring lights, with cameras flashing and microphones surrounding us, I envisioned the district attorney offering his "mea culpa." Maybe after that we could assure the public that all was now forgotten! My thoughts curdled with cynicism and I found myself going to a place that would be less than appropriate for a priest to express in public, in spite of the fact that I would have if I could.

Fr. Mike quickly squashed the district attorney's proposal to meet at his downtown office. He demanded that Mr. Harcleroad come to me privately, by himself, to St. Paul parish without press or cameras, to extend his regret. To my surprise, the district attorney accepted this proposal and agreed to meet on Wednesday morning, May 22. I recalled our initial encounter with him and found myself less than encouraged but the higher value of giving the man a chance, the benefit of the doubt, was the better part of the choices before us at this time.

That morning I paced in the parish office, but Fr. Mike was on the way and expected to arrive before the district attorney. Our parish secretary said, "Try to calm down, Father. Things will be fine."

"I know," I replied, "let's just get this over with." She nodded sympathetically. Not long afterward, Fr. Mike arrived. We agreed that he would take the lead and I could respond but should say very little. Yet, I thought to myself, why should I remain silent? This would be a chance to have my say. Yet, I didn't want to complicate the situation so I decided to leave this up to someone more knowledgeable in the fine points of the law. By now I had concluded that Fr. Mike was very much in control so I reluctantly agreed to his suggestion. I don't know that I ever had my call to Christian forgiveness and to say the least, my dignity and reputation as a priest and pastor so tested.

Then, I glanced out the window of the office and noticed something unexpected. Out of a large, black government car stepped out not only the district attorney, but a second man carrying a Bible. We soon learned it was Judge Michael Hogan, a local Federal judge known as a skilled mediator and one who was completely disassociated from this event; a neutral party. Judge Hogan was smiling, but Mr. Harcleroad's expression was somber. No television or newspaper reporters were present so I hoped we might have the chance to make our point once again in this second meeting.

As the two entered the open reception area, I found the scene uncomfortable, and, in myself, a mix of emotions between resentment and determination. I tried to shake off a feeling of manipulation. Yet I sensed the judge had good intentions from his smile, friendly handshake, and what appeared to be no other motive than to mediate the growing gap between church and state. How the more sedate district attorney would respond was unknown but this meeting seemed worth our efforts. Fairness demanded that polite handshakes be offered to these two officials, after which we escorted them down the hallway to the opposite end of the building into the conference room. I sat across from the district attorney and the judge; Fr. Mike sat to their right. The couches and fireplace gave the large room an uncharacteristic cozy feel. The air was tense and awkward.

Judge Hogan smiled, looked at Fr. Mike and myself, and then suggested we open with a prayer for understanding and forgiveness. He opened the Bible he had brought with him and read from the Book of Psalms. "Out of the depths I cry to you, O Lord; Lord, hear my voice! . . . I trust in the Lord; my soul trusts in his word . . . with you is found forgiveness, that you may be revered . . ." (Psalm 130).

His prayer was brief, then he stated that though he was not a Catholic we still shared common Christian values, and expressed hope we could forgive and settle the matter peacefully. As out of character as this felt to me, these two civil officials beginning with prayer, it seemed right in this situation. Judge Hogan was sincere in his efforts but I couldn't help thinking: We tried this three weeks before in our first meeting with the district attorney. We tried to come to some plan of reconciliation and reasonable compromise, so why are we here again?

Then Mr. Harcleroad spoke to me, "Someone told me I may have said something about your being a security risk at the jail. I don't remember saying this but if I did I am sorry.'

He looked my way as I gave my assent to his words. But, I checked an urge to ask if I could show him a video of the news report where he did state that the reason for the taping was for security purposes in the jail and in which he'd added, "Even priests and ministers have been convicted of serious crimes." While sadly it is true that a small number of clergy have been far less than the profession demands, and in some cases brought great scandal on the church and the priesthood, I was unmoved by his effort to place this incident in the larger context of routine security screening at the jail. There was no need to screen me for security as I visited Hale. The jail was well aware of who I was. Yet, I realized that anything more than to accept his words would have been excessive.

The district attorney continued as he looked at both me and Fr. Mike: "I was wrong to authorize that taping and I'd like to do what I can to see this never happens again. I've had many phone calls as I imagine you have. I've seen how unacceptable this has been and I'm frankly surprised by the reaction. What I've decided is this particular method is repugnant to a lot of people. So we're not going to do it again. I did not think about all the other things that have transpired in terms of the clergy-penitent privilege. We make a lot of legal decisions around here. I just missed that whole portion of it. I didn't catch it. We're human beings, and occasionally we don't make good decisions." He appeared stiff and his eyes darted about nervously as he spoke. I sensed his discomfort in this position but I wanted to see this through and remain respectful.

The state officials had gotten themselves entangled in a web of legalities. In this context, however, we decided not to push the issue of the tape's destruction because we never expected he would offer to destroy the tape, and certainly not at this meeting. Except for Mr. Harcleroad's verbal promise to do what he could to see that a secret taping never occurred again, there were no other expressions of regret or offers to support anything else the Church was asking, or anything in writing. He hoped we would simply take him on his word.

Fr. Mike reiterated the position of the Church, "We understand your words, Mr. Harcleroad, but we still have many concerns about the existence of the tape. There are many questions to be answered."

Judge Hogan broke in, suggesting we accept this apology and try to put the whole affair in the larger context of the responsibilities Mr. Harcleroad carried.

"I think we can all agree that the district attorney has been under a great deal of pressure to oversee this investigation," Judge Hogan offered. "Many are urging him to bring charges [against Hale] as quickly as possible. Hopefully, you can understand how difficult this investigation has been. The district attorney has come a long way here."

"Yes, it has been very difficult," I responded.

Judge Hogan made a commendable effort to bridge the gap between us but made little headway. It seemed to become an exercise in polite disagreement while what was not said struck me as more significant than what was. By now, I had become strangely accustomed to the surprising twists and turns in this case but my sense of resolve felt all the more bolstered. I began to recognize that the shock of the event was wearing off and I could think more clearly, albeit the emotions were not far from the surface.

While the duties of a district attorney are heavy indeed, as much as I wanted to give Mr. Harcleroad the benefit of the doubt, I believed that this was no mistake or misunderstanding. Neither I, nor church authorities would let this be reduced to a mere blunder. The description on the investigator's affidavit, which triggered the search warrant, stated that the jail authorities knew I was there to celebrate the Sacrament of Reconciliation. The pursuit for justice had to continue.

On behalf of the church, Fr. Mike thanked Mr. Harcleroad but refrained from any implication of our official acceptance at this time. The district attorney's words would need to be digested and there were further issues the church intended to pursue. In the end I realized we had only agreed to disagree.

Mr. Harcleroad had offered his apology and it was over. Nevertheless, we thanked the district attorney for his effort. We offered a respectful "thank you," then Fr. Mike opened the door and led us down the hall. I lagged behind, the last to leave the room, filled with a sense of incompleteness.

Fr. Mike and I knew this was not the end, but just one more development adding to the complexity of this case. As the well-intentioned judge and the district attorney hurried to their car, I could only guess what sort of conversation transpired between them as they drove away.

Fr. Mike looked grave as he closed the front door of the office. I asked sarcastically, "What was that? I feel more manipulated now than the original phone call from that reporter." I leaned back against the wall, not knowing what next to say. Was it my priestly identity that was offended or my sense as a citizen of this country? A presence of unfinished business haunted me.

"We might have to accept that," Fr. Mike said. I unhappily agreed. That no plans to destroy the tape or even acknowledge the concerns of the church were offered, it felt as thoughtless resistance toward the church's position. I knew that I had been used at the jail and wondered about the same after this exercise. I concluded it was more of an *apologia*—a defense. The only acceptable apology would have been to either hand over the original offense or to claim the contents of the tape as hearsay evidence. Or, at the least, propose a concrete plan to do either as soon as possible, so that it could be destroyed along with the written transcripts. That would have won great respect for the district attorney and the church would have made a public effort of praising him for doing so. Though the district attorney was bound by civil law to preserve evidence I never felt the church was asking too much too soon in demanding the tape be destroyed immediately. Instead, the transparent apologia felt to me as a body with no heart. The contrast between the judge's efforts and the near detached response of the district attorney struck me. Whether I was right or not, fair or not in my response, I could not deny what I perceived.

*   *   *

Following the apology, no mention had been made from the district attorney that he would go to the press but I knew it would be a logical next step since Mr. Harcleroad had first proposed his apology be offered in his office before cameras and reporters. I knew that my task was to reflect on and pursue the higher Christian value of forgiveness and to remain centered on the careful balance between what the church was seeking and what the state was offering. Later that evening, the step we expected the district attorney to take proved true—his apology was telecast on the evening news. As a public official, he could not remain silent.

Mr. Harcleroad sat in his chambers surrounded by three reporters and a photographer to make his statement and offer his official apology to the public at large. He sat at the same table we had sat around just one month before. He offered his official "mea culpa" by reading his written statement. He also made a point of mentioning that he had offered his regrets to me personally. The press statement was essentially what he had brought to us earlier. He leaned towards the cameras with his apology in hand and read from his written text.

"I was wrong to authorize taping that conversation. There are some things which are legal and ethical but are simply not right. I have concluded that tape recording confidential clergy-penitent communications falls within the zone of *socially unacceptable* conduct . . . It is important that our citizens have confidence in our justice system and the methods we employ. I believe that taping a clergy-penitent conversation in a jail shakes that confidence and must be corrected. I will be supportive of legislation revising Oregon law to protect such conversations.

"Regarding the tape: Our office will not attempt to use this information in any way nor derive any evidence from it whatsoever . . . Hopefully, there will come a time when it may be legally destroyed.

"At no time did I nor any of the lawyers in my office intend any disrespect to the Catholic Church or Fr. Mockaitis or to any people of faith. Our intention was to find the truth about the murder of the three young people. This is still our intention, but this method was wrong . . .

"The public discussion that has occurred over the last few weeks has been instructive, enlightening, and humbling. I am deeply impressed by how dearly Oregonians and Americans care about any infringement they perceive on their rights, including their religious freedoms." (End-District Attorney's press release statement).

As priest I had heard hundreds of sacramental confessions over the years. Those moments of reconciliation and self-revelation were nearly always times of inspiration. People come to admit responsibility out of a desire to grow to be better and more faithful disciples of the Lord. As I listened to the district attorney's apology, I could only hope that in some small way this civil confession would speed the process of litigation. I was anxious to hear what the official response of the church would be.

The written press was naturally eager to report on this and did so the next day in the May 23rd edition of *The Register Guard*. With a headline in bold print it read: **DA: Recording priest was wrong.** After quoting from the D.A.'s apology, it continued: " . . . The tape cannot be destroyed outright . . . He said he (the district attorney) doesn't know whether Hale may have any legal claim against the district attorney's office as a result of the tape-recording . . . I don't believe we have violated Mr. Hale's rights, he said . . . Harcleroad said deputy prosecutors who are investigating Hale proposed the taping after learning that Hale had asked to see a priest. He said his part in the discussion lasted 'two minutes' and he told the deputies to make sure the taping was legal . . . Officials of the Archdiocese of Portland said in a news release that they will study Harcleroad's statements and refrain from comment until a news conference today in Portland . . .

"Eugene lawyer Charles Porter had publicly called for a write-in campaign to protest Harcleroad's handling of the jail taping matter. Results of the write-in effort won't be known until next Tuesday . . ." Nothing ever came of this write-in effort which only contributed to the frustration in this process. It seemed to me the district attorney was untouchable and that the great burden of proof was falling entirely on the church, the innocent party. Then, very soon around this time, I heard from Hale himself.

*   *   *

I received a card from the Lane County Jail: the name Conan Wayne Hale was written in pencil at the top left corner of the envelope. (Conan was his street name, a name that struck me with a tough image the first time I heard it. One so well-known most everyone, including the district attorney, used it when referring to Hale.) I was stunned to find this envelope waiting for me at St. Paul and I had no idea what it would contain. I carefully slid the letter opener along the envelope's seal and found a pencil sketch on plain card stock inside.

It was the drawing of a waiter, a towel draped across his arm, pouring a cup of tea for a man seated at a table. The customer offered a smile of approval to the man serving him. Above them were the words of the waiter, "Would you like another?" The sketch was well drawn and I wondered if Hale had done it himself, but I was completely puzzled as to its meaning. Below the sketch Hale had written, "I'm very sorry about all the trouble this has caused. Thank you for coming to see me. I didn't know they would tape record."

I had trouble reconciling the apology with the somewhat eerie sketch. It was rare indeed to receive a letter from a penitent but this bizarre situation created strange twists and turns. For a fleeting moment I thought I might return to the jail for another visit. However, I considered the escalating publicity, coupled with my own good reasons for distrust of jail authorities, and decided it would not be wise. Although I didn't understand the meaning of the sketch, I appreciated his expression of regret and decided to accept it on face value. Perhaps the drawing was Hale's way of sending a message that he meant no harm. Whether it was meant to be sincere or not crossed my mind, but I had no valid reason to question his "I'm very sorry." I felt both sad and surprised—surprised at receiving this unexpected note but sad that he too, as penitent, was being pulled into this complicated mess.

Before long, though, the most poignant apology of them all touched me significantly for its sincerity. It was from Roger, my contact at the jail. He regrettably had resigned his ministry at the jail immediately after he learned of the taping—a ministry he loved and for which he had given years of his life in service to the incarcerated. I knew that Roger's sense of failure was tangible and that resigning his position after this event was a painful way to say goodbye but I could identify with with his reasons. In the weeks following the taping, I had become concerned about his health, and I soon discovered that the shock of the strange developments in the case had taken its toll on him.

I had met Roger when he first arrived in Oregon from California to be closer to his daughter about a year before the secret taping. Shortly after his arrival, this 83-year-old man asked if I would be the priest-on-call should inmates at the Lane County Jail ask for my pastoral services. Despite his failing health, Roger was an independent spirit who remained insistent about living on his own as long as he could so I made arrangements to visit him at his apartment in a refurbished older hotel in downtown Eugene.

Roger greeted me with a smile, "Good morning, Father, please come in." He appeared thinner and more bent over than I remembered, but he was gracious nonetheless. I couldn't help but notice the unmade bed, dirty dishes in the sink, newspapers piled in one corner, and the lingering odor of bacon and eggs. He apologized for the unkempt apartment, and then he carefully sat down across from me in a worn, dark blue lounge chair by the slightly open window that provided a cool gentle breeze.

He appeared in good spirits but there was certain heaviness to his gaunt body, now in need of an oxygen tank, which he had wheeled over next to his chair. Connected to the tank was a narrow, clear breathing tube that hung around his neck and looped over his ears as the oxygen passed through the nose attachment. He was not the same man I'd met a year before. Although he put on a strong face, I could sense he was troubled beyond his physical condition. I was not unfamiliar with visits to the sick at home and at hospitals but this one was especially personal.

He turned slightly toward me, "Father," lowering his head and gently shaking it, "I'm so sorry about what happened," he lamented. The disappointment in his voice was painful to hear.

"Roger, I am too but there is no need for either of us to feel guilty about this. You did nothing wrong." I did the best I could to reassure him that he was not to blame for anything.

"I just don't understand how this could have been done," he said. "I've never heard of such a thing!" More agitated, he began coughing.

"Roger, I don't understand it either," I said, attempting to comfort him as I placed my hand on his back. "It's a terrible offense but the church is fighting for the right thing."

He agreed but remained incredulous. As a life-long Catholic, he understood the iron clad confessional seal and the deep intrusion that had occurred.

"I should have been more careful," he said.

I sensed he was a man who would not hold grudges but might well remain completely baffled. While I did not belabor the point, I did my best—as I attempted for myself—that he should feel no personal responsibility for this. I wanted to be fully attentive to him in this moment as a pastor but I noticed he was growing more fatigued.

The rest of our conversation was small talk—pleasantries about his neighbor down the hall, the weather, his daughter, stories about his deceased wife, and fond memories of raising his family in southern California. Roger said he was thankful I'd come by and let me know, that in spite of his failing body, he was doing fine. His positive, independent streak served him well.

I could, however, see how much more tired he had grown in the course of our visit. I stood up, as did Roger, though a bit more gingerly than I. We shook hands, and with a gentle pat on his back I reassured him of our prayers. He smiled and offered the same. I left with some satisfaction but I didn't have much hope about his physical improvement. About two months later, his daughter told me that her father had died peacefully and received the final sacrament of anointing for the sick from the pastor of the downtown parish he attended. His remains would be taken back to Los Angeles and buried next to those of his wife.

His daughter was relieved her father had found peace, but later told me, "He never got over what happened at the jail." Roger's touching "I'm sorry," though unnecessary, was heartfelt and heartbroken. There was heaviness in me, realizing that I too would have to face the loss of my own father in the coming months. As so many times in our lives as priests we receive much more than we give from those we visit. My brief time in knowing this kind man became a sermon on the value of a life lived unselfishly.

Then, an entirely unforeseen letter was received from Judge Bryan Hodges, the same judge who had signed the search warrant to listen to the tape. This action had penetrated the seal of the sacrament further, allowing other ears to hear and recorders to transcribe.

On May 28, Judge Hodges wrote:

"Dear Fr. Mockaitis,

While I do not want to do or say anything to cause any adverse consequence to any party involved in any pending legal case, I feel a deep personal need to apologize to you . . .

"It was certainly not my intent to cause you anguish or grief in this situation, but I do recognize that effects can be just as real whether caused inadvertently or not.

" . . . I did not have any kind of knowledge that the taping was going to occur and absolutely did not, and would not, allow or permit or authorize any such taping to occur. Many people have accused me of such pre-approval, but that simply did not happen. My involvement did not begin until well after the taping had been done.

"Despite contrary appearances, I do have the highest respect and regard for spiritual and religious values in general and feel our society needs more, not less, of such values. For special reasons, I believe prisoners need clear and easy access to spiritual counsel and it is not my desire or intent to impede that in any way.

" . . . I will be among those asking the next legislature to amend current Oregon law so as to prohibit police and prosecution authorities from intruding on holy ground in any way similar to what was done in this instance.

"Sir, I am heartily sorry about all aspects of this situation, including my involvement in it, and hope to meet with you for further discussion as to the background and circumstances of this matter when the cases are finally resolved. In the meantime, I pray God's richest blessings on you and your wonderful work."

Sincerely,
(Signed-Judge Bryan Hodges)

I was taken-a-back by this unexpected letter since I never imagined I would receive such an apology. I wasn't sure what the judge was seeking. Yet, it did sound more sincere than the district attorney's efforts. While I didn't feel Judge Hodges had deliberately targeted the seal of the sacrament, he was, at the very least, aware of its significance—or so I thought. In this weird mix of apology and cooperation, I ultimately concluded some were "just doing their jobs."

However fair or unfair, I found I had become more suspicious of motives and reasons and had to remind myself that I was likely overly sensitive to people's intentions. These were unfamiliar feelings in my life as priest since our parishioners are often straightforward and respectful with us. However, to me, there was more in it than met the eye. While there was no malice in his letter, it added more fuel to the fire of my suspicions surrounding the real motives involved in the taping. The letter pushed my buttons. I found myself picking apart the words he chose and questioning the sincerity of this form of an apology. How could I put this unusual letter aside?

Judge Hodges wrote, " . . . my involvement did not begin until well after the taping had been done . . . ."

Yet, he had signed the search warrant on April 23, the day *after* the taping had occurred. I had to wonder about what sort of involvement he may have had beyond that date, although his name was never mentioned in any other context. I found his phrase, "Sir, I am heartily sorry . . ." to be a curious choice of words considering the traditional prayer offered by a penitent after the confession of sins begins, "O my God, I am *heartily sorry for having offended you* . . ."

The letter troubled me, but I needed time to reflect on this. I also felt his letter was an effort to defuse any accusation of guilt in the eventuality of a personal lawsuit for damages that I might initiate. At the time I had no plans to do so, but it remained a possibility. Besides, I doubted one could sue a judge under these or any particular circumstances. I did, however, know my personal desire for justice was interfering with my judgment therefore I concluded that his letter was a well-intentioned effort. Nonetheless, I was not able to let go of all doubts but I do believe the judge was seeking some form of reconciliation. His part was small in this process so I folded the letter back in its envelope and filed it away as one more strange development in this case.

*   *   *

After all this private, public, and printed apologizing, my thoughts raced in all sorts of directions. The protest of the Vatican, the United Nations committee on religious freedom, countless newspaper headlines, phone calls from television networks across the country, mention of this by national news anchors, and longer opinion pieces by respected journalists, such as William Buckley, indicated behavior well beyond socially "unacceptable conduct." While Mr. Harcleroad admitted his action to be an "unacceptable" intrusion of the priest-penitent privilege, he minimized this action by claiming his behavior was "legal and ethical," which struck me as a razor thin interpretation of the law based on allowing surveillance in a jail visitors' area.

I was also mystified by the matter-of-fact tone Mr. Harcleroad proffered in the words from his statement: " . . . legal and ethical . . ." If this was considered ethical behavior, what would be considered unethical? In the world of law, however, ethical codes and moral codes may not agree. Ethics reflect standards of behavior judged by conduct that involves, "dishonesty, fraud, deceit, or misrepresentation," or conduct that is, "prejudicial to the administration of justice." (American Bar Association).

The lighting rod was not that the clergy-penitent privilege was questioned by the state, a fact that took me time to discern, but was it appropriate to apply it in a jail setting considering the need to investigate a heinous crime? Far more attention was paid to the need to investigate the suspicions against Hale as that was their bottom-line explanation. That privilege was sacrificed for what was determined to be a higher purpose. The clergy-penitent relationship and the free expression of religious belief have been commonly respected throughout the history of this nation.

The autonomous nature of a Church, and the government's constitutionally protected mandate to not interfere in the operations of a religion was at the heart of the Church's stand in this case. The district attorney's public display of contrition, I felt was offered more to seek the sympathy of voters who had just returned him to office for another term the day before this apology was offered. Yet, I was emboldened to continue the fight for justice all the more.

*   *   *

It wasn't long before a contrary opinion from the public spoke out. A letter to the editor appeared in *The Register-Guard* written in support of the district attorney:

"My hat's tipped to District Attorney Doug Harcleroad for admitting that his decision to tape the priest/suspect confessional conversation was " . . . within the zone of societally unacceptable conduct." Everyone makes mistakes, honorable citizens admit them . . .

" . . . Clearly, the clergyman should be morally and legally obligated to report any information as regards the life-threatening safety and imminent welfare of others, not matter how said information is obtained. Sacrament of reconciliation, or otherwise . . .

"As both a medical doctor and doctoral student in psychology, I am required by law to report to the authorities if I even suspect that a case of child abuse has occurred. Verbal admissions are slam dunks, cans of corn, pieces of cake, you report! . . . The public is more sacrosanct than the individual. Confidentiality should have limits, don't you agree? . . . Why should the clergy/parishioner relationship be any more sacred than that which I have with my patients?"

The Church did not hesitate to respond with the same conviction. At an official Archdiocesan news conference, Fr. Mike echoed our reaction after the private apology with the district attorney and judge at St. Paul's:

"While we accept Mr. Harcleroad's apology and we are glad that he admitted he was wrong to authorize the recording, we don't feel he addresses two critical issues: destruction of the tape and a written guarantee that there will be no future occurrences. We welcome his apology, but this has never been an issue with Doug Harcleroad. This has never been about personalities . . ."

" . . . The suggestion that maybe we should be quiet on this in the hope that it may not happen again, well, that's the type of pressure that has been brought on other groups in history when they exercise their freedom . . ."

Public reporting carried the same theme in more forceful language. Through their consistency, I could not help be impressed by the now broad reach of this story. Two editorials appeared in Oregon's state-wide paper, *The Oregonian,* and *The Register-Guard* carried his apology in a front-page story with the headline: **Lane County DA Asks That Jail Tape Be Sealed.** *The Oregonian* entitled their commentary: **Apology Is Appropriate** and **A District Attorney's Confession.**

The Register-Guard stated: " . . . Mr. Harcleroad's apology was offered facing overwhelming public pressure . . ."

The Oregonian editorials took a more expansive view: " . . . The widespread reaction has been that the taping was wrong—if not because the law says so, then because conscience, tradition, church teachings and instinct say so . . . ."

The second editorial stated more emphatically: " . . . we have our doubts that this was legal . . . we hope Harcleroad joins the Archdiocese of Portland in asking the judge to destroy the tape and any transcripts of it. They are, after all, the shameful legacy of what he himself now calls 'societally unacceptable' conduct . . . ."

William Donohue, spokesman for the *Catholic League for Religious and Civil Rights* in New York reacted vigorously in an article from his journal *Catalyst* entitled: **Oregon D.A. Yields After Bugging Priest in Confessional:** "*The Catholic League* scored perhaps its biggest victory yet in pressuring the district attorney from Lane County, Oregon into apologizing for authorizing the bugging of a priest in the confessional . . .

" . . . We were looking for a statement that he was wrong legally and wrong morally . . ." (*Catholic League for Religious and Civil Rights.* Catalyst July—August, 1996.) These words supported what I felt was missing from the district attorney's efforts but it was best that it come from someone other than myself.

Then the *American Civil Liberties Union* spoke and felt the Church was taking a risk by insisting the tape be destroyed: " . . . If they lose, they run the risk of opening the door for other jurisdictions to make these tapes." (ACLU Oregon member Dave Fidanque).

Within a month, signs were now posted in the jail to notify visitors their conversations with inmates might be monitored. Since I had been given no indication of that at any time when visiting the jail, I welcomed this long overdue warning. I knew of no priest, however, either in Eugene or elsewhere in the state, who was ready to visit inmates for purposes of confession any time soon. Some were reluctant to visit at all. This was very sad, yet I could empathize with their reticence. However, the Archdiocese in a letter to priests asked pastors who may visit the jails and be requested to hear confessions, instruct the penitent to not verbalize their sin. They were to direct the inmate to silently reflect on their sin, express their sorrow and receive absolution. It was an unfortunate fallout from this affair and a form of the sacrament I had never experienced.

We were at a temporary impasse. The tape remained in Mr. Harcleroad's possession, but the more complicated issue had come from Hale's attorney, Ms. Terri Wood, who sided with the state in this matter. She too asked the tape be preserved for the integrity of the investigation and the upcoming trial of her client. It appeared that everyone's rights were placed in jeopardy.

While we knew the legal implications of this case stretched beyond Oregon and the Catholic Church, moral principals of privacy, conscience, and the value of the sacred were also at risk. Yet, I wondered how a sacrament of the Catholic Church could be considered evidence in any trial: admissible or not. What sort of complicated mess had now been created? My sense of personal violation as confessor remained strong so I needed to take this to prayer as I wanted to sort out the many thoughts and feelings which raced at me. Most of all, I needed to face the anger I carried which both troubled and emboldened me. It was time to take off my roman collar as such and just be myself before God.

*   *   *

By now I had concluded that Mr. Harcleroad, while not an enemy of the Church, nor a villain, nevertheless was responsible for this behavior due to his, at best, poor judgment in his approval for the secret taping. However, he had extended an apology, imperfect though it may have been, so it was right to not turn this into personal judgment. In the end, it was a sad self-created event in which the obstinacy of the state and the insistence of the church had taken this issue to a new level.

The promised prayers of many carried me through this, a support group of brother priests were sympathetic, but I had lost all respect for the district attorney and his officials. Though I remained determined to stay on task, I wanted to forgive so that I could more easily live with this. As a Christian and as a Catholic priest I had no other option but to forgive. It was not easy—deep forgiveness never is—and I began a long, internal quest to let go of negativity and personal attack, which would cloud the real issues before us if not dealt with.

If forgiveness meant "letting go of grudges" I felt I could do that. What I did know is that I wanted to inflict no harm, whether in legal action or in speech, while at the same time, to never forget the evil that had been carried out and not be denied right justice. I needed to come to the Lord and pray for healing in my heart so that I could stop letting my resentment eat away at me. The whole affair humbled me but I was struck by how my own pastoral advice to others as confessor or counselor would need to be applied for myself.

So one night I walked to the church, with the scriptures in hand. I took to prayer the names of the district attorney, the judge, and those who continued to perpetuate the strife between secular and religious issues.

As I entered the church, the large, clear side windows allowed artificial light from the street to stream through while the shadows before me offered a comfort in this familiar surrounding. It was good for me to be here but the red colored candle positioned in the sanctuary next to the tabernacle reminded me that I was not alone. Here I would find God but I wondered if He would remain silent.

I walked slowly down the aisle and entered the front pew, knelt down, looked up at the burning red candle light, and thought, "What next,

Lord?" My eyes darted to the larger than life-size crucifix on the back wall and I could not help but recall how this entire event had become a call to surrender myself in the midst of a yet unresolved decision. I then sought an answer in the Bible I had brought with me as I let the scriptures speak for themselves.

I sat down, picked up the Bible and opened to whatever passage would present itself. My eyes fell on a passage from the prophet Jeremiah and I then began to leaf through the entire book of Jeremiah. I marked those passages which resonated with my feelings: "Let me witness the vengeance you take on them, for to you I have entrusted my cause, (12:20) . . . Tell me Lord, have I not served you for their good? (15:11) . . . Go down to the palace of the king of Judah and there deliver this message (22:1)."

This collection, in the larger context of Jeremiah's writing, began to make some sense, however uncomfortable that became. After a time, I closed the Bible, placed it next to me, closed my eyes and rested my hands, open on my lap. I realized the anguish Jeremiah suffered. More than any other prophet of ancient Israel, Jeremiah revealed the affliction of his call to be prophet. With emotions far greater than what I felt, Jeremiah pleaded with God, over and over again, that the burden of a prophet was heavy but in the end he accepted his call to carry God's word to his people.

I began to see, though I was far from this ancient prophet, how this legal drama had become a Jeremiah moment for me. I had a great deal of anger to admit and I discovered that I had never decided where to place it: At the church for what felt like my day in court was denied? At the district attorney? At Conan Hale? At the media and news print reports? At our attorney? At God? At myself for causing this whole event?

I began to understand that part of my restless spirit was this free-flowing, unreasonable anger. While it gave me strength to carry this forward, I would only find peace if I could decide where to place this anger appropriately and allow it to not get the better of me. In the end, I didn't want to carry this at all but allow it to become righteous anger, which could be turned into a force for good. Here I began to know how that process had already begun. I then lowered my head in acceptance but concluded that would take some time.

After a period of time, I stood up, bowed to the God before me, slowly left the Church, and crossed the parking lot to my home. I left with a direction where I would find the power to forgive—not in my head alone but in my heart where God can be found. Still, I refused to deny the ugliness of what happened at the jail. Forgiveness would not mean to forget.

CHAPTER 5

Why Catholics Confess:
The Sacrament Made Clear

*   *   *

"And what did God do? First of all He left us a conscience, the
sense of right and wrong: and all through history there have
been people trying (some of them very hard) to obey it." (C.S.
Lewis—*Mere Christianity*)

*   *   *

I am aware that some readers may be puzzled or uninformed about this
Catholic sacrament entitled, *Reconciliation* (confession) and perhaps why
the state's violation was found to be so offensive. For those outside and
within the Catholic faith, who may have some need to work through this
idea of confession, the bottom line question which this case presents is:
What limits are appropriate, if any, on information that may be necessary for
public safety? While confidentiality is universal in the helping professions,
and is the professional expectation of other clergy as well, the sacramental
seal allows for no exceptions and is therefore considered as a privileged
conversation, at least by the church. Yet, what if a serious crime is confessed
with potential danger to the community? What of child abuse? Should such
crimes be an exception to "no exceptions?" Some wondered if indeed this
event at the jail was an isolated, one-time-ever intrusion, or is there some
historical footprint of similar face-offs between the rights of church and
state which have challenged the claim of this privilege? We need to look
back much farther than the beginning of this country.

In the early centuries of Christianity, those who were found guilty of serious offenses such as adultery, murder, blasphemy, or apostasy (the formal abandonment of the Christian faith) discovered their forgiveness was tied to a rigorous, public penance which sometimes lasted months or even years before those sins were deemed forgiven. The seal of confession, in this public sense, was non-existent since those who had committed such crimes were considered a danger to the community and must repent in a way that others will understand the seriousness of the punishment should they too fall in the same choices. Therefore, people would often delay confessing their sins until much later in their life—even until their deathbeds if possible. From this perspective, it was a tough time to be a Christian!

During the seventh century, however, Irish monks and missionaries traveled the countryside, bringing their familiar monastic practice of private confession to the European continent. Acting as both spiritual director and confessor for the penitent, public penance for sin was no longer required before one could be reconciled to the Church community. For obvious reasons, this practice caught on quickly and has been the norm ever since. Private confession opened the possibility of repetition of the sacrament, allowing Christians to receive absolution as often as they needed during their lifetimes with the guarantee of a confessional seal.

Before the Reformation (1500's), England was a Roman Catholic country and the seal of the confessional had great authority in the English courts. There seems to be no evidence which would cause one to doubt that a rule declared by the Church, including the seal of confession, would not have been universally respected because the Church declared it to be so. In fact for civil courts to disregard that expectation would have caused continuous conflict between two powers: civil and religious. Such a practice would have sharply diverged from the nation's religion. In fact, from the pre-Reformation times, there is not a single instance which suggests that the laws of evidence did not respect the seal of confession. The *History of the Laws of England* (1195) describes the presence of an archbishop, three bishops, and three archdeacons who sat in the Court of the King's Bench. From that same source we read:

" . . . *it is by popish clergy men that our English common law is converted from a rude mass of customs into an articulate system,* . . . *when the 'popish clergymen' no longer sit as the principal justices of the king's court, the golden age of the common law is over . . .*" In light of our present day system with the separation of church and state, this comment is intriguing.

Yet, after the Reformation a period of fierce persecution of Catholics broke out. Still, there is strong evidence that even in the post-Reformation period the common law of England recognized the privilege of confession, except in the case of treason. The greatest challenge to the seal was posed in the courtroom and the witness-box. Priest's themselves were excused from any punishment if they identified a criminal accused of high treason from information offered to them in the confessional. Treason seemed to be the only crime for which the seal did not apply.

The priest-penitent privilege in France and throughout Catholic western Europe received public notice at a very early date. Such recognition supported the sacredness of the confessional seal. In France it was a well established principle that a confessor could neither be examined in a court as to the content of whatever was revealed to him within a sacramental confession and if any admissions were disclosed from that conversation, it would neither be received nor acted on by the court, what today we may recognize as inadmissible or hearsay evidence.

From the Parliament of Paris in 1580, we hear that a confessor could not be compelled to disclose the alleged accomplices of a certain criminal if those names had come to the confessor within the sacramental conversation—this even if the criminal was going to the scaffold. Yet, even during the period of the Inquisition, one writer states: "never, in no interest," should the seal of confession be violated. The back and forth opinions are many between the safety of the state, the person of the King, and the rights of the church and religious freedom. Respect for the conscience of the penitent, whoever that may be for whatever he or she may have done seemed to be more respected in France than in England in the post-Reformation period.

By 1892, however, the French penal code states: "*The ministers of religions legally recognized are obliged to keep secret communications made to them by reason of their functions: and that with regard to priests no distinction is made as to whether the secret is made known in confession or outside it . . . the exemption from giving evidence is extended to priests with regard to the matters confided to them in confession . . .*"

Generally, then, it appears that the seal and its "no exceptions" clause has gone through a kind of evolution over time but effected in the realm of politics and the fight between civil and church authority. But, it seems that from the beginning the relationship between priest and penitent has always identified that privacy and confidence was part of the ethical obligation of clergy. In order to respect the conscience of the penitent and for their protection, whatever information had been offered during a sacramental confession was protected.

In the United States, the clergyman-communicant privilege is seen as both stemming from First Amendment protections and the common law. It appears as a reflection of both the English and western European experience but now with the present day force of Constitutional and statutory protections. All fifty states have adopted statutes providing that at least some of these communications are privileged. The challenge to the seal today arises mostly in cases of divorce proceedings and criminal (primarily child abuse) and ministerial misconduct cases. The established autonomy of a church in this country may be the strongest foundation on which the privilege is built.

Thomas Jefferson, in an 1808 letter written to a Rev. Samuel Miller, stated:

"I consider the government of the U.S. as interdicted by the Constitution from intermeddling with religious institutions, their doctrines, discipline, and exercise. Certainly no power to prescribe a religious exercise or to assume authority in religious discipline has been delegated to the general government."

From the viewpoint of the church, the purpose of the sacramental confession is the good of the penitent and the purpose of the sacramental seal is the protection of the Sacrament of Penance itself. As recently as a 1980 Supreme Court decision in Trammel v. United States, the court ruled that "the evidentiary privilege protecting private communications between a priest and penitent, attorney and client, and physician and patient . . . are rooted in the imperative need for confidence and trust."

In further discussion and similar cases to this one, although the specific circumstances of the jail-house taping were unprecedented, the definition of clergyman and the circumstances under which he/she were operating, in their professional capacity or not, and the intent of the penitent in approaching the clergy member, have been the greatest challenge in the delicate definition of privilege. Yet, the force of the First Amendment and the Church autonomy doctrine has held the greatest weight of protection in this country. One thing was clear from the moment we left the district attorney's office with his refusal to destroy the tape: this case would potentially bring the seal of the confessional under a never-before seen constitutional scrutiny and could lay the ground for either a new definition of the priest-penitent privilege, thereby affecting other private communications, or bring a new strength to the law. It was possible to go either way.

From that perspective, whether it is the King, the state, the district attorney, or a priest, an Archbishop, or the Vatican, the historical footprint of this case seemed to fall in line with the past. However, our present understanding of privilege and confidentiality offers a distinction which makes the subject of this book especially historical in this day.

The church and the legal team for the Archdiocese claimed that this was not a conversation subject to confidentiality alone but rather a legal *privilege* to be protected. The attempt before the district attorney to ask for the immediate destruction of the tape, reinforced by the Vatican itself, was a blatant demand in support of the confessional privilege.

In response, the state claimed that the conversation between priest and prisoner was at best, a confidential one and treated it as such, considering the right of those involved with Hale's case to be the only exceptions to the information on the tape. While confidentiality refers to the ethical expectation of several professions: medicine, law, religion, psychology, journalism, and others, the church demanded that whatever Hale may have revealed in his communication with the priest, is *privileged*, therefore not subject to a third party knowledge.

However, it is necessary to remember that this case was specifically about protecting the integrity of the sacramental seal, and its "no exceptions" clause. Not to compel a judge to rule that all communication between priest and individual, if offered outside of the sacrament, be also considered privileged. That lies within the realm of professional confidentiality but contains certain exceptions which could compel any priest to reveal. After all, this country is governed not by church law but by civil law.

While for many Catholics, this sacrament has a certain value, and in some parts, there are signs of a new appreciation for this sacrament, it is clear both in the religious and secular world, there is misunderstanding around the confessional seal and the necessity for the sacrament itself. In some parts, there is general indifference among some Catholics who, for a variety of reasons, make only occasional use of the sacrament today.

It is not uncommon for Catholics and those outside the Church, raised over the last forty years, to have the same questions: *Why does one need to confess, and why to a priest? Why can't you just ask for forgiveness from God directly? What do I confess?* To see these questions in the broad picture of modern day culture is helpful to understand what the church was up against and why the state felt it was justified in the act of taping. Some readers may hear a kind of apologia for the sacrament but my intent is not to convert, rather to provoke thought and perhaps to inspire.

*   *   *

The Catholic Church holds *sacraments* as a primary focus of religious life. At significant milestones of life such as birth, adolescence, forgiveness, community life, the union of marriage, the ordination of a minister, sickness, and death, the sacraments ritualize those moments when people come together for those transitions of human development. In faith, it is believed that Christ becomes present and that his ministry of healing, forgiveness, unity, and love are continued within the community of the church through those sacred rituals. There are seven sacramental moments and this particular violation, the subject of this story, was understood to blatantly interfere with the human conscience, in one of the most personal encounters we might find, where forgiveness is offered. These sacred rituals have been identified in number for almost 500 years, since the Council of Trent.

But, today we live in an age of moral confusion. We priests know that every Sunday we face diverse opinions about the church, politics, and everything in between. The concept of sin itself and personal responsibility have wavered. The secular gospel of today's popular culture has preached its message well in the name of tolerance. While the no-judgment acceptance of human diversity is in itself a positive moral stance, human behavior does call for a certain critical eye; a need to identify the truth. If everything is accepted in the name of tolerance or fear of political correctness, nothing is wrong. In the extreme, a person may deny the very existence of absolute morality in favor of a certain situational ethics. "It depends on what the situation is," might be a common opinion as the "situation" would depend on individual circumstances; a subjective judgment rather than an objective morality.

The pervasive attitude of self-determination and human arrogance in today's society shrinks from the truth of sin and its effect upon the larger community. "You have no right to impose your morality on me!" or "Who is to say what's right?" or "As long as I don't hurt anybody." or "I have a right to this, not because I need it, but just because I can." or "There is no right and wrong. It all depends on how you were raised," are common justifications.

Yet, our advanced age of technology and science has demystified the sacred and holy, claiming no reality outside the material world. The influential writings of Darwinian atheists such as Christopher Hitchens and Richard Dawkins who identified faith as "one of the world's great evils . . . a kind of mental illness," (*The Selfish Gene,* Richard Dawkins, 1989) dismiss the mystery of sanctity that can only be embraced through faith. The sacraments themselves are those spiritual gifts, human in their substance but mysterious in their power, that brings a sense of the sacred into our lives through religious ritual and provide a kind of stability in the midst of a changing culture. Awe and wonder touch deep within our fundamental, inner sense that reality is more than we perceive in this realm of time and space. When that basic religious sense is violated people of faith cry out.

But, our demand for answers to the unexplainable, in favor of scientific, technological, and intellectual proof, minimizes the willingness to accept interventions of the Divine. If a segment of our secular world is not dismissive of religion, it is often apathetic. Even some people of organized religion seek the easy way; the way that is not controversial; the popular way that places more emphasis on feeling good rather than seeking the truth. On a personal, individual faith journey, rather than a journey within the community of believers. The necessity and value of confessing one's sins to another can seem as a challenge to individuality.

While human behavior is anything but an exact science, today's persistent individuality causes many to brush aside sinful behaviors or questionable motives. The individual person is seen as the determiner of truth, rather than an outside code of morals and ethics imposed as a common rule of right and wrong which decide acceptable behavior.

As a result, we are losing a sense of the common good to the pre-eminence of relative morality. Truth is determined not by a universal standard but by social, cultural, historical, or personal circumstances. In such a case, personal accountability becomes less important than "moving on." The present narrative reveals an aspect of this morality as the state justified its behavior determined by the situation in the jail which was used to absolve the investigators of any responsibility since this was claimed to be in the normal course of jail house monitoring.

The church, however, judged the offense based upon a common code of absolute moral and ethical standards: the taping could not be justified regardless of the situation. The end desired by the state did not justify the means used to achieve that end which violated the higher ethic of religious liberty and personal privacy. The covert manner used to carry out the scheme would be judged as sinful in religious terms. Although "sin" is a religious concept, many label such harmful behavior as a "misunderstanding or poor judgment." As the district attorney stated in his apology, "We're only human. We make mistakes." So, if there is no sin, forgiveness is perceived as a kind of secular virtue which promotes order in society, rather than conversion of heart.

But, for people of faith, forgiveness is a transcendent virtue. Forgiveness of sin is among the most distinctive characteristics of the Christian faith, a value believers hold dear. Tied to this knowledge is our perception of God as judge, which touches on our understanding of eternal reward (salvation: union with God) and eternal punishment (eternal separation from God: hell). However, the Catholic Church does not view belief in heaven and hell as an indication of a vengeful God. To do so would be to imagine a scowling God ruled by strict justice with cold-hearted expectations who waits ready to punish even the most minor infractions; a tyrant God to be feared, not loved.

The God Jesus reveals to us is "Abba," a child's Aramaic word for Father more akin to Papa or Daddy—a merciful Father God who longs for his children to return and welcomes them home (Luke 15: 11-32). Christian forgiveness and its sacred trust is tied to this view of God's benevolence.

This is a God of love who offers us the gift of commandments or boundaries for behavior that promote order and harmony in society rather than the uncertainty of relative moralities. Forgiveness is viewed as an individual gift but one that is experienced within the context of the larger community. As a spiritual leader I have seen the force for good that reconciliation can bring.

If God is ever-welcoming, then, and eager to forgive, *Why confess?*—because we need to. This God of mercy is also a God of justice and our sins offend the justice of God, which disrupts the bond of unity with our brothers and sisters. In this sense, we bring the punishment for sin on ourselves, which is more specifically some degree of separation from God who does not interfere with our choices. God gave us a free will and he will not take it back. This leaves us free to love or not love; free to choose or not choose. Our ultimate destiny is up to us as we work out our salvation here on earth. But in the end it is our free choice, as is the decision to confess our sins and to face more deeply the duality of our human condition.

There is a story told about the famed Renaissance artist, Leonardo da Vinci that goes along these lines. When Leonardo began his painting of The Lord's Supper, his mural on a Monastery wall in Milan, Italy, he chose a handsome young man named Petri Bandinelli to be his model for Jesus. As it took the painter four years to finish his famous painting, the last character was Judas. Leonardo went into the slums and all of the dives in town determined to find someone who would embody the traitorous character described in the Gospels.

Finally, he found the perfect man who was willing to pose for Leonardo but later as he was painting he sensed there was something familiar about the man. He asked him if they had ever met before. "Yes, we have," replied the man, "but much has gone bad in my life since then." Leonardo was shocked to learn that his name was Bandinelli, and that it was he who was the model for Jesus years before.

✳ This duality of perception reminds us of sin and virtue at the same time; both saint and sinner lie within each of us. Confession allows us to recognize this duality, and in the process we receive the gift of greater self-understanding and much more. The sacrament is not only a means to forgiveness; it strengthens us to *want* to live our lives according to the high moral values Jesus has given us. To name our sin and replace it with virtue is the challenge we all face when we've stepped outside the boundaries established.

In the end, we are all called to live holy lives for it is virtue alone that inspires us; sin sickens us. The greatest among us, the saints, realized their human weakness and were quick to name their sickness. Often, at the center of identifying the sickness lies pride. Our obsession with independence—our pride—our resistance to surrender ourselves, or just simply the unwillingness to release our enormous egos is what Christian theology calls "original sin." These human egocentric challenges uphold the necessity for the Sacrament of Reconciliation.

✳ In light of that belief, this particular opportunity between priest and penitent whether behind bars in a jail cell, in a church, hospital room, home, or wherever requested, is a call to an interior conversion of the heart. In the simple ritual of confessing, we remember Jesus' invitation to be healed and to receive the strength of his merciful love. The foundation of Christ's moral teaching is that God *does* forgive sin and we are therefore called to forgive one another. Such extraordinary forgiveness is possible and we need not look far to find examples in our own day.

In October of 2006, a letter was sent to Pennsylvania newspapers from a member of the Amish community, Benuel S. Riehl. He extended condolences and prayers to the families of the killer of five Amish school girls at a one-room school house in Bart Township, PA. For this group, non-violence is a rule. Forgiveness is a necessity which avoids the endless angst of retribution and restores the process of one's own healing. The Amish have demonstrated the answer to violence is non-violence; the answer to hatred is love. It is possible for an entire community not to allow anger to become rage. This amazing example, and others like it, though rare, gives us all pause.

The late Pope John Paul II gave us a further amazing example. After his recovery from the failed assassination attempt in St. Peter's square on May 13, 1981, the Pope sat face-to-face with the very man who had intended to take his life, Mehmet Ali Agca. Sitting in Agca's jail cell, the Pope forgave him for what he had intended to do. It is alleged that Agca said to the Pope: "Why are you still alive?" No condemnation, only the gift of forgiveness and love was offered by the Pope. What transpired in the mind of Agca is unknown, but the Pope exhibited a power which the Gospel challenges us to embrace: "Love your enemies and pray for those who persecute you." (Matthew 5:44.)

But why confess to a priest? It is important to note that Catholics do not believe any individual priest, no matter how virtuous or saintly, has the power to forgive sin. That power belongs to God alone. But God, in Christ, has chosen to exercise his power through the Church in general, and in the priesthood specifically. Yet, every priest is basically faceless to the penitent and the promised seal of the sacrament is the unqualified guarantee of respect for the one confessing. As priest and penitent meet, both recognize this holy moment and instinctively bring an expectation of the most sacred privacy to the interaction.

When one confesses to the priest, who represents the community of believers and the person of Christ himself, the confidence of the sacramental seal creates an environment in which telling the truth is possible. For both priest and penitent to know, with certainty, that their exchange within the sacrament is forever sealed, is the only way in which the courage of personal revelation would be possible. The faith of the penitent and priest, expressed within this setting of trust, offers a freedom to respond to God's grace of mercy and forgiveness. I had no reason to believe that my conversation with the inmate was monitored and therefore, a certain freedom was assumed. The appearance of confidentiality was tangible as it has always been throughout my pastoral life.

This begs the next question of what to identify as our sin. *What do I confess?* The verbal naming of sin first demands an informed conscience and an understanding of one's place in the community of believers. Conscience guides our behavior based upon the lived experience of our Christian faith, personal prayer, that "inner voice" which speaks to our hearts day by day. Through correct information taken from the scriptures, for Catholic Church teaching is rooted in the scriptures, and from the lived experience of our faith, better known as tradition.

Moral choices are "lived" within the human family, and as such, they are balanced against where we stand in light of those relationships according to our understanding of God's law rather than individual, personal moralities. Countless Christians of various denominations agree on this sense of absolute morality. Yet, while we are not responsible for what we do not know, we should not hide from what is more certain to be sin in our lives.

However, culpable ignorance, as moralists may explain, is the failure to exercise ordinary care to acquire knowledge. If I fail to inform my conscience when the information is available to me, for that failure, I would be held responsible, but not for lack of knowledge through no fault of my own. Sin is committed through free choice guided from a rational mind, which violates a properly informed conscience. Virtue, in the same way, respects the conscience and divine law.

Our sins may take form in behaviors that erode the unity of the Christian and non-Christian family in many ways. There is a social dimension to sin that we often overlook. Catholic people have a great sense of community life in which our mutual relationships hold important value. In today's modern world, that social dimension is particularly significant due to the impact our behaviors have on the world community: the illicit use of drugs is among behaviors or addictions that harm our own bodies and damage relationships with those around us; the horrendous crime against the innocent: the sexual abuse of children and other questions of modern medicine challenge the ethical use of science—because we can do something does not mean we should; pollution of God's creation and the social and economic injustices of our times are all among the ways in which our flawed humanity expresses its less than virtuous nature.

We know that crimes and grievous offenses need to be confessed, but gossip, vengeful thoughts, exploitation of others, dishonesty, lack of forgiveness and the unwillingness to let go of past offenses against us, are but a few behaviors that can lead to repeated or greater sin, and therefore more of what "sickens" us. Often these sins stem from pride as do disrespect for the sanctity of human life in all its stages of life or a resistance to surrender ourselves and confess to what we know is contrary to the will of God. Once we confess, the burden of sin is lifted from our shoulders and God's forgiveness opens the door to conversion in our hearts. It is understood as a grace given to resist such behavior in the future. It flies in the face of today's individualism and recognizes that my actions, my choices, damage more than just myself.

The confession of sin to another brings us to a healthy responsibility for correction in our lives. Sometimes a priest will suggest combining words with action in the form of penance which establishes the principle of justice necessary to correct any damage done by our choices.—something beyond a specified number of Hail Mary's or Our Fathers. He may suggest combining action with words of prayer, such as recommending a penitent embrace greater kindness or tolerance to remedy the cause of a particular occasion of sin, or reflect on specific passages from scripture, or to go and be reconciled with someone who has been offended. When appropriate, the Church encourages this sort of extended spiritual direction. Within this shared sacred offering of words and action we are not only forgiven, but set free and guided more specifically to live better lives.

St. Paul, who never hid his feelings about things, in his letter to the unruly Galatians chapter 5: 16-26, offers a wonderful examination of our conscience as he contrasts the works of the flesh and the fruit of the spirit: "Now the works of the flesh are obvious: immorality, impurity, idolatry, hatred, rivalry, jealousy, outbursts of fury, envy, drinking bouts . . . the fruit of the spirit is love, joy, peace, patience, kindness, generosity, faithfulness, gentleness, self-control . . . ." If one wonders what they should confess, just read these words and ask, "Is this me?"

There is no magic ritual or formula that compels God to forgive. He forgives us because he chooses to do so, and we need to seek that forgiveness both in and outside the sacrament. Since we believe in a God beyond ritual, forgiveness is not restricted to this sacrament alone, but the sacrament offers a unique moment to face our sin and hear the healing words of reconciliation. And, as one would never act as his own doctor, or as her own lawyer, it is wise not to act as your own confessor. The fact that we have all failed at times, does not mean that we are bad people. We are a people who should be struggling against our fallible nature, wanting to be better than we are. And in that struggle alone; in that sincere desire to be better, there is virtue. In that light, it is understandable why those in jail or prison, with such limited freedom and "surrounded by darkness" as Conan Hale once put to me in a later conversation, have a particular right to exercise their faith if they so choose.

God does not give up on us. Time and time again he renews his covenant with us. Within every confessional encounter, we have the opportunity to accept Christ's gift of renewal, to embrace conversion of the heart.

*   *   *

The value of this privileged relationship, with the guarantee of respect for the penitent, made the violation committed at the jail even more grievous since this inmate had no other choice. In our earlier conversation with the district attorney we were determined to find an answer. But the gulf between church and state had become deep and the stage was set for more intense public reaction. With the arrival of the new Archbishop, the issue was taken higher.

CHAPTER 6

Public Confession

*   *   *

"Real forgiveness means looking steadily at the sin, the sin that is left over without any excuse, after all allowances have been made, and seeing it in all its horror, dirt, meanness, and malice, and nevertheless being wholly reconciled to the man who has done it. That we can always have from God if we ask for it." (C.S. Lewis-*The Weight of Glory*)

*   *   *

When Bishop Francis E. George arrived as the newly appointed Archbishop of the Portland, Oregon Archdiocese near the end of May, many wondered how this newly appointed spiritual leader would handle the delicate legal and religious issues no Bishop had ever faced before. He soon proposed a way to exercise our First Amendment rights so violated by the surreptitious taping: a public celebration of the Sacrament of Reconciliation would be the key as a way to affirm the continued value of this privilege and to offer this public statement as a reaffirmation of religious liberty.

Parishioners at St. Paul felt honored to be among the first parishes in the Archdiocese to welcome the newly appointed Archbishop and particularly grateful for his specific support in the case. In the eyes of the Catholic Church, and many others, there was no difference between a public reconciliation service and the private confession of inmate Conan Wayne Hale. So, on a Saturday afternoon in early June, we vested in long white robes with knee-length priestly stoles draped over our shoulders, and then we gathered outside the church entrance to greet congregants.

By now the church and Archdiocesan officials used words such as "clandestine, surreptitious, conspiracy, eavesdropping, unconstitutional, illegal" when referring to the case. By contrast the state's description as, "legal, ethical, evidence, compelling reason, conversation, within our rights," created a legal tangle no one would have imagined. Now, St. Paul Church would be at the center of such descriptions, much less the continued focus of a media blitz.

Archbishop George was a man with an impressive, scholarly mind, an engaging smile and ready handshake. He greeted everyone warmly. The Archbishop wore the familiar miter—a tall white hat with two pointed panels front and back—which symbolizes his responsibilities as high priest of the local church. He stood with Bishop's staff in hand, called a crosier, marking his position as chief shepherd of the Diocese as we waited for the opening hymn.

Standing nearby, I overheard parishioners express their sorrow and confusion over events at the jail. For life-long Catholics, this was seen as a personal affront as well as an attack on the Catholic Church. The Archbishop, however, remained upbeat and smiling for he knew that the Church was not about to give up its fight—no matter what lay ahead.

To the sound of soft reflective music, the last of the congregation took their seats. Although surrounding area pastors had invited their parishioners, until the actual service no one was sure how many would come out on this sunny early summer day. By the time five other priests, the Archbishop and I had assembled, I was encouraged to see over 200 people already had arrived. Although not an enormous crowd, it was more important that this service be held for its symbolic value. No particular public expression or words were organized by civil authorities which made the lack of opposition noticeable. The state players remained silent outside the courtroom or legal briefs.

Piano and flute began to swell as the choir opened with the words of a familiar hymn, "Come back to me with all your heart . . ." The congregation stood and joined in song. We priests then processed side by side down the center aisle with Archbishop George entering last. We bowed toward the altar in the sanctuary of this simply adorned church, entering the front pews on either side, while I, as pastor, and the Archbishop took our places on a raised platform behind the altar. The music then ended.

Archbishop George moved his hand in the sign of the cross and proclaimed, "In the name of the Father, and of the Son, and of the Holy Spirit." He then extended both hands toward the people and said, "Peace be with you." The community responded, "And also with you." The new Archbishop welcomed everyone and thanked them for coming in light of such an unusual state of affairs. After his opening prayer, which plead for God's mercy, as everyone sat for the reading of the scriptures, all eyes turned toward the lector who stood at the pulpit.

The silence was pierced by the voice of the reader who proclaimed two passages, one from the prophet Hosea and the other from St. Paul. Both readings offered reassurance of God's mercy and our victory in Christ. The choir followed with the "Alleluia," and everyone stood for the proclamation of the Gospel. The parable of the Prodigal Son was the Gospel story. There I read, " . . . we must celebrate and rejoice, because your brother was dead and has come to life again; he was lost and has been found." (Luke 15: 32). I returned to my seat as Archbishop George approached the pulpit. The congregation remained silent as they sat; not even the occasional cough was heard. The Sunday Mass one month earlier with Fr. Mike and his passionate words echoed this moment. Archbishop George spoke directly to the people about the tense situation foremost on our minds. In a clear voice he stated:

"That taping was morally very wrong and probably constitutionally wrong in a country that prohibits interference with religion." Archbishop George reinforced the Church's demand for destruction of the tape and he reassured parishioners of the confidentiality they rightly possessed in the sacrament of reconciliation. He referred to the taping as " . . . the most important issue in the Archdiocese." Barring something else, it would remain crucial until the matter was settled.

He described the sinful nature of the secret taping, then further emphasized that making amends for wrongdoing is an essential part of forgiveness. "Amends must be made." He then added forcefully, with the gesture of his hand, "That tape must be destroyed. It was wrong to make it, and it is wrong to play it." He warned that the taping, if allowed to go unchallenged, would set a very dangerous precedent, and not just for Catholics. "I ask you to pray that justice be found here."

Then, he balanced his strong comments with a reflection on the forgiving love of Christ expressed in this most sacred of privacies—confession, and encouraged the congregation to continue their prayers for the pending legal fight. "The Church must forgive the moral wrong that has been committed. We _must_ forgive." He reminded everyone about the proper Christian response in the face of such a blatant offense. Speaking as a pastor, he invited us to approach the sacrament with complete confidence in faith that the protected status quo would be maintained. In such surroundings, this sacrament would not be violated. It was time to seek the forgiveness we are promised in the sacrament.

As he closed his remarks, we all knelt and joined in a communal reflection on our offenses against God and neighbor. This collective "examination of conscience," in which we identified the duality of our human nature, brought a litany of reflections reminding us of our sins before God and each other. I gazed for a moment at the congregation assembled with familiar faces I had seen under very different circumstances and was reminded about my own need to repent. Though I was their pastor, neither I nor any priest is immune from human weakness.

When the communal examination of conscience ended, the Archbishop, other local priests, and I went off to more isolated areas of the Church to hear parishioners' individual confessions in private spaces, out of earshot from others.

Throughout the church, people waited in lines as they reflected silently on their lives to confess to any one of the priests or to the Archbishop himself. Soft, soothing music played in the background to enhance the contemplative atmosphere. In this public service of reconciliation, visible exchanges between priest and penitent are evident but the seal remains in place for no words are audible to those in line who maintain a respectful distance.

After one has confessed, a brief discussion between priest and penitent often takes place in the form of brief personal counseling or spiritual direction. It may be advice the priest himself was given in his own search for forgiveness. As a matter of justice and to heal the harm confessed, the priest then assigns the appropriate penance, as was described in the previous chapter.

Penitents are then invited to express their sorrow through a specific prayer, or they are free to pray spontaneously. The specific prayer, formally referred to as an "Act of Contrition," may be as simple as, "Father," (addressed to God the Father), "I have sinned against you and am not worthy to be called your son/daughter. Be merciful to me, a sinner." It also could be a more lengthy prayer or a reading of Psalm 51 for example. The point is that we express our sincere sorrow and resolution to do all that is possible in our efforts to avoid sin in the future; to resolve to do the best we can day-by-day with whatever supportive sources or methods are available to us.

Acting in "persona Christi" *the person of Christ,* the priest then raises his hand over the penitent and prays the words of absolution, calling on God the Father and the Holy Spirit to bring pardon and peace to the penitent. He then prays: " . . . *I absolve you from your sins,* in the name of the Father, and of the Son and of the Holy Spirit." Then, a short proclamation of joy may be offered by the priest, "God has forgiven your sin, now go in peace." As is the nature of this sacred privacy, these exchanges will forever remain between the penitent and Christ himself,

The joy of forgiveness whether felt or convicted in faith, may be analogous to other gratifying or blissful feelings we experience when we hear good news: Your physician tells you that you're healthy after your exam; so too does this divine physician, in the voice of the priest, declare you forgiven. One spouse forgives another and they embrace; they are reconciled. A jubilant parent rejoices in the safe return of a lost child.

Penitents usually leave one by one while a sense of gratitude prevails. The conversation between Jesus and Peter is a poignant reflection in gratefulness. Peter asks Jesus, "How many times should I forgive my brother, seven times?" Jesus responds, "Not seven times but seventy times seven times." (Mt 18:21-22). This extravagant forgiveness is the mercy of God that we take hope in as we live our lives between saint and sinner.

In the sacramental "I'm sorry," heightened by the presence of Archbishop George and my brother clergy at the public service of reconciliation, I also felt encouraged to delve more deeply into the process of my own need to forgive and to move my anger to a force for right justice. I had looked evil in the face, I called it what it was, I was not excusing it. I also needed to admit I did not wish well to those who were responsible for the act. I had been both priest and penitent while I felt something inside was sustaining me.

As parishioners completed their individual private confessions on that day in June, the impact of the ongoing media blitz softened for me but I also knew that the protracted legal battle before us had just begun.

*   *   *

By now, Fr. Mike Maslowsky had become the carefully worded voice for the Church's position in this case. County authorities had no intention of changing their position. Neither did we. We would need to go higher in the court—probably to the federal level. Meanwhile, the Vatican added another voice to its protest. Secretary of State, Cardinal Angelo Sodano spoke unequivocally, " . . . The Holy See considers it reprehensible and unacceptable that this tape could be used in any way."

Still, I wrestled with the desire to have "my day in court." There was a part of me that felt this event was somehow ripped away from me from the beginning as church authorities very early stepped in. However, this was not a battle I could win on my own. Though I sensed some resentment, as priest, I wanted to remain a loyal "son of the church" and found I was torn both ways. Jesus teaches the Christian ethic to "love your enemies and pray for your persecutors . . ." (Matthew 5: 44). I knew this well, for I gave the same advice to many I had counseled and my earlier time in prayer and reflection was a foundation on which I stood.

Yet, much more than my personal feeling was at stake here. While the Catholic Church is a recognizable leader among religious bodies of this country, for the sake of defending our American way of life where church and state have lived together in relative peace for more than two hundred years, the legal drama was worth pursuing. It was no surprise that the ACLU with its strong defense of privacy rights, a secular organization, early on spoke out in defense of the church's efforts.

All the more, the broad implications of this event were reinforced in personal ways. In the midst of all the news swirling around, I received signs of solidarity from other Christian congregations. Fr. John Hondros, a local priest of the Greek Orthodox faith, sent these kind words as he echoed our sentiments and offered support:

> " . . . Forgive me for not approaching you sooner, but I want you to know you have my prayerful support. Though we have some theological differences regarding the sacrament of confession, as an Orthodox I empathize with your Church for the lack of reverence and dignity given from public officials.
>
> "From the onset of the Church, Christians have been encouraged to 'render to Caesar what is Caesar's' namely to be obedient to the laws of their land . . . . Christians have been willing to die to protect the integrity of their faith . . . Justice is not served by injustice, but by integrity and decency. True Christians remain faithful to God and the state, but not to godless justifications and spurious justice."

(End Letter)

We live in a day of competitive morals and ethics.

CHAPTER 7

Confession Goes on Trial

*   *   *

"Men do not differ much about what things they will call evils;
they differ enormously about what evils they will call excusable."
(G.K. Chesterton: *Illustrated London News*—1909).

*   *   *

By now, just a month after the taping, a grand jury had indicted Conan
Hale for aggravated murder. Archbishop George and our entire legal team
were determined to move forward with our case and found ourselves in a
delicate position of not wanting to interfere with the state's interests in the
prosecution of the case against Conan Hale now made all the more definite
by his charges. The art of diplomacy, as we priests often need to exercise in
this helping profession, is essential when faced with a conflict of opinions.

But for the church, accusations against Hale were not the issue. Willful
interference on the part of state officials created an entanglement of
Constitutional proportions. On one hand, I felt hope that our efforts would
be successful; on the other, I remained cautiously suspicious due to the
opinions expressed by the district attorney and those responsible for the
future trial of Mr. Hale. Who did what and when became the focus of legal
exploration as religious principles were juxtaposed to that of the state as
our case was likely pushed to a higher level.

To that end, in a separate proceeding, Tom Dulcich sent a letter to
Judge Jack Billings, Circuit Court Judge in Lane County, Oregon, who was
appointed to try Hale's case. The letter included the petition and supportive
materials requesting the tape's destruction. For the state, the admissibility

of the tape as legal evidence in the homicide investigation was the crux of the issue and would have to be settled.

Judge Billings responded to Tom's petition but ordered the tape and transcript preserved. The court decided it would not accept any intervention on our part since our request did not present a "justiciable controversy" and therefore had no standing. In his letter the judge wrote:

> "Dear Mr. Dulcich,
>
>   " . . . To the extent that the Petition which you have submitted on behalf of the clergy attempts to intervene in the pending criminal case involving the above-named defendant, that is not permitted by law. To the extent that the documents you have presented to the Court represent an effort to commence some separate proceeding, they do not state a justifiable controversy. They are therefore not suitable for filing. Accordingly, I'm returning your papers to you, together with your filing fee.
>
>   "Finally, I enclose for your information a copy of an Order . . . Please be advised that except upon further motion of one or both of the parties, or upon directive of some higher court, this Court will not consider, under any circumstances, the action which your clients desire."

While Judge Billings was not involved in the jail taping his uncompromising attitude was frustrating. To be dismissed outright was unconscionable to me. This level of what felt to me as dismissive of our interests was new ground to be sure in my life as priest. While respect is something that we need to earn with our people, such indifference to religion was a reality check that reinforced the need to be all the more resolute.

The church now had no other choice than to push this case to the Federal level. As the media blitz continued, the existence of the tape itself remained a public controversy, but the state held tightly to its position that our case did not meet the standard of "justifiable controversy," despite ongoing negative reportage.

Therefore, our attorney Tom Dulcich filed a complaint listing seven requests with the Federal District Court. The wishes were unequivocal and left no doubt as to the position of the Church:

1. A judgment mandating that defendants provide the names of all persons to whom the contents of the tape have been divulged, a description of all forms of copies or transcripts made of the tape, indicating when and by what means the copies or transcripts were made and what disposition has been made of them.

2. A judgment that defendants Judge Leonard and/or Judge Billings order that the tape and transcript of the Sacrament of Penance and all other printed or electronic progeny be destroyed or turned over for destruction.

3. A judgment enjoining defendants and all agents, employees and all persons acting in concert with them, either directly or indirectly, including all John Does and Jane Does, from further publishing or disclosing in any manner whatsoever the contents of the tape or transcript.

4. A judgment enjoining defendant Harcleroad as the person responsible for the Lane County District Attorney's Office, and all of the employees and agents thereof, from future interception of taping of the Sacrament of Penance and similar confidential religious communications at the Lane County Jail.

5. A judgment declaring that the specific Oregon statute concerning the priest-penitent privilege violates the First and Fourteenth Amendments to the United States Constitution and/or the appropriate sections of the Oregon Constitution, if used to monitor, intercept or record the celebration of the Sacrament of Penance or other confidential religious communications.

6. Such preliminary relief by way of restraining order or preliminary injunction, which might be necessary.

7. A judgment in favor of plaintiffs to reimburse the Archdiocese for all of its legal costs relating to this case.

These non-negotiable requests while separate from Hale's process were inextricably woven within it. I stood in this mix of demands and legalities, and found myself going along in a world far from my pastoral life. The usual day to day responsibilities aside from this process became an island of sanity in the midst of this indecision. Then, days before we carried this forward, a momentary setback caught us off guard.

* * *

On the morning of July 31, a few days before our scheduled appearance in Federal Court in Portland, I received an unexpected request: "Father Mockaitis, I think you need to come join Fr. Mike and myself as quickly as possible. We have a phone call into Terri Wood's office and plan to speak to her tomorrow. This is worth a try." It was Tom Dulcich whose voice expressed great urgency.

As counsel for Hale, Ms. Terri Wood had filed a motion for discovery; it included a request to listen to the taped conversation. Judge Billings had already moved to seal the tape as requested by the district attorney, but the Judge and the state did not oppose the motion from Ms. Wood and Judge Billings expected her to appear before him with a request to listen to the tape. Tom feared the outcome but sought a temporary restraining order to prevent Ms. Wood from listening to the tape until we were able to explain our position. The meeting in Portland would be our first effort to speak directly to her and explain why playing the tape once again would make the offense more grievous. I was determined to be there and did what I could to rearrange my time. The next morning I found myself returning to the law firm in Portland but wondered if the effort would be worth our while.

Despite my doubts and inner resistance, I stepped determinedly from the underground parking lot into the morning sun. A blast of fresh air helped to ease the tension, until I glimpsed my somber face mirrored in the glass and chrome doors of Tom's office. I was troubled. Our attempt to put off Ms. Wood felt desperate.

It was 9:45 a.m.—long enough for Tom and Fr. Mike to fill me in before our 10:00 o'clock. We clarified our objections and prepared to begin a dialogue with Hale's counsel for the first time. I wondered how Ms. Wood would perceive us. Tom believed she had not heard the tape, only that she felt she had a right to hear it. As advocate for Hale's interests, she certainly had a right to examine any potential evidence. Yet, why was she asking for this now? Perhaps she feared we might be successful in having the tape destroyed. Yet, Hale's trial was not imminent; it was scheduled for nearly a year from now. Did she think we were meddling in her client's case where she felt we didn't belong? Hale had pleaded, "Not guilty." The new paralysis between the interests of state, defendant, and church made this all the more intricate.

We entered the conference room, closed the door behind us, and sat down around a large oval table. The round, flat telephone-like device with a multi-directional speaker, placed at the middle of the table, was apparently designed for use by several participants on conference calls. Tom dialed Ms. Wood's office.

"Ms. Wood," said Tom, "Tom Dulcich here with my client Fr. Mockaitis and also Fr. Mike Maslowsky, who is representing Archbishop George."

"Hello Gentleman," she stated flatly.

"Ms. Wood," continued Tom. "We need to discuss a few things with you in regards to the disposition of the taped confession between your client, Conan Wayne Hale and my client, Fr. Mockaitis."

"What sort of things?" she inquired.

Tom and Fr. Mike explained why the church continued to demand the tape remain sealed. As of May 22nd, on orders of the district attorney, the tape had been sealed by Judge Billings, who knew it was not to be listened to and its contents not to be used in any trial. Was this gag order a guarantee that the tape would remain sealed?

After further discussion on the merits of our case and the sacramental value of the tape itself, Ms. Wood, who spoke with self-assurance, reminded us of her responsibilities as Hale's counsel and why she felt the tape was relevant.

"That tape recording would be the best evidence of what was said during that conversation," she remarked. "Hale's recollection is circumstantial evidence of the contents of the tape. The statements he made to Fr. Mockaitis are material to guilt or innocence. I have been told the state intends to seek the death penalty if he is found guilty. My client has a constitutional right to evidence and the state defendants' have a constitutional duty to preserve it."

She questioned the efforts of the church to intervene in this case. "The state is the adversary and the only party which may object to Hale's use of evidence at his trial."

"Ms. Wood, while we understand your position," Tom Dulcich responded, "This has become a very delicate and complex legal case. We felt this would be the best time to explain our position to you. The interests of the church have been made clear around the religious nature and purpose of Fr. Mockaitis' visit to your client. It is our contention that the gag order imposed by the district attorney should be left in force. This would give everyone some time as we wade through all the legal issues facing us. Not the least among those are likely constitutional violations. Mr. Hale's trial may not be for some time now and we are set to appear in federal court for a hearing in just three days."

Then, she challenged our attempt to claim a tape we did not own. But, Fr. Mike responded without hesitation:

"No one owns that tape!" Fr. Mike shot back as he leaned forward toward the phone on the table, "Hale doesn't own it; we don't own it. If anyone owns that tape, it is God himself. And it must be returned to God."

Then she startled us and admitted, "Well, I've already listened to it."

A collective sigh of frustration filled the room as she calmly admitted the tape was heard again. Tom and Fr. Mike soon composed themselves and firmly expressed their objections. I said nothing as I sat back, angry and resentful. Terri Wood had got word of the impending restraining order filed by Tom Dulcich, so she took advantage of an early opportunity to listen to the tape. She felt justified in her action by the urgency of her situation and the interests of her client. Ms. Wood's skillful coup in listening to the tape felt rude and offensive. Her behavior reinforced the state's belief that the church was interfering in the homicide investigation.

Between "the tape must be destroyed" and "the tape must be preserved," I found this ongoing tune wearisome. But, now the tape was used regardless of the church's request. Staying one step ahead was our game plan and it seemed to be the defendant's as well. I wondered if Tom and Fr. Mike shared my irritation. They were clearly not happy about it and I joined them in that thought.

We were likely to have a much better chance for a fair hearing before the federal judge with the hope that the concerns of the church would now be treated fairly and of relevance to this case. With this hope, our meeting was essentially over. Apologies from Tom and Fr. Mike were offered for calling me to Portland in what they had hoped would be a more positive outcome.

As I left the law offices, the late summer morning felt heavy. Far from any semblance of priestly life as I felt this affair had now turned, I found myself lost in thought. I walked down the sidewalk, reflecting on how low this attempt to investigate charges against Hale had gone and how I could not flee my direct involvement in this legal web. I sat on a nearby park bench. The sun was warm but shaded by the trees and I found the cooler air welcome. I turned back to an earlier time in my life, far removed from this bizarre situation yet strangely related to it. It was an easier time, less complicated but was at the root of our efforts to defend the right of religious liberty. I wrote down thoughts which helped to center myself in this undesirable mix of sacred and secular.

Anyone who attended Catholic school in the 1950's and early 60's can likely recall their first experience of confession. After careful preparation by the Nuns, our second grade class was ready to name our sin, confess to the priest, and enter the confessional for the first time. As we stood in a single file line along the walls of the Church, one by one we entered a dark room about the size of a hall closet, closed the door, and knelt down facing an opening in the wall the size of a small window, behind which sat the priest in a similar size booth waiting to slide back a wood covering over his side of the window, which remained covered with an opaque cloth so the anonymity of the penitent could be respected. I began to review my sins as I waited for my classmate on the other side of an adjoining booth to finish her confession. I remembered how I disobeyed my parents, told a lie, maybe called someone an unkind name, or was selfish in my behavior. And, I had to be sure I had the correct number of times for each sin listed properly.

Then, the priest drew back the wood covering as light from his side caught my darkened eyes with a momentary glare. I dutifully began, "Bless me Father for I have sinned. This is my first confession . . ." I remember speaking with exacting numbers about the types and frequency of my sin. As the priest patiently listened, he offered his response in a soft voice, just loud enough to be heard but never with anger or admonishment. His suggested penances of "Five Our Fathers," or "Three

Hail Mary's" were expected. After leaving the confessional booth, I would join my classmates and kneel with hands folded in silence in the church pews to fulfill my penance. I found myself filled with a sense of relief, as much as an eight year old child was capable, and the knowledge that I was free of something that held me down.

As thoughts of our present day odd experience returned, I wondered if anything significant might come of our time before the judge in Portland. Far from any appearance of my life to this point, I stood up, and determined my call to priestly service would carry on despite the uncertainty of the future.

The drive back to Eugene was a simple one, the traffic relatively light. The monotonous low rumble of the tires lulled me into a mood of passive resignation. I buried my negative thoughts along that familiar stretch of highway and was distracted by radio chatter as I longed to return to the more familiar and reassuring parish life.

There was another matter, however, on a more deeply personal level, over which I had no control whatsoever. My father's health had deteriorated to the point that my family and I recognized the end was not far away.

I found myself conflicted, both for my mother's future and what life would be like for all of us without this man. My dad was a down-to-earth, practical businessman who had looked at life in mostly black and white terms. His persona had become part and parcel of who we were as a family and to our friends. Everyone admired my father for his hard work, honest business dealings, and enterprising spirit. I held tight to those memories.

But now, his deep, commanding voice, and tall, large frame were diminished by his thinner, weakened body. As a family, we knew the chances were unlikely that my parents would see their fiftieth wedding anniversary to be expected in about two months. Keeping my father comfortable now was primary to my mother's and my family's concerns. My father was at peace about his condition. Despite the welcome compassion of Hospice volunteers my mother insisted on being present for him until the very end. An only child, she had missed that chance when her mother died and said she would not let it happen again. While I shared my families' concerns, for me the hearing in Federal Court was on the horizon.

CHAPTER 8

Challenge on Disputed Facts

*   *   *

"In the old days it was supposed that if a thing seemed obviously true to a hundred men, then it was probably true in fact." (C.S. Lewis—*God in the Dock*)

*   *   *

After the upsetting action of Hale's counsel, it was troubling to know the church was aware of the extent to which information from the tape had been made available to others as it had now to Ms Wood. Although this was usual procedure with any criminal investigation, it was clear that by now the unique circumstances surrounding the tape made this anything but a routine piece of evidence. As part and parcel of my pastoral life, confidentiality and ethical standards of behavior are rightly demanded by the people we serve. To have this tape thrown around from person to person with no regard for the church's concerns at this point was a mockery. We were far apart, church and state, on the value of the tape and as one who appreciates fairness and tries to be so in my ministry, I could not help but be scandalized.

The tape was transcribed into a typed document and we had been given the names of those who had already listened to the recording: Joseph Kosydar and Patricia Perlow, who were Deputy District Attorneys in Lane County and Jeffrey Carley and Brandy Selby, employees of Lane County, had either some or full knowledge of the contents of the tape. In addition, on Hale's behalf, Terri Wood's co-counsel Steve Miller had listened to the tape.

Briefs presented by the defendants had the full support of the state's Attorney General and Assistant Attorney General as well as counsel for Mr. Harcleroad and Judge Billings. As we neared our time before a Judge, the position of both sides was clear.

The church never challenged the importance of a fair trial nor questioned the value of law in this land. Rather, it was the proper use of that law, established in our Constitution, which the church was seeking. The founders of this country were wise enough to see value in crafting autonomy for a religious body where its citizens are free to worship as they please without government interference. I realized how naïve I was and possibly so many Americans on the presumed safety of this right granted to us in this nation. Any look at history reminds us that this right was not won easily and in so many parts of the globe, has often been either limited or abolished all together. This began to shape up as a real test of our Constitution and carried with it more ominous implications.

The state pointed to the aggravated murder charges and the possibility that Conan Hale may face a death penalty. But the greatest new claim of the state was their fear of, " . . . a devastating effect both on the state's ability to prosecute Hale . . . for heinous murders and on Hale's ability to defend against such charges and avoid the death penalty . . ." Further, in agreement with the state, the issue for Terri Wood remained her same concern for a fair trail.

Whether Hale's trial would be "devastated" by the destruction of the tape was a cause for debate. Right now, the action was centered on the church's response to the state's efforts as legal briefs and affidavits were prepared. Our chances of gaining any respect for the sacred felt tenuous.

In fact, in a challenge "on disputed facts" submitted for this hearing, the state wrote:

> "Although Fr. Mockaitis' encounter may have been clerical, it was
> not sacramental . . . Plaintiffs presented no evidence to establish
> the allegation in their complaint that, in fact, Fr. Mockaitis ever
> administered the sacrament to Hale . . . (court brief).

I was puzzled by this stand which allowed the state to consistently refer to my encounter with Hale as a "conversation, not a sacrament." Was this a role reversal on who has authority to determine a sacrament? While this may indicate the distinction between legal and theological terms, as conversation or sacrament, the signal sent by the state was to dispute the church's theological position. Though the state did not challenge the broader sacramental theology of the Catholic Church, the stage was set for someone to determine, in a court of law, whether the theological position of the church or the secular position of the state was definitive. It was a weird mix of the sacred and secular.

Yet, the Archdiocese had already offered a reliable explanation through the affidavit of a well-known Canon lawyer who was the best source to explain the autonomous nature of the Church and to articulate its sacramental theology. Fr. Bert Griffin was a well known voice among clergy both locally and nationally so his opinion was sought and respected.

The Reverend Bertram Griffin, J.C.D., came with impressive credentials: a doctorate degree in Canon Law from Lateran University in Rome; adjunct professor of Canon Law at Catholic University of America in Washington, D.C. He had also served as president of the Canon Law Society of America and Judicial Vicar of the appeal court for the religious courts in Dioceses throughout Alaska, Idaho, Montana, Oregon, and Washington.

Fr. Griffin explained:

" . . . The seal (and corresponding duty of confidentiality) comes into existence wherever a penitent indicates to a priest his or her intention and desire to confess sins. With that expressed desire for reconciliation a 'sacramental forum' is established. The establishment of the 'sacramental forum' means that everything communicated to the priest comes under the sacramental seal of absolute confidentiality. This seal . . . applies to everything which is communicated within the 'sacramental forum . . . The seal binds even if all the elements of the sacrament are not fully present. Once the 'sacramental forum' is established and the Sacrament of Penance is begun and confession of sins initiated, everything revealed by the penitent falls under the sacramental seal of confidentiality.

"It is for the Church, not governmental instrumentalities, to determine what constitutes acts of worship in general and the Sacrament of Penance in particular . . . The Church regards as outside the competence of civil, secular authorities a determination of what constitutes the seal of the confessional and other aspects of church religious doctrine.

" . . . The continued existence of the tape and transcript . . . sends the message to Roman Catholics and other persons of religious faith that the governmental authorities may intrude upon a ministry which is by religious doctrine meant to be confidential and the state can make the encounter non-confidential. It is not necessary that a penitent be a member of the Roman Catholic faith for the seal of the confessional to apply to and bind a priest, or for the Sacrament of Penance to be performed . . .

"In all my years as a Canon Lawyer I have never heard of another instance in which governmental authorities with foreknowledge of the event intentionally and surreptitiously monitored, intercepted and recorded a priest-penitent communication, without telling the priest that this would be done. This event has caused grave concern among my fellow priests within the Archdiocese of Portland in Oregon, Catholic scholars, religious and lay persons outside of Oregon, and church officials at the Vatican in Rome, about the freedom to practice our religion without government interference in our sacramental lives, in particular the Sacrament of Penance . . ."

I wondered if the defendants had ever read Fr. Griffin's opinion since citing the claim about the legal and ethical nature of the action in the jail. In addition to Fr. Griffin, Fr. Mike and I gave our affidavits, as did the investigator who requested the search warrant for the tape, and Ms. Wood added her request on Hale's behalf.

In her affidavit, Terri Wood was in agreement with us concerning the privacy issues: " . . . Hale and plaintiff Mockaitis were similarly aggrieved by the actions of law enforcement . . . Hale never consented in fact to the recording . . . no one can know at this time how the evidence will unfold at Hale's trial . . . We pray this case not be remembered as a 'case where humans are sacrificed in the name of religion.'" (Wood, affidavit).

Church and state had drawn a line in the sand on disputed facts as the interests of both sides weighed heavy. In the face of opinions, neither side rested. The church was not posturing to be antagonistic but only to be respected and heard in defense of itself. The state was fixed on pursuing justice.

*   *   *

Now three months into the process, on the morning of August 4, I woke to the familiar rhythm of this legal drama. While I felt duped into this cycle I had no choice in leaving it. Clothed in my clerical garb of black trousers, black shirt and white Roman collar, I added my black suit coat, my "power suit" as a parishioner had once referred. I smiled half-heartedly as I recalled this comment and thought if there were ever a time for the right use of power, now would be the time! I never imagined that my priestly, pastoral role in offering this man sacramental forgiveness, would be turned into a liability. Why was all this time and effort spent on hearsay evidence? I inhaled deeply in front of my bedroom mirror then walked out into the still warmth of this mid-summer morning.

I prayed the day would go well, a prayer that under these circumstances I had never prayed before, as I backed my car out of the driveway. My mind was numb—saturated with too much information. Through this entire ordeal I was learning to surrender that which I could not control and recognized that I was being invited to take my faith to a deeper level. I often preached to my parishioners, "Trust in God," or "Have faith" or "Hard times can be a moment of grace for you." This was indeed a time to practice what I preached; it would be a good test for there was a greater good than my own at stake.

As I traveled north, the brown, sun dried fields on either side of the freeway with the low ring of the Cascades to the east and the coastal range foothills in the distance to the west were a familiar sight. A tractor plowed up clouds of dust under the bright August sun. The car radio confirmed the larger world—reports of political elections, the grinding war in the Middle East, and of course reports on the state of the economy. Everything around me held some parallel meaning to the secret taping. The state claimed a devastating effect on their efforts but I drew a strange comparison to another event that same year.

That year the Olympics were held in Atlanta, Georgia. It was a peaceful effort to promote harmony among athletes and, by association, nations of the world—a sacred pursuit. But, in the third week of July 1996, a bomb at those games killed one person and injured over one hundred. The violence shattered a dedicated effort to promote peace and cooperation between human beings through these Olympic Games. The sacred had been dishonored in the midst of an effort to maintain a sacred harmony between potential enemies. I quickly turned off the radio for some blessed silence. Two polarized positions were held firm as we moved to our hearing in Federal Court.

As I neared Portland, the freeway traffic grew dense. I slowed and turned to the downtown area, then parked in the same underground garage which I'd entered just five days earlier when we'd experienced our disappointing conference call in Tom's office with Hale's attorney, Ms. Terri Wood.

Archbishop George, Fr. Mike, and our resident Canon lawyer and theologian, Fr. Bert Griffin were waiting with our defense team. All were dressed in their appropriate power suits: black clerical attire and white collars mixed in with the professional suits and ties of attorneys. Added to the priestly garb was the obvious sign of Archbishop George's position as chief shepherd in the Archdiocese: He wore a long, bright gold chain around his neck with a simple gold pectoral cross attached—the sign of a Bishop's authority over the local Church. I was surprised that Fr. Griffin appeared unusually tense; his facial expression tight, his posture stiff. I could empathize with him. Surrounded as I was by these heavy hitters, my role here felt more symbolic: *the* priest/*the* penitent. We were all feeling the strain.

Still, we managed to share small talk and disarming laughter, all the while maintaining confidence in the proceedings ahead. It was time to move forward with resolve. We left the law office and strode out into the summer sun, crossing downtown streets toward the imposing stone Federal Courthouse just a few blocks ahead. Our walk was brisk with Fr. Mike leading the way. By the time we reached the front steps, a hungry pack of news reporters had gathered. They waited on the steps, directly in our path. We quickened our pace to the mixed chorus of "Archbishop! Fr. Mockaitis! Fr. Maslowsky!" Archbishop George only acknowledged the reporters with a slight smile and wave of his hand, "Good morning everyone." We quickened our pace up the stairs, in the front doors and completed the security ritual through the metal detectors just inside. The elevator to the third floor was just down the hall. Relieved, we then walked calmly, our footsteps echoed on the dark tile covered, concrete floor.

When the large oak doors of the courtroom were opened, I noticed that the sunlight streaming in from side windows formed shadows on the jury box and its twelve empty chairs. On the other side sat the state attorneys, Hale's counsel, and the jail personnel dressed in their tan and dark blue sheriff's and police uniforms. Surprised for a moment, I saw the female officer who had been at the reception desk outside the visitors' area of the County jail on the morning I had heard Hale's confession. I'd seen her infrequently before that notorious visit since there were others who would sit at that desk so I wondered for a moment why she was there. Then I surmised she would have been the only eyewitness to my entering the jail that day so her presence here was logical. Though I had been going to the jail for only about nine months, I didn't recall her name for I was more focused on the reason for my visits. This mix of prime players created a kind of surreal moment.

Our attorneys identified this incident as a "case of first impression," which is a case or controversy over an interpretation of law never before reported or decided on by a court. We had no inkling what this first day of hearing on disputed facts before judge and attorneys would bring. I hung on a hope that maybe we would receive some respect and our positions and concerns would be taken seriously. It was nearly 10:00 o'clock.

Side discussions filled the large room as we repositioned our chairs, arranging ourselves in the proper places. I sat between Archbishop George and our assistant attorney Brad Nye. Fr. Mike and Tom sat next to each other to our far left. Parties for the State were seated in a similar grouping, according to their order. We heard, "All rise," and stood in our places. The judge appeared, Judge Owen Panner. He was a thin man with gray hair and sharp facial features. He glanced our way, smiled, and invited us to be seated for this "first impression" hearing.

Polite but hurried, I surmised the Judge wanted to begin straightaway in order to confront the fewest objections, and settle any disputes early on. Would my conversation with Conan Hale be determined sacramental and confidential based on the facts of this case or would the state resort to some strange twist in which church teaching would be minimized as irrelevant? This was the fundamental issue we faced in the beginning. I hung my hopes on the protection of our First Amendment rights and the good wishes and prayers of many parishioners with whom I had grown to feel a kinship as this case developed.

"Good morning," greeted the Judge from his bench above lawyers, priests, and Archbishop. "Where do we stand now? Apparently Mr. Harcleroad is prepared to concede that it was a confidential communication." And so the debate began between Greg Chaimov, State's attorney, and Tom Dulcich, attorney for the Church. Mr. Chaimov surprisingly took a somewhat conciliatory position.

As he stood, Mr. Chaimov added, "Beyond that, your Honor, we were willing to concede as the plaintiffs have alleged that this conversation was subject to the seal of the confessional which, as I understand it, is a significant obligation imposed on Fr. Mockaitis."

"Well by the Church not to talk about what happened during the conversation," Judge Panner continued, "I understand also that the plaintiffs have conceded that the person making the confession has a right to have it disclosed if he wishes to do so; am I correct about that?"

"Not quite, Your Honor," said Tom Dulcich as he stood by his chair. "The distinction is very important to my client." The he turned to face each of us as he introduced us to Judge Panner: Archbishop George, Fr. Mike Maslowsky, law associate Brad Nye and me.

"Good morning," said Judge Panner as he nodded in our direction. Tom then continued his explanation around the status of the sealed sacrament and its relationship to the penitent.

"It is allowed under canon law, the rule which governs the Roman Catholic Church, for a penitent to speak outside the sealed confession as to what occurred; however, the penitent cannot release the priest from his inability of testifying in church court nor in civil court about what occurred within the context of a conversation between himself and any particular penitent."

Tom's point, by emphasizing the sacramental seal, challenged the objections of the state that my encounter with Hale was not sacramental. I sat there in silence but knew that for the state to object to this would be interpreted as the government objecting to the religious discipline of the Catholic Church, a place I assumed they couldn't go.

Tom objected to a two-line statement in the last paragraph of the State's brief, then read that statement:

"If, as plaintiff now asserts, the contents of the tape are irrelevant, we would expect them to drop their allegations that Fr. Mockaitis administered the sacrament." Tom looked up from his paper and continued:

"I might state for my client, as I am required to say, we cannot say my client did not celebrate the sacrament since the only client of mine which was involved was Fr. Mockaitis. Archbishop George knows nothing about the communication; Fr. Mockaitis cannot say what occurred. So, we cannot say whether there was absolutely or not absolutely." I never thought such a private moment would become so public.

Mr. Chaimov responded with a further implication: "As I understand, the Church is alleging and intends to assert in their case that because this tape includes the administration of the Sacrament of Penance, what to the Church is a communication between a person and his God as mediated by a priest, is so important that it outweighs what right Mr. Hale has to a fair trial."

Tom rose from his chair and raised his hand as he clarified:

"Again I must speak, your Honor. As I note from the brief submitted this morning, we say that a sacrament of penance occurred."

Judge Panner explained, "I think it is going to have to be done based upon what I find in the law or based upon the nature of the communication at the outset, rather than what is contained in the recorded statement."

As I realized earlier, the matter of whether the sacrament was offered, as strange as it felt, would be established by a Judge rather than by a religious leader. Judge Panner offered this respect to the church and seemed he would accept this based on facts rather than any need to play the tape or any further explanation of Catholic theology.

I wondered about the need for further proof, however. Who might be called to testify that this particular encounter was sacramental? As I was briefly distracted by this thought, I heard "We call Fr. Mockaitis." Tom walked toward me as I caught my breath for a minute. I had no idea what sort of questions would be asked or how deeply the state would probe. My greatest fear was that I would inadvertently break open the sacramental seal. I felt as if I was on trial for doing the right thing! Tom leaned over with his hand on my back and reassured me the questions would be brief and he would jump in where needed.

I stood up and approached the bench with resolve to reaffirm what I knew was true.

With my right hand raised, I stood before the uniformed officer and "swore to tell the truth, the whole truth and nothing but the truth." Then, I added forcefully, "So help me God!" The officer broke into a smile at my extra words.

Mr. Chaimov, attorney for the state, stood before me and began the questioning: "Father Mockaitis, in your affidavit, you testified that you found Mr. Hale prepared to celebrate the sacrament of penance. Upon what facts do you base your opinion that Mr. Hale was so prepared?"

I looked directly at Mr. Chaimov and answered: "When I was called to the jail to celebrate the sacrament of penance with Mr. Hale," I explained.

"I was told by the individual who had called me there several times before for the same purpose and for only that purpose, that he had prepared Mr. Hale for the sacrament; so I presumed that he was prepared."

Chaimov returned: "Did you form an opinion about whether Mr. Hale is a member of the Catholic Church?"

"I object, Your Honor." Tom Dulcich stood and quickly broke in. "That question is going to require Father Mockaitis to break the seal of confession. May I ask a question in aid of an objection?"

"You may, "agreed Judge Panner.

"Fr. Mockaitis," said Tom as he approached me, "did you have any communication with Conan Wayne Hale of any kind before you met him in the jail on April 22 for the purpose of taking his confession?"

"No, I did not," I said.

"Did you have any information from anyone else as to whether or not he was a member of the church?" asked Tom.

"No, I did not."

Then, Mr. Chaimov, the state's attorney, resumed questioning:

"Upon what facts do you base your claim that you administered the sacrament of penance to Mr. Hale?"

I repeated: "On the facts of why I was called there," I clearly stated. "My intention in going to the jail was for that purpose only; and I fully intended to administer the sacrament of penance to the individual. Beyond that, I don't think I can say anything else."

"That's all the questions I have." Mr. Chaimov rested and backed away.

Judge Panner looked at Tom, "Any further questions of this witness?"

"No, Your Honor," said Tom.

"You may step down." Said Judge Panner as he looked at me, then turned back to the attorneys. My face felt solemn as I returned to my chair and I was relieved the questions were brief. Archbishop George offered a supportive smile as I sat down. These proceedings had taken on a surreal sense for me. It was like a parable about the search for truth and justice.

Who knew what and when would be at the root of all this. The next witness to take the stand was Cindy Sarnowski, the receptionist at the jail on the day I'd heard Hale's confession and the primary eye witness to my visit. She was dressed in the same dark blue uniform she wore on the day I saw her—her face stern, though otherwise expressionless. The state attorney began his questioning after Ms Sarnowski was sworn in and seated.

"Thank you for coming, Ms Sarnowki," said Mr. Chaimov as he approached her, "where do you work?"

"I work at the Lane County Adult Correction Center."

"What's your job there?" asked Chaimov.

"My job consists of receptionist and control duties at the jail," she stated flatly.

"Do you know Father Mockaitis?" queried Chaimov in a raised tone.

"Yes, I do," she stated.

"How do you know him?" questioned Chaimov.

With a more lively voice, she answered, "From previous contact with Mr. Mockaitis dating back a couple of years. He has been called upon to come in and speak with inmates on various occasions in the past."

Chaimov continued, "Were you working at the jail on the morning of April 22 of this year?"

"Yes, I was."

I paused for a moment in my attention and wondered, what previous contact dating back "a couple of years?" I didn't even know this woman's name until today. Her statement struck me with confusion and I wondered about the quick exchange between "Father" and "Mister."

"What were you doing that morning?" asked Mr. Chaimov as he looked at her.

With a hint of pride she answered, "My duties as receptionist."

As he calmly walked past her, Mr. Chaimov asked his question, with head raised but looking forward, "On the morning of April 22 did you have any contact with Father Mockaitis?"

She responded confidently, "Yes, I did."

Please tell the Court about that," encouraged Mr. Chaimov.

"I was expecting Father Mockaitis. We had been advised by a volunteer approximately a week prior that he was going to be coming in on that date to hear the confession of Conan Wayne Hale. We had a written request from Mr. [Roger] Lederer that we work with Mr. Mockaitis to make sure that he received prompt access to the inmate.

"Father Mockaitis arrived a little bit late. I had already been phoned by the volunteer asking me if Fr. Mockaitis had arrived yet. I said no, Roger, he has not. I told him I would call him when Mr. Mockaitis was finished. When Fr. Mockaitis arrived, he was directed in and the conversation took approximately a half an hour, I believe, forty-five minutes perhaps; he came out."

I leaned back in my chair, still puzzled by her testimony and as I listened to her. She never looked my way, her eyes fixed on her questioner. Perhaps as a non-Catholic she may be confused about the proper title for a priest but the "Father/Mr." mix in the same sentence was curious. It felt intentionally disrespectful but I wrote it off as unimportant. I found her previous statement more troubling.

I leaned over to Archbishop George and quietly stated, "I've only been going to the jail for about nine months not 'a couple of years.'" I didn't even know her name and she doesn't know me except in this context."

The Archbishop looked puzzled. "Why would she say that?" he asked.

I shrugged my shoulders, shook my head, and said, "I have no idea." As I leaned back in my chair, I felt the same indistinct feeling I'd had at the jail when I'd been surprised by her unusually curt demeanor. Was something more at play here? I wrestled with the thought of a conspiracy yet I wondered if that image was too strong. At the very least this entire affair was poor police work. However, did she have knowledge of the secret taping and was she part of what appeared to be a setup? I could only speculate.

Tom began his cross-examination about Hale's procedure to request the visit of a priest.

"You mentioned . . . a written request. Is that called a kite?"

She answered, "I am not familiar with the absolute procedure for an inmate to request to see a clergy member. We have instances where a clergy volunteer would have access to the housing. They make a verbal request or they can also write a kite, an inmate request form, to our program staff and they will follow up on that."

"Are there posted orders out in the waiting room where visitors come before they are allowed to see inmates?" Tom asked as he leaned towards her.

"Yes, there is a brief overview of the visiting rules." Ms Sarnowski said, "They pertain to social visits."

Mr. Dulcich continued, "Is it a sign that is about three feet high or so?"

"Approximately," she stated in a routine tone.

"Among those posted orders, is there a statement, 'no recording equipment allowed?" as he looked directly at Ms. Sarnowski.

Then, Mr. Chaimov interjected before this witness could complete her answer since he felt this line of questioning on posted rules was off the subject. The answer would have been "Yes," there was a line which stated, **No Recording Equipment Allowed**, as had been established earlier.

Was this a prophecy come true? Was this proof of parishioner Judge Coffin's comment made to me two months earlier about how "They created the illusion of confidentiality . . ." in the jail? Of course at that time I didn't know exactly who "they" were and I speculated again about a possible conspiracy.

While this was hardly the KGB or some CIA plot hatched in darkness, as the facts unfolded I could only consider why secrecy was so important to the success of this plan. If this was a legal act, as was being claimed by the state, why was I not warned about the possibility and why were no signs posted informing visitors of their privacy rights and why was something legal done covertly? But, the intent from the beginning was to take advantage of a situation that could only be successful without my knowledge. If I knew, it would have blown their cover. Judge Coffin's insight about the illusion of confidentiality, I concluded, was more than mere conjecture and I felt a surge of determination to continue our search for the truth.

But the illusion of confidentiality with the implication of a deceptive setup sent darkness through me. I never had the chance to rebut Ms. Sarnowski's story and no one challenged the accuracy of her testimony. My priestly life had never felt surrounded by such uncertainty. This was hardly a routine exchange between priest and parishioner.

Judge Panner was anxious to settle this matter so he moved forward with his comments on the nature of my encounter with Hale. The Judge continued:

"The question is, is it confidential based on the fact? The facts are that the state has admitted that Hale asked for the Sacrament of Penance and it is clear that Fr. Mockaitis went there to give the Sacrament of Penance. The most serious question I have now is whether, in light of the state judge's ruling already, am I too late to do anything? So, where are we?"

Mr. Chaimov looked up from his papers and asked the Judge: "Your Honor, I believe that we are still disputing whether what occurred on the tape was the administration of the Sacrament of Penance as I understand the Church is arguing."

Judge Panner with hurried firmness said: "It seems to me the parties can now complete that stipulation of facts without controversy so this matter can be decided by this court as quickly and as reasonably as possible and get this matter on to further appeal and if necessary or terminate it if possible. It appears to me that the Sacrament of Penance was the intent of Fr. Mockaitis and was the intent of Hale. Based on that I am inclined to foreclose that issue and get on to the other issues in this case.

"I am not going to read this recorded statement to determine whether this was a Sacrament. Based on that, I think it is confidential. So, that is going to be my ruling. Let's get on with this case. You've got a lot of other arguments that I need to hear, such as whether I can do anything at this time in light of what has already happened in the state court. This issue I think is resolved factually. Anything else?"

The Archbishop remained quiet as a secular ruler in this land of civil law had the final say on a religious sacrament. Although Judge Panner never challenged Church doctrine, it still seemed peculiar to be sitting next to Archbishop George, whose theological knowledge far outweighed any explanation a judge or attorney could ever present in the realm of Church teaching. By now it was clear that church and state remained as adversaries.

Still, the defense requested an additional witness be called, which struck me as a desperate attempt by the state to push the sacrament issue further.

Mr. Chaimov addressed the Judge, "I would like to call one additional witness. I believe it bears upon the finding that you are going to make."

Judge Panner answered, "All right I will be happy to hear it, call your next witness.

"Call Mr. Kosydar," Mr. Chaimov stated as he turned to face him. Joe Kosydar, lead investigator and additional participant in our initial meeting with the district attorney months before, approached the bench. I remembered the proud explanation of his autobiography in the district attorney's office and his determination to move Hale's investigation forward. I wondered if this testimony would accomplish anything.

He was sworn in, then Mr. Chaimov stood near and asked, "Mr. Kosydar, where do you work?"

"At the Lane County District Attorney's Office," he answered.

'What is your connection to Conan Wayne Hale," queried Mr. Chaimov.

"I am the prosecutor of him along with another attorney in State court."

"What faith are you?" asked Mr. Chaimov.

"Catholic," Mr. Kosydar answered confidently.

Mr. Chaimov followed, "What is the extent of your catholic education?"

"I attended Catholic grade school," said Mr. Kosydar.

Mr. Chaimov speculated: "And, as part of your catholic education, did you learn how to perform the sacrament of penance?"

"I learned how it was performed, yes." Mr. Kosydar agreed.

"Do you know the contents of the tape recording of the conversation between Mr. Hale and Fr. Mockaitis on April 22 of this year?" asked Mr. Chaimov.

"Yes, I read the transcript." Kosydar answered with a stern face.

Mr. Chainov asked, "Are you aware that the Lane County Circuit Court has ordered those with knowledge of the contents not to disclose them?"

"Yes, I am," answered Mr. Kosydar.

Mr Chaimov sped up his questions as he looked more directly at Mr. Kosydar, "Do you believe the order from the state court permits you to testify about what is not on the tape?"

"Yes, I do," stated Mr. Kosydar.

"Is the Sacrament of Penance on the tape?" Mr. Chaimov questioned.

Tom Dulcich abruptly rose from his chair as this enticing question was asked:

"Your Honor, may I ask a question in aid of objection?" he said as he raised his hand.

"Yes, you may," agreed Judge Panner.

Tom walked over to Mr. Kosydar and then faced him directly. Kosydar shifted in his chair.

"Mr. Kosydar, do you have any training in Catholic theology?" Tom stressed the word "any."

"None," answered Mr. Kosydar more softly.

Tom Dulcich pressed, "Have you taken any course on penance?"

"None."

Tom continued, "You have not attended seminary?"

"Correct," said Mr. Kosydar.

Tom pushed further, "You are not an ordained priest of the Catholic church or any other faith?"

"That's correct," Mr. Kosydar answered as his voice dropped.

"So what you are prepared to offer is your personal opinion as a lay person about what you heard or didn't hear on the tape." Tom stated.

"Correct," Mr. Kosydar said.

"But you don't have any specialized knowledge," Tom continued.

"Correct, Mr. Dulcich, I do not,"

Mr. Dulcich stated: "Thank you, Mr. Kosydar." With a quick and dismissive wave, Tom turned around and said: "I object to this testimony. He is not competent."

"Well, other than competency," Judge Panner commented, "it seems to me that testifying about what is not on the tape is also a violation, if there is a violation in the first place."

Mr. Dulcich, with a slight nod of his head, said: "Yes, your Honor. Thank you."

Judge Panner speculated: "I don't see how he can follow the State judge's order not to disclose what is on the tape by testifying to what is not on the tape. That in effect is disclosing, at least by implication, something that is on the tape. I will sustain the objection."

But "who knew what" in regard to my coming to the jail, was Tom's further questioning:

"I will ask you to hand the witness Exhibit 105." Tom raised papers in his hand and questioned, "Mr. Kosydar, do you recognize Exhibit 105 as the search warrant affidavit—the search warrant and the return of the search warrant prepared for the tape that is in question in this case?"

"Yes, I do,"

Mr. Dulcich continued, "Did your office assist the Lane County Sheriff Department in preparing this document?"

"Yes, I believe I had some input," said Kosydar.

"So it was known in advance that the reason Fr. Mockaitis was coming to the Lane County jail was because he had been requested as a Catholic priest to do so by Conan Wayne Hale?"

"Correct."

As he handed the papers to Mr. Kosydar, Tom briefly paused, and began: "If you could turn over to the third paragraph which reads, 'I know from my experience and training that the Catholic confession is an integral part of Catholicism. It is a sacrament. The basic tenet of confession is that a person is absolved of his or her wrongdoing upon making a full and complete acknowledge of what that wrongdoing is. After the person gives that acknowledgment of what he or she has done wrong, the priest prescribes a penance. Upon performance of the penance, a person is absolved of his or her sins.'

As Tom leaned into the short wall before the witness stand, he looked at Mr. Kosydar: "Is that consistent with your understanding of this sacrament?"

"Yes," said Mr. Kosydar.

Tom pressed on: "When your office prepared this affidavit, did anyone ask the affiant to include that paragraph that the sacrament confession is also deemed to be entirely confidential by the Catholic Church?"

"It was deemed confidential. And, that is included in here," said Kosydar with a tone of hesitancy.

"It is?" Tom asked.

"I guess that is not included in this document." Kosydar responded. "I don't believe it is. I haven't read the whole thing today; but I don't believe it is."

Tom pushed him further: "Have you spoken with Fr. Bertram Griffin who is here and provided an affidavit for the court about the essentials of the Roman Catholic doctrine on the sacrament?"

"No, I haven't," stated Mr. Kosydar. (Court transcripts).

This was a desperate attempt to push the point further. This man, with what appeared a fundamental knowledge of Catholic theology, was placed against men such as Fr. Griffin and Archbishop George to defend the state's claim that what Hale and I had shared was not sacramental? I decided to let Mr. Kosydar's testimony rest on its merits. The very fact that we were discussing such a matter as a point of legal probing was indeed extraordinary.

*   *   *

Down in Eugene, and unbeknownst to us still witnessing arguments in Judge Panner's courtroom, a protest in front of the Lane County Jail was underway. A hundred strong, Eugenians had gathered in support of the Church's position. They peacefully stood on the sidewalk, waved to passing traffic, and held their signs high. "The Persecution of Christians Is Here!" one sign read. Disgruntled parishioners from St. Paul Parish and a smattering from other parishes joined them. Some waved their signs with conviction, leaving no doubt of their endorsement for my position and for their Catholic faith.

Among the more vocal was a woman named Mary who stated, "We're standing here as a presence, saying we support the leaders of our Church and we are opposed to the initial taping and to any further listening to the tape. There are people in this community who want to see justice. It's our right to practice our faith without interference. This was an invasion of our right to worship. We want that tape destroyed!"

Jean Marie, an older Catholic of seventy-five, had joined this protest as her first public action. She proclaimed, "The sacrament of reconciliation is a most treasured gift for a Catholic who uses it to unburden their souls. For someone to tape-record that is not only offensive, it's terrifying."

As the Eugene protest neared its end, objectors put down their signs. They formed a circle, joined hands, and then they prayed for the Church—for all of us.

*   *   *

Back in Portland, Judge Panner finalized his opinion, bringing any further discussion on the nature of my conversation with Hale to a close.

"It is my finding," said Judge Panner with a more definitive tone, "that Fr. Mockaitis intended to give the sacrament as alleged by the plaintiffs in the case. It is also my finding that Mr. Hale himself intended to make a confession and participate in the Sacrament of Penance.

"Beyond that, I think it becomes a question of argument and law. Are we now prepared or do you need any other fact findings in connection with anything that has happened this morning before you submit to the Court a stipulated fact in this case so the matter can be decided?"

Tom said. "Not on those issues you just addressed."

"We need a prompt decision here." Judge Panner stressed and quickened his pace. "We have a criminal trial that is pending in Lane County. We have a judge down there who is under extreme pressure. We have the prosecutor who needs to know what to do. So I am going to insist that we get it done. If there are any other factual issues to be decided, I want to hear about them and we will try to get them moving."

Tom added, "My client appreciates your ability and willingness to move promptly. I would point out to the Court, the criminal trial of one of the criminal defendants is not set until next summer."

"That doesn't matter, Mr. Dulcich, you know how long appeals take." Judge Panner sounded irritated.

Tom rested, "I understand. I don't mean to argue."

"Let's move it," said Judge Panner with an urgent tone.

Serious allegations of a wire tap charge pointed to a covert plan which specifically targeted the moments between priest and penitent—outside the normal course of jail-monitored conversations. My experience as confessor, priest, and pastor was so far removed from this event that to imagine wire-tap charges being laid against a sacramental confession was deplorable. How long this effort to obtain evidence would be justified was unknown.

Mr. Dulcich said, I was going to examine " . . . on the contention that Lane County jail personnel intercepted and recorded Fr. Mockaitis' conversation with Hale in the ordinary course of their work as law enforcement officers."

Judge Panner interjected, "Well, frankly that's a matter of their intent. I don't know that it has anything to do with the issue, does it?"

Tom added, "We do have a claim in the case for violation of Federal wiretap statute. There has been an affirmative defense raised by the state defendants."

"It is my understanding," Mr. Chaimov countered. "That if the jailer is monitoring all conversations, then that counts as an ordinary course. The fact that is what happened in this case militates in favor of the state being able to argue for that exception."

Judge Panner: "All right. Why do you object to that, Mr. Dulcich?"

Tom said: "I don't' know whether he did or didn't and there is a question as to whether all Hale's conversations were taped."

"Does it matter?" Judge Panner wondered.

Tom explained: "To us it doesn't because there is no evidence that Fr. Mockaitis had knowledge he was being taped." (Court transcript). This bizarre charge was basically dropped for the time being.

This brought the day's testimony towards an end but I found myself more convinced by what I would say was a set-up. They knew that Hale's "confession" could potentially contain statements of self-incrimination while I was objectified as the necessary means to that end. We pastors and priests enjoy the respect of our parishioners and though we should never presume it is automatic, that we need to earn the trust of those we serve, such objectification challenged my whole sense of competency. While I refused to feel helpless or weak, since I knew that many were supportive of me in this process, my anger was finding a more specific target.

As he was about to close for the day, Judge Panner requested both attorneys decide, " . . . The only issue that will remain essential is whether this was in the ordinary course of business."

Tom explored some final clarifications, and then Judge Panner declared, "We will be in recess." The next hearing would take place two days later at 10 a.m.

Surprise had filled this day and I wondered, in the end, if we had made much progress. What image might emerge from this now frozen state? I recalled a story from the Renaissance about Italian sculptor Michelangelo. He had a theory about the powerful, twisted figures he would present to the world. He believed they were held captive in the formless marble blocks before him. Through pounding, carving, and chipping away at the stone, he would release these beings from the confines of their frozen state so they could be given life. The disputed and agreed upon facts of this unprecedented case felt more like a jigsaw puzzle.

The courtroom hearings chipped away at the question of a sacramental confession as admissible evidence in a trial. Still, I was grateful this was not turning into a direct attack on the privilege itself. The church hoped to push that clergy-penitent privilege to a more equal level of protection in line with the understanding of church law. Not to seek any particular rights for a Catholic priest but rather to protect all members of the clergy and their similar expectation of privacy. In this tense mix, this encounter between God, penitent, and priest, the free exercise of our religious beliefs, which is a hallmark of our American tradition, and the inherent right to personal privacy, were on trial. What form would ultimately be released? One person had that power—Judge Owen Panner.

*   *   *

Next morning, a full-blown report in *The Register-Guard* came as no surprise: **Taped Talk Ruled a Sacrament.** The *Register-Guard* article recounted the basic find of Judge Panner about the conversation between myself and Hale. But, Fr. Mike's opinion was helpful:

"This ruling is important to the Church's case because it recognizes the nature of the tape recording based solely on the statements of the individuals who were recorded. It also recognized a legal tradition that blocks judges from deciding for an individual what is or is not religious."

Judge Panner had agreed with the position of the church but what if he had ruled otherwise? Would that trump Catholic theology? Mockery on my part, yet this complex case struggled for a precise legal description.

On the Eugene protest, Fr. Mike commented, "It's very important for Catholics, as citizens, to express their indignation when they feel their rights as citizens have been violated."

Those were welcome words and I was grateful this first hearing was over. Yet, my family's concerns were ever more on my mind.

*   *   *

I was not encouraged by the condition of my father whose health declined at a steady pace. My brother Mike had arrived from Chicago, so I looked forward to being with the family for a few days as soon as I was able. Due to the health of my father, and my mother's all-consuming attention to his needs, I refrained from sharing my legal concerns in much detail. I spoke in general terms about what was unfolding, not wanting to add more worry on top of what my mother and the rest of my family were facing. Still, the cloud of another court hearing occupied my mind.

CHAPTER 9

Who Knew What and When

*   *   *

"Nothing can destroy a government more quickly than its failure to observe its own law." (Justice Clark: Mapp v. Ohio—1961)

*   *   *

Two days later I noticed a different mix of participants would mark this hearing in Portland. Archbishop George was not present but two priest representatives, the Vicar General, the highest official in the Archdiocese after that of the local bishop, and the Vicar for Clergy would join us in the courtroom. Fortified with renewed determination, we walked outside and headed for the courthouse under an overcast sky, the breeze stronger than a few days before.

Hurried morning pedestrians rushed by us with occasional glances, their coffees and newspapers in hand. They sometimes brushed an arm against mine; I could pick up the faint scent of freshly ground coffee beans and some sort of spicy cologne or floral perfume amid bits and pieces of serious conversations about the latest investment, stock value, or simply laughter in delighting over stories about their children. But I remained reflective as I stood in a world I felt no one understood.

As I walked with mixed emotions, I silently reflected on the upcoming day. Then, in my mind's eye an entirely different scene flashed before me. *I was struck with an image of Jesus, the accused and innocent, standing before Pontius Pilate in a search for the meaning of truth. As the case was argued, I could only see Pilate questioning Jesus. It was then, in that brief moment, that I was granted an acute understanding of the meaning of innocence. Our Lord was self-confident as he stood before the government authority—because of His pure innocence. He is truth itself; all the rest are shadows. Pilate questioned Jesus and Jesus answered Pilate: "... the reason why I came into the world is to testify to the truth ..." Pilate responded, "Truth! What does that mean?" (John 18: 37-38).*

In today's court of law stood the ancient truth of the Catholic Church: the dignity of the human person and the promise of forgiveness. Jesus Christ, who is truth itself, was confronted by officials of the government and called upon to defend himself. The innocent identified as guilty, as the state pointed a finger at me and by association, to the church itself as the one who should have known better. I rested in these thoughts as we approached the courthouse.

On the front steps of the courthouse, Fr. Mike, who had gone ahead of us, now stood deflecting the attention of reporters with an update on our progress. Fewer reporters than at our first session were present, although they were no less eager for information. They glanced as we passed but Fr. Mike kept them attentive to his information.

The overcast sky diffused a dull light from the side windows in the courtroom. The mood was distinctively more solemn as two days before. Judge Panner took his seat at the bench.

First to speak, Ms. Wood, dark haired and dressed in a simple white blouse, navy blue skirt, and a muted yellow scarf around her neck, stood to express her disagreement with a statement I had made in my affidavit. With paper in hand, she read the paragraph from my statement to which she objected:

"As long as any copy of tape or transcript of the Sacrament of Penance I administered on April 22, 1996 remains in existence, I feel uncomfortable in administering the Sacrament of Penance [Reconciliation] in the Lane County Jail. My religious duties as a priest require me to respond to people who ask me to administer the Sacrament of Penance, even outside of the physical structure of our parish church building. This is especially important for people who may be in a state of serious sin and therefore in particular need of the Sacrament ... As long as the tape and transcript remain, I will have doubts about the ability of Catholics to practice this important Sacrament as it is meant to be performed." (Fr. Timothy Mockaitis: court affidavit).

She put the papers down on the table before her and addressed the Judge:

"For defendant Hale, Your Honor. We dispute that because we are under the impression that Lane County Sheriff's Office has made a special room available where there wouldn't be any recording."

Judge Panner responded with some irritation, "But, this is just his opinion. You are not going to dispute how he feels regardless of what the facts are. I am not going to worry about that.

"You can argue about his feelings if he goes on the stand. I can understand why you can claim it is not relevant to my decision; but—

Ms. Wood interrupted: "I just dispute it. And I dispute to whatever extent it claims he was in a state of serious sin."

"You want to hear him say that?" said Judge Panner sounding more irritated as he gazed at Ms. Wood.

Judge Panner with finality in his voice, returned, "Well, it doesn't so imply." A surprising statement, I thought, for an attorney to make reference to an alleged "serious sin," a religious term, of a client.

The emotional exchange between judge and lawyer ended. Ms. Wood sat down in her chair and appeared deflated. But, the order of the jail was to remain in the visitor's area. No other option was offered.

Legal counsel for an alleged accomplice of Hale's was also present in the courtroom. An intricate layer was introduced in the question of confidentiality as Mr. Michael Phillips spoke out:

"I don't agree that he had no reason to doubt the confidentiality. There is a state statute that would give him reason to doubt that Oregon evidence code provision.

Judge Panner volleyed his remark: "What is going to happen is if we have testimony on this, he is going to say he didn't have any reason to believe it wouldn't be confidential."

"Then we would find out what information he relied on," said Mr. Phillips.

"He says he had no reason to believe it," commented Judge Panner.

"We will make it so it will read 'prior to communicating with Hale on April 22, 1996, based on facts which he had knowledge, Fr. Mockaitis had no reason to believe his communication with Hale would not be confidential'" (Court transcripts).

Although returning to the stand was the last thing I desired, I wanted to fight and prove the point on confidentiality by saying, *look at history and precedent!* There was, however, a stronger part of me that felt it wiser to sit quietly with my startled thoughts.

Judge Panner then sounded further disturbed as he questioned the legal team who stood below his bench.

"A Judge from Eugene called this morning to advise that the tape would not be here. I don't know who subpoenaed it; but, to think it could be subpoenaed without either an order from this court or an order from the Lane County Circuit Court. It surprises me that any lawyer would do that. Who subpoenaed the tape or tried to?"

Ms. Wood slowly stood, "Your Honor, I subpoenaed the tape. I did so, and I didn't learn until 4:30 yesterday that the plaintiffs were going to dispute the fact that the tape had any bearing."

Without a moment's hesitation, Judge Panner stressed his words and glared at Ms. Wood:

"Why did you think the tape would be here just by issuing a subpoena when there is a Lane County Circuit order precluding it?"

Ms. Wood said, "Well, Your Honor, the subpoena was the only method that I had to try and get it here. If the Court wants to proceed this morning, I took the only effort I could take at that time."

"In any event, it won't be here today," remarked Judge Panner abruptly.

Ms. Wood responded, "Your Honor, I understand the Court's willingness to say it could go either way; the record that I am trying to make on Mr. Hale's behalf, your Honor, is that this tape is evidence that he is entitled to under the fourteenth amendment."

Judge Panner became more impatient upon Ms. Wood's further persistence.

"That may be. I will accept that argument. That is something you can argue with me about and absent some other privilege, he might be entitled to it. That's the end of that."

Ms. Wood questioned further, "But the Court will take notice of that so that is a fact in the record?"

"No, I won't. And I am not going to until we determine whether the tape is going to ever be released. That has not been decided now," answered Judge Panner in an urgent voice. "We will determine whether it is to be unsealed or destroyed. That's my job."

Ms. Wood pressed on, "Would the Court grant me leave to have a copy of the transcript entered into the record in this case as evidence?"

"No." Judge Panner quickly stated.

The Judge released his exasperation in a self-controlled manner but it exposed the pressure he was under to finish with this matter. After the unexpected aside, we turned to the testimony of two key witnesses. A detective and a captain with the Lane County Sheriff's office were called to testify.

Detective James Carley, whose affidavit spurred the search warrant signed the day after the taping, was called and approached the witness stand in a deliberate manner. I glanced to my left, and was distracted by Brad Nye, another of our attorneys, who leaned over in my direction, lowered his head and whispered, "What they fear is that Carley could be sued."

I slowly turned my face in his direction and queried, "Sued by whom?"

"Who do you think?" Brad replied, stating what he felt I knew would be the obvious.

Although I had contemplated an independent lawsuit, everything had moved so quickly, that no appropriate response to his enticing statement came to my mind. I felt pulled both ways and wrestled with this whole idea. How often would a priest sue someone? Yet, how often does such an egregious action take place? I certainly had cause as a tax paying, law abiding citizen of this country but as a Christian and a Catholic priest, I needed to ponder this. Many in my parish had urged me to consider it seriously, however. All things being equal, a large part of me did feel it would be right to do so, not out of revenge or for money but for justice.

After Brad's brief comment, I caught up with Carley's testimony. State's attorney, Greg Chaimov, opened the questioning. Carley sat poker-faced, stiff in the witness chair. Mr. Chaimov got right to the point.

"What is your connection with the criminal case against Conan Wayne Hale?"

Carley answered, "Lead investigator in the case that he is a suspect in and having been charged with."

Chaimov continued, "Were you aware in the spring of this year that Lane County was monitoring Mr. Hale's conversations with visitors?"

"Yes," said Carley abruptly.

Chaimov approached closer to the witness stand and asked Mr. Carley, "In an affidavit that this Court has already submitted you testified, 'Conan Hale is aware that his visitors are being recorded.' What facts support that testimony?"

Carley explained, "In monitoring his visitors, his social visits, he demonstrated that by holding up a piece of paper indicating to the visitors—Do you have that, remember don't say it over the phone."

Chaimov said, "By phone, was Mr. Hale referring to the communication device in the security visiting tier?"

"That's right," agreed the detective.

"Have you listened to recordings of Mr. Hale's conversations with visitors other than Fr. Mockaitis?" asked Chaimov.

"Yes, I have."

Chaimov concluded, "Thank You. That's all the questions I have," and he turned away from Carley.

Judge Panner addressed Tom, "You may cross examine."

Tom stood, approached the witness stand, adjusted his tie and faced the detective for a moment, then turned to the green chalkboard to his right. Tom calmly leaned over, lifted a piece of white chalk from the base of the board and turned to the detective as he asked:

"Detective Carley, I'd like to give Judge Panner a little bird's eye view of what the Lane County Jail visiting facility looks like and in particular, the place where the inmates come and speak through the glass in person."

Tom began to outline a sketch of the visitor's area, then continued:

"I will put a 'D' up there. Then there is a wall and plexiglas and a seat on either side of this and then a handset device is on each side; is that correct?"

"That's correct," agreed Carley as he studied the drawing.

Tom continued, "At the podium or where the detective is, (the "D") there is a place for the detective to monitor the communications that are going on between the visitors and the inmates?"

"That's correct."

Tom pressed, "And explain to Judge Panner how it is that those can be taped?"

Carley explained, "Well, I know there is an intercom system. When they built the place, they wired it so we have the ability to tape conversations."

Tom asked, "Is there a tape machine here where the deputy sits at the podium at all times?"

"It's a portable machine," revealed Carley. "I don't know if it is there all of the time."

Tom moved closer to the witness, "In fact, it requires that when a decision is made to tape the machine has to be brought to the control board, near where the deputy sits. It has to be clipped on to the wires of the intercom system?"

Carley appeared anxious but answered, "I don't know—I don't work in the jail. I don't know if the recorder is there at all times. It does have to be specifically plugged in, I believe, or clipped on. I don't' know what the exact procedure is."

Tom queried, "So it is accurate to say all conversations of all inmates are not recorded?"

"That's correct," admitted Carley.

"All conversations of Mr. Hale were not recorded?" pressed Tom more firmly.

"That's correct."

Tom asked further, "And how did you come to learn as you indicated in your affidavit that Fr. Mockaitis, a Catholic priest would be coming to visit personally with Mr. Hale in the jail on April 22, 1996?"

"I received information from Sergeant Bud Spencer at the Lane County Jail."

"So, Deputy Carley," continued Tom, "you learned from Sergeant Spencer on or before April 16th that Mr. Hale had arranged to have a Catholic priest visit him?"

"That's correct. I don't recall if he said Catholic priest; he said a priest, and I assumed he meant Catholic," said Carley.

Tom asked, "For the purpose of making a confession?"

"Correct," affirmed Carley.

Tom continued, "From your training, you were aware that a 'Catholic confession is an integral part of Catholicism?"

"Yes, that's correct," said Carley.

"It was a Sacrament?" Tom emphasized.

"That's correct," answered Carley with less strength.

"You made special arrangements to make sure that conversation between Fr. Mockaitis and Mr. Hale would be tape recorded?"

"That's correct," said Carley.

"Did you seek a court order of any kind before making arrangements to make sure that the communications between Fr. Mockaitis and Mr. Hale were going to be tape recorded?" Tom pressed on.

"Negative," affirmed Carley.

"That's no?" as Tom raised his voice.

"No," Carley answered with assurance.

Tom continued as he glanced at the Judge, "During April of 1996, can you tell Judge Panner if there were other inmates whose communications with a priest or other clergyman were recorded by tape by Lane County authorities?"

Carley answered, "Not to my knowledge."

Tom looked at Carley intently, "So, would you say this was an unusual circumstance?"

"I would say that, yes." stated Carley confidently.

"Not in the ordinary course of business?" Tom pushed.

"That would be correct," continued Carley with the same assurance.

Tom backed away, looked up at the Judge and closed, "Thank you, Your Honor. Nothing further." (Court transcripts).

Detective Carley's testimony painted a picture of disrespect and at the very least, ignorance of the sanctity of conscience. To feel so violated in this sacred trust touched me further on both a personal and professional level and stirred up those uncomfortable memories of the original phone call from the reporter. Now, with these specific facts before us, the violation seemed all the more real. What could have turned out to be an isolated incident of poorly calculated investigative zeal, had turned into a very public challenge to our Constitutional rights as American citizens. For that implication alone, this case was significant. Implied on another level was the fear that this behavior might be repeated if the same circumstances presented themselves. Though it was unfeasible to imagine such conduct would be tolerated in this country elsewhere, this was post April 22, 1996 and that inviolable wall of privilege had been breached. For the sake of precedent, this needed to be faced with tenacity.

While this was the posture of the church it was a delicate spot we found ourselves in. The church tried not to appear insensitive to the victims of the triple homicide and their families but found itself caught in this complicated litigation. The state upheld its responsibility to prosecute a serious crime and the church fought for its right to religious liberty. Yet, it was increasingly clear that one power had overstepped their responsibility in a way never before breached. I could not help but notice the solemn facial expressions of all the participants as I surveyed the room. We were writing legal history.

The next witness called was Benjamin Sunderland, a Captain with the Lane County Sheriff's Office. Sunderland was Director and supervisor of the Adult Corrections Division. His role in this plan was unclear so our anticipation was tangible. In his position at the jail, he was likely a key player. The state opened with its questioning along similar lines of Deputy Carely:

Mr. Chaimov addressed Captain Sunderland: "Mr. Sunderland, would you please describe for the court the device that inmates at the jail use to communicate with visitors?"

Captain Sunderland sounded eager: "Yes, the visiting that is done is in an area that is referred to as secure visiting. The device that's located there is a phone handset. But it is like an intercom. It is a stand-alone independent separate system that functions just in that area."

"Does the jail have confidential visiting rooms?" Chaimov asked.

"Yes."

Mr. Chaimov continued, "For whom are those rooms available?"

"They are available to anyone who has an approved pass to make use of those rooms. They are available routinely to attorneys and to law enforcement officers," explained Sunderland.

Mr. Chaimov asked: "For what purpose does Lane County monitor inmates' conversations?"

"It might be a number of purposes," added Sunderland, "dependent upon the source of the request: the need might be for safety security; it might be for compelling interest to the community; it might be pursuant to an order or directive from a court."

Chaimov looked at Sunderland directly: "Do you know why Lane County monitored Mr. Hale's conversation?"

"Not specifically, no." A curious answer, I thought, considering his position as Supervisor.

Then, my memory was jostled as I recalled the first words spoken by the district attorney a few days after the taping: " . . . even priests and ministers have been accused of serious crimes. Sunderland had stated the taping might be done, "for safety security" and the district attorney's early explanation indicated a similar rationale. I recalled meeting another member of the clergy on one occasion in the visitor's area who left shortly after I arrived. Was he considered a security threat? It felt a confused reasoning. A thought of manipulation grew stronger and I sat uncomfortably in those memories as we passed from one attorney to the next.

Tom began his cross-examination of Capt. Sunderland. He moved toward the green board he had stood by earlier and pointed to the visitor's area diagram:

"Captain Sunderland, The purpose of the handset device in the visiting area as I diagramed here on the board, is for the purpose of allowing the inmates and the visitors to have oral communication with one another while still being separated by the glass?"

"That's correct."

Tom walked over toward Sunderland, "If an inmate wants to make a telephone call outside the jail, there is a different facility for that?"

"That's correct," agreed the Captain.

"So there is one facility for telephone calls and then this facility where Fr. Mockaitis was recorded is for oral communications?"

Sunderland continued, "Yes, it works like an intercom."

"Captain," followed Tom as he looked intently, "are inmates at the Lane County corrections facility told their telephone calls, outside the jail, may be monitored?"

"Yes," answered Sunderland.

Tom pressed the point to the next level, "Was Conan Hale told his oral communication, in the jail visiting area, was to be monitored?"

"Not that I am aware of," remarked Captain Sunderland.

Tom briefly smiled and added, "Do you have any information, Captain Sunderland, that Fr. Mockaitis was told that his visit to Mr. Hale in the jail visiting area on April 22, 1996 would be monitored?"

"No, I don't."

"Or recorded?" Tom added.

"No, I don't have that information," Sunderland answered with tone of assurance.

"Is it accurate, Captain Sunderland, that for oral communication in the jail's visiting area, a tape recording device has to be brought to the area of control and hooked up to wires underneath the top?" Tom's voice sounded confident.

"That's correct."

"And, you have no information that Conan Wayne Hale consented to have his communication with Fr. Mockaitis recorded?" questioned Tom.

"I do not have that information."

Tom continued, "Are there any signs in the visitor's area of Lane County Jail that would indicate to Fr. Mockaitis that his communication with Conan Hale was to be recorded?"

"No, there was not at that time," voiced Captain Sunderland.

Tom probed deeper. "Do you have any information on whether any of the communications with Mr. Hale and any other clergy were recorded, other than Fr. Mockaitis?"

"I do not have that information." Captain Sunderland stated convincingly. (Court Transcripts).

Mr. Chaimov posed no further questions.

I found the Captain a reliable witness but I couldn't help speculate: Did Hale have any knowledge of this taping? And what of his own attorney? Such outlandish guesswork weighed down my thoughts as I tried to connect the dots of who knew what when.

Clearly, the testimony of these witnesses revealed that I and the Sacrament of Reconciliation (Penance) were premeditated targets. It was clear we all felt the stress of a day, which uncovered much about intent, but nothing about the ultimate fate of the tape. We hoped this time in court would ultimately bring an end to this saga and I had no doubt Judge Panner was anxious to end this story as well.

"I will give you some findings of fact" the Judge told us, "so that we can get this case decided promptly. Then after I do that, we will set a time for briefing and argument next week so there can be a final decision.

" . . . All right now, I want to schedule a time to conclude this matter, to give you an opportunity to file briefs and to argue this case. Will you be available by 1:30 on Monday?

"I think this needs to be resolved and to expedite that hearing also . . . Then we will be ready and I will attempt just as soon as I can after I have absorbed your arguments to give you a final decision. Anything further at this time?

Hearing no answer to his question as he gazed at the lawyers, the Judge concluded our day. "Thank you all very much." I sat back for a moment and let my body release its tension. (Court transcripts).

Attorneys would present their closing arguments the following Monday, August 12. I held cautious expectations that we were coming to the end of this dilemma, which Judge Panner understood and appeared to be sympathetic. If the tape was handed over with the transcripts and then destroyed, the privilege of privacy between clergy and penitent reinforced, and the balance between church and state as supported in the First Amendment re-established, it would be a victory for both sides. However, I wasn't sure Archbishop George, Fr. Mike, and our legal team shared my degree of optimism. The Archbishop approved a move to go higher should this not fall in our favor—to the U.S. Supreme Court if necessary.

As I reviewed the disjointed facts revealed in the courtroom, part priest and part detective, I attempted to connect the dots: the confused testimony of the jail receptionist who claimed she knew me for several years, the Lane County sheriff's detective, the convincing testimony of Captain Sunderland that he had no knowledge of routine taping in the visitor's area, and earlier statements by the district attorney about his claim of the legal nature of this action and the assistant district attorney's admission of his direct hand in gathering evidence as lead investigator. Most seemed absolutely aware of this plan at some level, and their testimonies painted a foreboding and dark image about the approval that had allegedly been issued to conduct the surreptitious taping.

So, much was left unresolved after day two before the Federal Judge. There was no closure worth celebrating. Where would the line be drawn between investigation and privacy if the church were defeated at this level and this sacramental intrusion allowed as evidence? If overlooked, what would be next? Others likely had contemplated conversations with clergy as a hypothetical opportunity but sensed instinctively the unethical and immoral nature of such behavior. Yet it appeared this plan had been perpetrated with forethought.

*   *   *

The First Amendment's free exercise clause echoed in our collective consciousness:

"The free exercise clause prohibits the government from intruding on individual religious choices . . . the establishment clause gives greater latitude to an individual's exercise of religious choice, and by committing religious belief and practice to the realm of individual choice, the free exercise clause reduces the possibility that religion will become an area of state power." *(Law 101.* Oxford University Press 2000. Jay M. Feinman. Copyright 2000. P. 71).

Among the leading words of the First Amendment are named two fundamental rights as our most protected: religion and freedom. Why? Not because the authors of the Constitution feared dominance by religious bodies but because they saw its value for society as a whole. Faith, morals, religious expression, and privacy are high moral absolutes that maintain order and respect among persons. The incarcerated are person's who deserve certain protections and for those who generously give themselves to this important ministry I knew they too felt as I did. It was not long after the news of the taping first broke that I received letters from various prison ministry groups around the nation.

However, wiretapping, conspiracies and plots to deceive are the stuff of spy thrillers and undercover agents. But this was real life. We were left at best with cautious hope. Although prepared for whatever Judge Panner ruled on Monday, August 12, I wondered how far the government would be allowed to interfere and for what ends and by what means?

CHAPTER 10

A Dangerous Precedent

* * *

"He who surrenders himself without reservation to the temporal claims of a nation, or a party, or a class is rendering to Caesar that which, of all things, most emphatically belongs to God: himself." (C.S. Lewis—*The Weight of Glory*).

* * *

No matter what the opinion would be at this final hearing I knew this saga would not die easily. An authoritative decision was beyond Archbishop George or any attorney's power. If the judge ruled in favor of the church, his decision would need to be enforced along with a procedure for destruction of the tape. If he ruled in favor of the state, an appeal to a higher court was our only recourse. Still, I had no doubt the church was right in this and I found myself sustained by an inner sense of resolve to see this through. While I wanted to trust my inner more positive emotions about the outcome, I soon began to think more pragmatically. We were not due back in Judge Panner's court until 1:30 p.m. so by mid-morning, I set out for Portland in a more guarded mood.

The familiar two-hour drive passed quickly. I arrived in Portland, found the well-known parking garage, left the car and headed cautiously toward Tom's office. The day felt lighter; afternoon sunlight had cut through the city haze, which gave life and color to the city park. Might these scenes foreshadow grateful news later this day? Once inside the office, I greeted our team and sensed Archbishop George, Fr. Mike, and our attorneys were optimistic. They engaged in light conversation and some laughter though appeared tempered and prepared for any possible outcome.

We moved outside along our route toward the courthouse; passersby took little note. Media, however, had gathered on the front steps of the courthouse, a larger group than at the last hearing, and Fr. Mike promised them his impressions after the judge issued his ruling. We passed by, up the steps, and entered the Federal Courthouse without interruption. While my parishioners seemed to appreciate having me around, they understood my need to attend to this matter. A matter I prayed would be ended here.

The sun shone through the windows in the courtroom, and the atmosphere took on a tangible presence of expectancy. The dark wood of the judge's bench struck me as alive with power. Yet, my head and heart were in tension between confidence and pragmatism. We took our seats as the legal team for the district attorney and Judge Jack Billings did the same.

Judge Panner entered at 1:30 p.m. sharp; we stood, were seated, and then listened with cautious hope for his next words. He invited final comments from representative attorneys on both sides. Tom Dulcich stood and spoke first as he summarized the established facts.

"Mr. Harcleroad said on May 22 that he authorized the taping of a private conversation between Fr. Mockaitis and Conan Wayne Hale at the county jail. He didn't say it was a public conversation. He didn't say it was a conversation in which Fr. Mockaitis should not have had an expectation of privacy. He didn't say that it was a conversation in which Fr. Mockaitis should have been expected to be intercepted or monitored. Mr. Harcleroad called it a private conversation and we wholeheartedly agree.

"Second, Mr. Harcleroad said, 'I was wrong to authorize the taping,' and that, 'I have concluded that a tape recording of a confidential clergy communication falls within the zone of socially unacceptable conduct.' Note the words that Mr. Harcleroad used, that it was a 'confidential' clergy communication that was tape-recorded. He didn't say it was a communication that Father Mockaitis was aware of or should have been expected to be aware of, and we wholeheartedly agree.

"Mr. Harcleroad also said on May 22 of this year: 'It is important that our citizens have confidence in our justice system, and this tape recording shakes that confidence."

"With that statement, Your Honor, we wholeheartedly agree, and we're here today to ask you to correct that error. Mr. Harcleroad concluded that privacy was vital, and we believe the privacy interests at stake are vital as well.

"First, my clients asked him orally and by letter to destroy the tape. My clients then attempted to apply to the Lane County Circuit Court for the same relief, but received a letter from Judge Billings with their papers and filing fee, so we were never able to have the request we bring before you today considered by the state court system.

"The defendants raise many issues and Your Honor noted the paperwork. Let me touch upon five of those points." Tom moved around his desk, turned a profile to the Judge and spoke both to him and to the courtroom participants.

"First, it's contended that what occurred was no violation of the right to the free exercise of religion.

"I don't think you need to argue that," Judge Panner interrupted. "I'm prepared to accept that."

"Thank you, Your Honor," said Tom as he turned to Judge Panner. "Another thing that is suggested is that the remedy that is requested is extraordinary. We disagree. The Civil Rights Act, the Religious Freedom Restoration Act, and the Anti Wire Tap Act all suggest a . . ."

"Have you found any case in any way close to the facts of this case?" Judge Panner again interrupted.

"No, your honor, we haven't," said Tom confidently, "And we believe that's extremely significant. Nobody has had the audacity in this nation to go as far as what happened in Lane County on April 22. That's the only reason.

"The Supreme Court in the Church of Scientology case, which we have cited to you, gives you full authority to do what we ask. We are not seeking an extraordinary remedy.

"There's also a contention that there's no continuing violation of the religious or privacy rights by the existence of this tape. Your Honor, each time that transcript is reviewed and every time that tape is played, Father Mockaitis is, in effect, forced to disclose what his religious beliefs are and to violate the seal of the confessional. Each time the tape or transcripts are reviewed, his rights to privacy are further violated.

"Another contention that is made quite strongly in the briefs is that the taping was legal. The state claims that Fr. Mockaitis' should have been aware that Oregon law 'authorizes' interception and taping of priest-penitent communications that occur in a jail setting. But, it is clear that visitors do not relinquish their Fourth Amendment rights at the prison gates. Prison or jail visitors retain their right to be free from *unreasonable* searches and seizures.

"They knew it was to be a privileged communication, they knew Father Mockaitis was a priest, and they knew his mission was solely religious. They knew because he had visited before and signed in. They knew that his duty was confidential, they knew it was sacramental, and there was no warrant for the Court to tape-record the statement. Under the First and Fourth amendments, this was not legal or constitutional, and the remedy that we've asked is appropriate."

Tom stood before the judge and articulated his points with skill and enthusiasm. All this talk about Constitutional amendments and the fine points of who said what made me uneasy in a world I had never been. But, the Fourth Amendment's "search and seizure" issue felt correct as this was a blatant invasion of privacy. I leaned forward in my chair and listened more intently as Tom continued his summary to Judge Panner:

"There are other ways in which the defense tries to avoid the implication of the Wire Tap Act. They claim that Mr. Hale consented to this. We've cited and explained that point in case, which is a Ninth Circuit case. There is no evidence of implied consent by Mr. Hale to the taping of his conversation with Father Mockaitis. As Detective Carley and Captain Sunderland made clear, this was not in the ordinary course."

Tom assured Judge Panner that there was no reason to not order the tape destroyed and the state's claims about our interference with the future trial of Hale should be left to "the court system that is in place to determine that."

The Judge asked Tom: "If I destroy the tape and record of it that would not be available in the event they did decide something different."

"That's correct," Tom answered.

Judge Panner wondered, "Have you studied the Perez case, a Supreme Court decision in 1971, at all?"

"I have not, Your Honor," said Tom.

Judge Panner cited a case entitled, *Perez v. Ledesma* from a 1971 United States Supreme Court ruling. In *Perez,* the federal court plaintiffs had an adequate opportunity to present their constitutional defenses to the allegedly illegal seizure of property in the criminal proceedings. Nonetheless, they sought to circumvent the state court criminal case by seeking an injunction in federal court.

Judge Panner found a similarity in that case to our own. But, in our case the church appealed to a higher court rather than deal with this in the lower court since Judge Billings had essentially dismissed the church's attempt.

However, attorneys for the church alternately relied on a case from the Church of Scientology (1992) in which the United States Supreme Court had determined that the return or destruction of property seized in violation of the Fourth Amendment may provide an effective remedy for the constitutional violation. The parties disputed the government's possession of tape recordings of privileged conversations between Church officials and their attorneys. The government contended that the controversy was moot because there was no longer a threat that the tapes would be used against the Church but the Supreme Court disagreed. Justice Stevens:

" . . . A court *does* have power to effectuate a partial remedy by ordering the Government to destroy or return any and all copies it may have in its possession . . ." (Plaintiff's brief). While Judge Panner took his approach, our attorney felt the Scientology case was the stronger.

Tom concluded his summary, sat down and gave deference to the defendants.

Judge Panner next invited the attorney for the state, Greg Chaimov, who stood by his table, looked to the Judge, and was about to begin. However, Judge Panner looked directly at Mr. Chaimov, and questioned: "Wasn't it illegal to take it?"

Chaimov responded, "It was not illegal, Your Honor."

Judge Panner looked somewhat puzzled and continued: "How do you respond to the arguments made by Mr. Dulcich?"

Chaimov defended his words: "The folks in Lane County that did the taping, under the law, did so in a jail so long as it wasn't between an attorney and a client. And the folks in Lane County got legal advice about whether they could do the taping before they did it. Under those circumstances, it is under the law to make that tape."

Judge Panner moved on: "Is there any written record of that kind of advice knowing what they knew? It's clear they knew that it was a priest and that it was a confession. That's what he went there for. It's also clear that there was no security threat in any way with a priest. Was there some written advice that it was legal to make that recording?" We all shifted for a moment in our chairs.

"I don't know of any written advice, Your Honor." said Mr. Chaimov. "I wouldn't be surprised to find that the advice was simply oral."

"It's very disturbing to me that any lawyer or giver of legal advice would advise that it was legal to do that under those circumstances." The Judge sounded perplexed.

The hand of disrespect toward my purpose in visiting Hale sat heavy on me as Judge Panner pushed the issue of "legal advice" the state claimed they obtained for the taping. Such disrespect was far from my experience since people of faith have a great sense of reverence for things holy. It was clear to me that this entire affair was covertly planned and I was used as a gateway to its success. Detective Carley's earlier admission that he was not aware of tape recording other conversations Hale had had with ministers of religion, only this one, chilled my confidence. It appeared they had moved ahead with little, if any, research or search warrant to support their action. The defendants knew, as they took pause before the taping, that their plan was out of the ordinary course of action. Yet, in the interest of conducting this clandestine action swiftly, it appears they simply did it.

Mr. Chaimov then continued:

"A person has no reasonable expectation of privacy in conversations that the law allows to be intercepted. In this case, Fr. Mockaitis is charged with knowing that Oregon statute 165 authorizes the monitoring of any jailhouse conversation by an inmate with anyone other than his lawyer. Likewise, a person who communicates with an inmate can have no greater expectation of privacy than the inmate, which is none."

"The identity of the person with whom Hale conversed does not take the interception out of the ordinary course of the county's work. A jailer's interception of an inmate's communications is within a jailer's 'ordinary' duties. To preserve institutional security, jailers routinely monitor inmate conversations. The search warrant suggests that a purpose for intercepting the conversation between Hale and Fr. Mockaitis was to gather evidence against Hale. Plaintiffs have presented no evidence to suggest that, unlike a prison guard, Lane County's jailers also gather evidence for use in trials.

"The issue in this case is not whether this tape ought to be destroyed, but *when* the tape should be destroyed. The answer to that question is after the criminal trial is over (that of Hale) but it ought not be destroyed now." Chaimov moved around the table and gestured more emphatically as he continued.

"This court should resist plaintiff's attempts to 'pigeonhole' this case. The facts of this case are unusual. The 'complex of considerations' surrounding a federal court's intervention in a capital-murder prosecution, over the objection of the prosecutor, the state court judges, and the criminal defendants, is immense. Plaintiffs ignore that 'complex of considerations,' and make no mention of the principles that underlie the doctrines of abstention. Anytime a federal court case is so inextricably entwined in a state criminal proceeding as is the present case, the federal court must consider the concerns of federalism." (Court brief, p. 20-21).

Mr. Chaimov concluded his testimony with claims contrary to that of the church:

"I would like to leave the Court with these thoughts. The state very much wishes that the tape did not exist, and the state feels very sorry for any hurt that it has caused the plaintiffs. But the fact is, the tape does exist, and the state has to preserve that tape. The tape is being preserved by the state court judges pursuant to statutory and constitutional obligations that override any concerns that plaintiff may have about the continued existence of this tape. We'd ask that you leave the matters where they stand; in the hands of the state court judges."

Despite a request of the church, a copy of the alleged search warrant to authorize the taping was never produced. All that was discovered was a search warrant, signed by Judge Hodges, permitting investigators to listen to the tape. That warrant, and the reporter's phone call to me, will forever stand out as a "somber moment" in my ministry.

Hale's attorney Terri Wood, then intervened as she stood up and raised her hand:

"Your Honor, the only thing I want to tell the Court is that in conversation with my client we'd ask the Court not to destroy the tape. We submit that plaintiffs don't have a case that requires the Court to destroy the tape and that the Court could grant part of the relief sought by plaintiffs and yet allow the tape to be preserved." She felt the continued existence of the tape was necessary for the integrity of Hale's future trial. Hale's attorney, in particular, felt the tape must be preserved in order to give credibility to any information Hale or the state may claim was taken from the tape. But, would it ever be played in court?

Judge Panner calmly stated, "Thank you."

*   *   *

At issue was a legal theory entitled the "Fruit of the Poison Tree." This legal term, essentially used to describe evidence gathered with the aid of information obtained illegally, was floated by the state, Terri Wood and others concerned with the upcoming trial of Conan Hale. The state could declare a mistrial since this tape could be declared improperly admitted evidence thus bringing other evidence into question. If the tape is declared illegal evidence due to a Fourth Amendment violation, as the church was stating, then any use of information taken from the tape would more than likely be excluded.

Adding more complexity, Michael Phillips, attorney for Hale's alleged accomplice also asked that the tape be preserved. In an earlier moment, he spoke in defense of the death penalty and the preservation of all potential evidence. Speaking to Judge Panner, he said:

"The State of Oregon has an interest in having an effectively applied death penalty adopted by some 75 per cent of the Oregon voters and by the legislature since 1985. Oregon has built into the application of the death penalty some principles designed to protect the citizens of Oregon as distinguished from the accused. Every matter that may affect the judgment of jurors with regard to the position of the death penalty should be brought before the jurors."

*   *   *

The competing interests of so many touched by this affair incited an unparalleled test case in legal history. The obvious stalemate between church and state was substantial. While the murder of three teenagers was a tragic event that cried out for justice, and no one minimized the sadness of that loss and the suffering for the families involved. Inevitably, however, the church was criticized by some for its singular focus in demanding the destruction of the tape. This uncertainty was part of side discussions and I began to understand the real concern of both sides. It had become a standoff, a "legal nightmare," as Richard Cossack of CNN had labeled it.

By this time, my personal crusade had become an effort not only to defend my profession but in the midst of this "legal nightmare," I wondered when it would all come to an end. Though implied otherwise in the state's brief, I resisted the temptation to second guess myself as a member of the clergy who came naively, as the state had claimed, to celebrate a religious ritual with an inmate. Were the investigators so desperate in the case against Hale, the amassed evidence so lacking, and the circumstances around this case so singular that they needed to resort to this unparalleled secret taping or was it really a total disregard for religion and its value in people's lives? These thoughts had become both a question and a challenge to overcome and as we sat in the courtroom before Judge Panner I could not help but imagine what my future life as priest and pastor would be like.

Would I be able to empathize with victims of personal violation or would I just want to forget this entire affair? Would my anger serve to be a strength or turn me bitter? Open to all, patient, understanding, prayerful, skilled administrator, inspiring speaker and strong leader are among the expectations of a priest and pastor. I concluded that so much of what unfolded in this case, could be turned to a force for good: I could learn to be vigilant, determined, and grow in compassion for victims, and overall be a more affective pastor. That was a hill I could climb.

Yet, I found myself having little patience for weakness and incompetency, wanting to deal with the truth rather than dance around it. That too could serve well to be a form of growth if tempered with understanding. However, I knew this would always be a lonely ride, it would be *my* story, since the interests of Archbishop George and the Church as a whole, were far beyond myself. I knew the institution of the Church was not here to defend me alone for the Church had its own interests at heart, so God was inviting me to enter this experience in the midst of its loneliness, as a form of conversion to greater compassion, sensitivity, patience, a desire for truth. I began to see these as signs of hope in the midst of still unresolved questions. I knew I had probably a lifetime to absorb these lessons but I hoped these new positive insights would serve me well. I loved the priesthood, as I know the vast majority of my brother priests do as well, I felt privileged to share in this ministry, so I knew the grace of conversion was still possible. God uses the events of our lives to achieve much good if we only let him.

So, as we moved to the Judge's decision, I hoped my emotions were correct and that Judge Panner, at least, was "getting it." After closing summaries concluded from attorneys for plaintiffs and defendants, Archbishop George, our attorneys, and I listened with rapt attention to Judge Panner's every word. We held our collective breath and hoped for a cause to rejoice.

*   *   *

The judge sat up straight in his chair, reached for his reading glasses, and then leaned forward with his hands clasped. He paused for a moment, briefly gazed at us, and began speaking in a clear but somber tone. His speech, however, was rapid.

"Well, I think I share the feeling of Mr. Chaimov that I wish the tape did not exist. This is a difficult case. It's a very unique case. I have been unable to find any case even very close to the point.

"It is extremely unfortunate that it was recorded. The Defendant Harcleroad has admitted it was wrong and unacceptable conduct for whatever reason and I certainly agree with that. Whether or not it was legal or illegal I don't believe is necessary to my decision. It was knowingly and purposely recorded. It was a confession between a penitent and clergy, and I can think of no excuse that it was so done. I suspect that Mr. Dulcich is correct that the reason that I don't find any cases on point is because nobody has had the audacity to do such a thing.

"I commend District Attorney Harcleroad for his admission that it was not the right thing to do. The very able state trial judge (Judge Billings) properly sealed the record and prohibited its disclosure. Unfortunately, it had already been disclosed, which is part of the problem that occurred when it was taken in the first place.

"Two defendants are faced with a possible death penalty. The state court trial judge is faced with making a determination—If I do not order the tape destroyed, the state court judge is faced with the determination of deciding what, if anything, to do, or when, if ever, to allow that tape to be exposed further . . . The relief requested by the plaintiffs in this case is exactly opposite of the state court's order already to the extent that the plaintiffs would have me order the tape destroyed . . .

"I understand the concern of the plaintiffs. Father Mockaitis has done nothing wrong. The plaintiffs have a real concern about the confidentiality of future activities and confessions. The plaintiffs have done everything possible in this case to protect that confidentiality, and I hope that the public and the media outcry that have come from all over the country about the injustice together with the district attorney's and the court's actions will help somewhat in that regard. I can't concede that it will happen again. If this is the first incidence in the country, let's hope it will be the last.

"I'm amazed at the comments I've received from all over the country about the case in the short time it's been before me. The plaintiffs make strong and valid arguments, but I must say that as I look at the Perez case, and some of the other cases, and draw the closest analogy I can find, I must say that I just can't, consistent with the duty to protect the rights of the two defendants in the murder case, order the tape destroyed in advance of the trial. It's up to the state trial judge to make that determination.

"I think it would be a serious abuse of the deference that federal courts owe to the state courts for me to order it destroyed as much as I wish that it had never happened and perhaps would like to have it destroyed. But the state trial judge has that responsibility. It may very well be that the state trial judge will order the tape never to be used. I don't know the answer to that. It may very well be that ultimately it will wind up being destroyed. It's going to be first up to him in that murder case to make that decision. The federal courts owe that type of deference to the state courts.

" . . . It's been a very hard decision for me, and I thank you all. If you determine on behalf of the plaintiffs to appeal it, you understand that the granting or denying of an injunction is ordinarily a further basis for expediting the matter so it can be heard promptly. Not that I think you'll have any success. I would have decided otherwise if I thought you would, but I've been wrong before." (Court Transcripts) Judge Panner's words fell on me like a cold towel slapped in the face and I sat stunned. No doubt they affected Archbishop George and our entire legal team with the same amazement.

The judge dismissed everything the Church had requested with the exception of concluding that the conversation Hale and I shared was confidential due to the expectation of penitent and priest. It should be respected as a religious ritual. That alone was the only concession to the church yet it accomplished little for the overall concerns. The vast importance of the state investigation remained a powerful competitor.

While I understood Judge Panner's reasoning, it sat heavy knowing that the protracted process would continue. Back at the parish I was prepared to deal with my parishioner's disappointment and puzzlement. This was a story I knew they followed closely and my take on it was something that many were eager to hear.

With uncharacteristic irritation, Tom Dulcich, in an effort to salvage some hope, then requested a decision about "declaratory and injunctive relief" concerning further authorization of the tape recording. But the judge disappointed further.

"Well, in light of what the district attorney has said," Judge Panner commented, "what the Court has said, and what the public and media outcry has been, I don't believe that it is appropriate for me to do that. You can raise that also in the appeals court if you wish, because I decline to do that."

Panner admitted he knew this was a "disturbing" opinion but felt his written opinion would outline his reasons and be legally sound. With a speedy wrap-up, and the bang of the gavel, the judge closed the hearing with the expected, "We are in recess."

This last rapid blow left the suggestion for appeal as the only glimmer of future resolution. I reminded myself how wrong I had been about feeling somewhat confident at the close of the last session. I sensed the judge would make a bold and unprecedented move to bring justice to our cause. Caught in a tough position Judge Panner appeared sympathetic to the church but this could have been an opportunity to decide the issue with certainty. Judge Billings in Eugene would be trying his first murder case in that of Hale and that judge was not sympathetic to the church in this matter. I thought we were back on first base.

Nothing more than a slap on the hand to state authorities was offered as relief for the church. Still, I was further astonished the judge was amazed by the international outcry to the taping when it was first revealed. Those in the Catholic world and beyond had shown overwhelming respect for the privileged nature of this relationship between a member of the clergy and their parishioner and were collectively mortified.

After what seemed more than a minute but likely much less, I gathered my papers and walked from the courtroom along with Archbishop George, Fr. Mike, and our attorneys Tom Dulcich and Brad Nye.

*   *   *

Judge Panner cited *Younger v. Harris* from a 1971 U.S. Supreme Court case as a basis for abstention. *Younger v. Harris* was a 1971 case in which the United States Supreme Court held that United States federal courts were required to abstain from hearing any civil rights tort claims brought by a person who is currently being prosecuted.

The viewpoint of the state was clear on the *Younger* application:

" . . . Fr. Mockaitis alleges he 'feels uncomfortable' administering the sacrament in the Lane County Jail as long as the challenged audiotape is in existence . . . In *Younger*, the plaintiffs who were not parties to the state criminal proceedings alleged similar 'chilling effect' of their constitutional rights . . . In the present case, the types of harms alleged by plaintiffs are similar to the 'feel inhibited' and 'being intimidated' types of harms that were insufficient in *Younger*. . . This court should reject plaintiffs' argument that no 'ongoing state proceeding' exists . . . the trial of Mr. Hale is an ongoing state proceeding . . . (Court brief).

However, the Church was confident in its viewpoint:

"Abstention under *Younger* is proper only where: There is an ongoing state judicial proceeding, the proceeding implicates important state interests, and the proceeding offers an adequate opportunity to raise constitutional issues. In *Younger* the Supreme Court recognized that abstention under the principles enunciated in that case may be improper where a party may suffer irreparable injury in the absence of federal court action." (Court brief).

In the church's view, the continued existence of the tape was felt to cause "irreparable harm" to the First and Fourth Amendment rights of both myself and Archbishop George, not to mention the fallout upon future ministry to the incarcerated. I wondered if the secure experience of parishioner's confessions would be colored by this entire legal journey. As I sat each week in the room reserved in the church to welcome parishioners who came to seek forgiveness, it was as if my opinion on the value of this sacrament was ever more intense. Though Judge Panner's decision was both a disappointment and a surprise a sense of regret only caused to energize our efforts to press on. Our position remained the same. It was more than a recording. It was a living desecration which had no right to exist so our appeal was on the move.

Soon after we'd emerged from the hearing, Tom wasted no time. He made a quick phone call to get the appeal process underway. As he stood outside the courtroom, with phone in hand, I could hear his determination along with that of Archbishop George and Fr. Mike.

As we left the courthouse, Fr. Mike offered scant information to the reporters but prepared them for a more detailed response at a later time. The world around us seemed surreal, out of step with our three days in court—the city went about its business, the warmth of the day and the scent of summer air continued to exist, people relaxed on benches in the park as they drank their ice teas and sodas or licked ice creams, children's laughter echoed from the fountain across the park, and two young men threw Frisbees in a game of catch with an eager golden retriever. The low rumble of Friday afternoon traffic surrounded us. I had nothing to say to anyone at this point.

*   *   *

Predictably, the volley between news reporting began. The next morning in a story headlined: **Judge Protects Taped Confession**, Oregon's state newspaper *The Oregonian,* reported on the ruling. It highlighted the main points at play and expressed Archbishop George's deep disappointment. George said the Church would appeal: " . . . If this dangerous precedent stands, our relationship to the state will be different from what we had assumed it to be. This is a cause of great sadness and concern."

Tom was quoted with a familiar point that each time the tape or a transcript of it is reviewed, I would be forced to violate the intended seal of the sacrament.

While Tom's point may be taken by some as symbolic, it had weight nonetheless. As the tape is played, the inviolable seal of the sacrament, which any priest is absolutely forbidden to break, my voice is heard, that seal is broken without my consent or control, and thereby could be interpreted as an unwilling violation of the sacramental seal. I could not imagine the deep sense of betrayal on the part of any penitent should they find the content of their discussion with the priest revealed as public knowledge. How could they ever trust again?

Although Greg Chaimov, lawyer from the Oregon Department of Justice and attorney for Mr. Harcleroad reminded his hearers that the tape would be destroyed after the trial, I could only question, what does "after" mean? What does that bode for further potential public violations of the tape itself? Would I be hearing my own voice and that of the penitent on the evening news? Despite the decision, we still maintained hope that Hale would indeed be given a fair trial.

Soon, *The Catholic Sentinel,* our local Catholic newspaper, added its voice and published an editorial asking Catholics and all people of faith to do their part in helping everyone to understand the sacred value of the church's efforts:

"This is a case that confuses many of our un-churched friends and even some of our brothers and sisters from other religions . . . This is the moment when we can proclaim our faith to those who seem poised to hear it. How is this violation like the betrayal of any confidentiality between clergy and faithful? How is it different? What does the sacrament mean to Catholics . . . It is not enough that the church responds as an organization. We must add our individual voices to the proclamation."

But *The Oregonian* responded with a counter editorial entitled, **Judge Right To Save Tape:** " . . . Judge Panner's decision showed respect not just for the state courts, but more broadly for the capacity of the criminal justice system to achieve the proper balance between society's interest and the rights of suspects. To destroy the tape now would upset that balance."

That balance was already upset and it was not the church who caused it. Our camp was surprised by the *Oregonian's* support for Panner's decision since it had been fairly supportive and sympathetic to the church; yet an opposite point of view was understandable since other papers from the secular press offered occasional contrary reactions to this event. Other newspaper headlines reflected outrage such as *The Denver Post*—**A Bayonet in the Confessional.** Were all these commentaries just so much hot air? In the post-Panner decision, I attempted to absorb this mantra of viewpoints but stood, thankfully, on the confidence of our consistent opinion.

In a later statement to the press, Archbishop George put our legal battle in its current context: "Citizens of all religions should be dismayed that the state may now with impunity violate fundamental religious practices." We also knew religious and civil rights issues had been further sacrificed by this decision and each had equal weight. The Constitution is meant to endure; its mere existence sets the fundamental structure for our society.

To some, this case in the larger context may seem to like an overstatement—an event unlikely to ever happen again; a singular violation of the sacred or an isolated incident. Yet, the world had reacted appropriately as the countless reactions of outrage had indicated. This violation was like a crack in the dam—should it be repaired or ignored? I knew I had my own repairing to do, however.

My ever present struggle to forgive those who perpetrated this action but not forget the seriousness of what was done, coupled with the whirlwind of litigation, taught me that forgiveness would be a long journey to discern right from wrong and to separate the facts from my emotions. I concluded this was not a direct personal attack on me as I believed county authorities would have done this regardless of who the priest was. However, the very fact that I *was* targeted, the sacrament deliberately violated, and the inmate and his future trial placed in possible jeopardy, was enough to sort through in my head and heart. If I could achieve peace of mind I could say I was on the road to forgiveness for of this I was certain. What had the potential at the very least to demoralize my sense of confidence as a member of the clergy, I wanted to use for growth. However, such idealism can only be given life through prayer and trust. A move in that direction was my hope.

*   *   *

Our next step would be the Ninth Circuit Court of Appeals. I was out of my league with the Court of Appeals and just placed my trust completely in the hands of attorneys, Archbishop George, and the heart of God. The appeal included a request that this case be "expedited," handled as quickly as possible. But, a case submitted to the Ninth Circuit could take as much as two to three years to unfold.

CHAPTER 11

Uncertainty Reigns

* * *

*"If you look for truth, you may find comfort in the end: if you look for comfort you will not get either comfort or truth." (C.S. Lewis—*Mere Christianity*)

* * *

Still at odds, the interests of church and state continued unresolved as Archdiocesan attorneys concentrated on getting our case expedited by the Ninth Circuit Court of Appeals. Our concerns about privacy, civil rights, and the place of religion in public life were also at play in the less polarized election year of 1996 than we saw in 2008. While the war in Iraq, wire-rap surveillance, continued hostilities in the Middle East, and fears of terrorism trudge on in our time, so did similar news at the time of this breach of privacy.

Though it had been a month since Judge Panner ruled on the case contrary to plaintiff's desires, press coverage continued unabated. The unresolved issues remained in a kind of legal limbo. Newspaper articles from *The Oregonian*, quoted Fr. Mike: "The tape has no practical value to Hale's defense or to the prosecution . . . This tape is a present reality. We will continue to seek, within the judicial system, the destruction of the tape."

The Ninth Circuit Court's reputation for making decisions that were often challenged did not give me confidence for a speedy response or victorious outcome. Even though attorneys requested this case be taken quickly, there was no guarantee the Appeals Court would agree to our request.

Meanwhile, state officials remained silent on the issue and only expressed their concerns within legal briefs and planned court hearings. The district attorney had said nothing more since his televised public apology. Then, a well-known case being litigated that same year posed a curious comparison.

Seen in the context of its time, the whirlwind of events in late October, 1996 around the O.J. Simpson civil trial, brought me to the conclusion that an aspect of that trial paralleled our case. The Simpson case dealt with the issue of right justice for a wounded family, whose daughter had been brutally murdered. In the charge against Hale, anguished families were standing on the side awaiting a resolve of their suffering.

But, more specific to our church interests, Rosie Greer, a lay minister at the jail where O.J. was held, had visited with the former football star and certain information was reportedly overheard by jail guards. It was quickly determined that the information was hearsay and inadmissible in the trial because of the religious nature of the conversation.

I had to wonder: Why was this celebrity granted the respect of privacy but Hale and I were not? The guarantee of non-interference in religious ritual by the government was supported in that case. Why not ours? For the church, the broader issues of religious integrity, free expression, privacy, and the sanctity of the human conscience became a fight to the next level as concerns circulated about whether the information on the tape, obtained in a far more deceptive manner than the method with Rosie Greer, would also be considered not acceptable.

*   *   *

As the litigation temporarily slowed to a quieter pace, I had time to rest and turn back to some familiar parish life. Plans for baptisms, funerals, weddings, and the day to day phone calls and requests were never so welcome. My parish had a school and to be around lively, happy children was a healthy diversion. They provided a routine pattern that also gave me the luxury to think and reflect from where we had come and to where we hoped to go.

In our particular case, both the *right to know* and the *need to know* were certainly at play. How much should the public know and how much should remain sealed? The issue of privacy and confidentiality affects all of us and was a fundamental apprehension throughout this extraordinary litigation. The state needed to collect concrete evidence for charges in their investigation and felt they had both the need and the right to undertake their action against the church and to consider whatever information was contained on that tape.

But the church had a right that was equally important—to resist the dissemination of whatever information was contained on the tape recording. Further, the church felt the state had neither the right nor the need to know whatever information was shared during the confessional encounter and, in like fashion, the church had neither the right nor the need to know the contents of the tape. The tape had to be destroyed.

Similarly, with our present day concern about the public's right to know what it is the government is up to, such as an explanation of our homeland security, in their rush for the presidency that year, President Clinton and Senator Robert Dole reflected our tensions as they clarified their position on the Freedom of Information Act in debates before Election Day.

Senator Dole remarked, "If the public has the right to certain information, then it should get that information and government should not attempt to mask its actions. Its actions must be, from the start, clean and honest and within the law. If government sticks to these principles, then there will be nothing to hide and no reason to fear . . ."

President Clinton stated his position, "The more the American people know about their government, the better their government will be." Society on the whole would not be better off, nor well served in the future, if the tape were allowed to live.

Searching for an outside perspective on this case, in his preparation for the hearing before the Circuit Court, Tom Dulcich sought the opinion of a well-known professor who, at that time, was from the University Of Texas School Of Law, Douglas Laycock. Professor Laycock's opinion was mixed:

" . . . In essence, they are saying they can commit any outrage on a church once, promise not to do it again, and there is no corrective remedy. The only way to correct what they have done is to destroy the tape . . .

" . . . I don't know if there is any way to back out of this, or any face-saving way to settle for some slight additional concession. But I would be thinking of damage control at this point. I certainly would not try to get this appeal expedited. The best possible outcome may be for it to sit for four years in the Ninth Circuit and then become moot . . ."

Tom was unsatisfied. We could not wait four years for the Ninth Circuit Court to take this up since the case had already been filed with a request for a speedy hearing and the legal momentum was unstoppable. Archbishop George, our attorneys, and I felt time was *not* on our side. We needed to bring this to final closure, to find this intrusion illegal as a violation of the Constitution, and execute an order for the tape to be eliminated. The state also felt the pressure of time in their pursuit to initiate Hale's trial. By this time, civil law, religion, and ethics were bound tightly in this bizarre mix of concerns as attorneys for both sides outlined more facts and new perspectives on well-known opinions already filed, took shape in briefs and affidavits. Finally, October brought good news.

Our appeal to the Ninth Circuit Court was accepted and a hearing before a panel of three judges in Seattle, Washington, was set for December 12. We had moved from the appeal to acceptance to a date for the hearing within a two-month period. The apparent Constitutional and religious issues—though apparently lost on state officials—would be addressed by the Ninth Circuit Court. The pace at which they had responded was impressive, and to me this indicated that they understood the urgency of our case. It seemed the judges of this Circuit had followed developments in this incident on the State and Federal level and were well aware of the issues. As we prepared, I wondered what further information would be collected by the defense (the state) for greater impact. Now it was time to once again move from the comfort of supportive friends back to the uncertainty of the courtroom.

* * *

I regularly received faxes and mail from our legal team as the wheels of justice rolled on towards the December date. The fine points and details of these documents I left to those more familiar with the law. I was both enlightened and wearied, but as I read through the new briefs, certain positions came to the forefront.

State defendants presented their position. The case was often referred to as, *Mockaitis vs. Harcleroad.* To forever be associated with a man whose position I respected but found this particular district attorney to be, for me, less than admirable, was all the more disturbing. I was called to separate the person from the behavior and was struck to see this as the same fundamental task within the sacrament we were fighting to protect.

The state continued to identify my visit with Hale as a "conversation," despite the ruling by Judge Panner two months before. The position of the state litigators remained the same: there was no interference in the free exercise of religion and there was no undue burden caused by the continued existence of the tape. We were never sure whether the D.A. listened to the tape or read its transcript but I presumed he did. What was done was done.

The state fleshed out how the efforts of the church were harmful to theirs: "The defendants' interests in the underlying criminal actions clearly are diverse, but all of them as parties in this case strongly agree that plaintiffs' attempt to interfere in the state-court prosecutions is seriously detrimental to their interests in ensuring the criminal defendants obtain a fair trial . . . federal courts must refuse to intervene in state criminal proceedings to suppress the use of evidence." (Court briefs) The state was emboldened by Judge Panner's decision to abstain from interference in a lower court criminal proceeding.

The state's brief claimed Archbishop George's interest was subjective: "Archbishop George's standing is based upon his subjective concern that other priests of the Roman Catholic faith may 'feel uncomfortable with administering the sacrament of penance in the Lane County Jail.' The Archbishop offers no explanation for his belief that priests will feel uncomfortable in the future, given the facts that Lane County has agreed to cease taping clergy conversations . . . and the district attorney has agreed that he has not used and will not use the contents of the tape in any manner . . . Plaintiff's suit for prospective relief has become moot because the alleged official action has been discontinued, and there is no reasonable expectation that it will recur."

More to the point, I was characterized by the state as "foolish or exceptionally naive" due to my expectation of privacy in a jail setting. I had never found myself labeled as foolish in my service as a priest so while the jail is certainly not a church or a confessional, it was clear to me that we were dealing with an overzealous law enforcement agency. I could only speculate why this had never come before a court of law in the past or what made this particular case so remarkable from others that this governmental agency considered this unprecedented method to gather evidence a justifiable "compelling" reason to invade a sacred religious ritual. While the death of three young teenagers was a heartrending event that the state had a right to investigate, it seemed a definition of the "compelling governmental interest" would be a challenge to the courts from both sides. Therefore, I continued to believe the state took advantage of this opportunity and violated the civil rights of myself and perhaps the prisoner.

While my feeling "uncomfortable" may not have been enough to establish a constitutional violation, much more was drawn in than just my emotions.

Meanwhile, the church pointed to Constitutional violations setting the event once again in its broad implications:

"Nowhere else in modern America has a state actor trampled so flagrantly upon the religious and privacy rights of a clergyman . . . The provisions of the First and Fourteenth Amendments to the Constitution of the United States as well as Sections 2 and 3 of Article I of the Bill of Rights to the Oregon Constitution, require the destruction of the tape and transcript . . ."

Sections 2 and 3 of the Oregon Bill of Rights say accordingly: "No law shall in any case whatever controls the free exercise and enjoyment of religious opinion, or interfere with the rights of conscience."

First Amendment offenses were explained: " . . . The clandestine taping and continued existence and preservation of a record of the secret taping of the confidential, sacramental duties of the priest place a 'substantial burden' upon plaintiffs' exercise of their religion . . ."

The Fourth Amendment was brought into play: "The right of people to be secure in their persons, houses, papers, and effects, against unreasonable searches and seizures, shall not be violated . . ." and the further offenses against the wire-tap law, mentioned earlier before Judge Panner, were presented to support the destruction of the tape.

The church brief continued:

"Whenever any wire or oral communication has been intercepted, no part of the contents of such communication and no evidence derived there from may be received in evidence in any trial, hearing or other proceeding in or before any court, grand jury, department . . . or other authority of the United States . . . 'oral communication' means any oral communication uttered by a person exhibiting an expectation that such communication is not subject to interception . . ."

This was to me an obvious explanation of why the tape cannot be used or played. Perhaps, I thought, among the Church's strongest support was this defense but whether it would hold weight was yet to be seen.

Essentially, the church claimed the religious ritual of the Sacrament of Reconciliation, in particular the *seal* of the sacrament, falls under the protection of secular law. The taping was unconstitutional and illegal due to its interference in the free exercise of religion. " . . . The interference can be remedied effectively only by destruction of the offending record and an order prohibiting further disclosure of its contents." (Court brief)

*   *   *

It had become starkly clear to me that so many of us have naively assume that our freedoms simply exist since we've never known otherwise. We live in the luxury of distance from the days when such freedoms were not so automatic; before church and state stood as two entities in co-existence under the protection of one common law. But, by now I had been hit through this litigation with the sober realization that those rights carry a price and demand vigilance. Complacency brings defeat so the Church was determined to push the issue of harm to the sacrament and the free exercise of religious faith. Doing so would protect the interest of privacy and that of any future penitent. Still, the central point remained: To whom does the tape belong—the church or the state? Adding to this problematic web were the interests of the inmate himself.

Despite his status as a jailed inmate, Conan Hale or any other prisoners do not discard their fundamental human rights outside the jail cell. Though prisoners do not have a reasonable expectation of privacy in their prison cells, as they are subject to shake-downs and searches for weapons and illegal drugs, freedom to worship does not disappear.

The American Civil Liberties Union has fought hard to maintain the integrity of prisoner rights as have other institutions. Beliefs that are sincerely held and religious rituals are protected by the Free Exercise Clause of the First Amendment to the United States Constitution. Mainstream belief systems such as Christian, Jewish, or Islam and less non-traditional faiths, which may or may not be recognized as religions, still offer prisoners certain religious rights nonetheless: "to practice their religion, obtain and keep written religious materials, communicate with a religious leader, and obey the rules of their religion that do not endanger security in the prison." (http://law.jrank.org)

Nor may the government impose a substantial burden on the religious exercise of prisoners unless that burden is "in furtherance of a compelling governmental interest; and is the least restrictive means of furthering that interest." (ACLU National Prison Project).

Therefore, Hale needed to convince prison administrators that his beliefs were sincerely held and that he was honest in his desire to see a Catholic priest. He was not asking to do anything outside the mainstream practice of the Catholic faith and his extreme restriction offered him no other option at the time. That was established by the Sheriff himself in the affidavit that spurred the search warrant to unseal the tape.

Likewise, members of the clergy, Christian and non-Christian alike, particularly within a jail setting, hold a common professional bond with an expectation of respect and privacy granted to them in their professional capacity. This issue touched many with the common fear of invasion of privacy.

Further, Terri Wood, Hale's counsel, explained her further concerns about the extent of the news reporting and its affect on the community:

" . . . The story of Hale's confession has attracted national and international press and it is reasonable to conclude that members of the Lane County community will be among the potential jurors . . ." (Court affidavit)

This complex of interests and opinions stood ready to be presented in print and word before the judges of the Ninth Circuit Court. But, what guarantee remained that privacy would be upheld? Further, I was still dealing with a personal sadness and had been reminded that the case was not my only concern.

*   *   *

In my personal life, uncertainty reigned as well. A few weeks after our hearing before Judge Panner, my father's health had deteriorated further, and by late August the end appeared close for him. Though my Father's condition was far removed from the secret tape, the concern and now inevitable outcome, allowed me to connect on a human level with my family and friends. For the time being, I could leave the sterile, somewhat monotonous atmosphere of legal briefs and courtroom hearings, and be genuinely myself as son and brother. Although sickness and terminal illness was nothing new to me in my service to parishioners, I need not be professionally distant and objective with my Father and family. Here, though sad, I could step away from being "Father" and just be a supportive son to my Dad and in particular to my Mother whose own private sorrow was mixed with gratitude for fifty years of marriage. It offered me a humanizing moment and taught me that gratitude is expressed not only when times are joyful but to be thankful also in the sadness of loss and the comfort of faith.

Hospice volunteers provided compassionate support, as they do for those dying who wish to remain in their homes until the very end. Their support was a most welcome blessing for my family. While my father's death that year would be a loss expected, the death of three teenagers in the woods, the crime the state was so vigorously investigating, was a tragedy for families never anticipated. Both were sad.

When my father lost consciousness, we felt it humane to let him leave this world as God intended, which is what he had requested. Medical science, ethics, and church teaching are not meant to be adversarial. Both should realize that there are limits and we are not meant to be here forever. Two days before, I had offered him the sacrament of the seriously ill and dying, the Anointing of the Sick, so I knew he was spiritually prepared.

Three days later at the funeral, the stressful events of the preceding months seemed far behind me. For my nephew Alex, whose second birthday we celebrated on the day of my father's funeral, it was a time of true innocence. The morning was sunny and clear and we were grateful that over two hundred people had attended. My father had been a very practical, straightforward businessman, a true product of his generation, who had owned a retail store in the southern suburbs of Chicago. I remembered again the man whose hard work and steady hand became the strength of our family life, and I sighed in gratitude.

Yet, even at the reception questions and comments came from guests and family. "How's that case going, Father?" "Isn't that terrible!" "What's the latest?" "How are you doing?" I must admit that I appreciated their interest and support as the case remained very much a part of my day-to-day reality.

The drama of this event felt more as a Greek tragedy than part of this modern day battle between church and state—a kind of *Antigone* in the battle for higher principles above that of human law. Many agreed that the legal and moral lessons to be learned from this case were far too valuable to minimize. For, by now, I had come from a stage of initial shock at the first news of the taping, to a frozen affect, to a simmering anger with an irrational sense of personal guilt, but a resolve to reach above the negative feelings. I felt pity for the perceived blatant disrespect of religious faith on the part of law authorities, in particular for the incarcerated. Still, through the prayers of many I found an inner resolve that emboldened me to keep moving forward. I continued to seek solace in prayer and the company of others who generously shared their support with me and I relied on an inner sense of determination that sustained my hopes.

*   *   *

Those not sympathetic to the religious issues involved in this case continued the demand that all information should be made known and preserved but the trial of Conan Hale was yet to be scheduled. Church and state had both "shouted out" their positions but Christmas was on the way and I wondered what sort of gift would be given by the court after the hearing in Seattle.

CHAPTER 12

The Sixty-Minute Countdown

* * *

"As Christians we give in too much. We are tempted to make unnecessary concessions to those outside the Faith. There comes a time, when we must show that we disagree. We must show our Christian colors, if we are to be true to Jesus Christ. We cannot remain silent or concede everything away." (C.S. Lewis—*God in the Dock.*)

* * *

Throughout this process, I could not help but connect some spiritual dots that gave me confidence we were not alone. December 12th, the day chosen for our hearing before three judges of the Ninth Circuit Court of Appeals, was for me a date not purely coincidental.

In the Catholic liturgical calendar, December 12th is the Feast of Our Lady of Guadalupe which commemorates a sixteenth century apparition to a native convert, Juan Diego. The event is a story of hope in the midst of disunity and injustice among a culturally diverse people. The vision of a woman standing before the sun, dressed as an Aztec maiden, who spoke tenderly with Juan Diego and whose image miraculously appeared on his tilma, an outer cloak made of cactus fiber now more than 500 years old. That primitive cloak is enshrined in Mexico City and has become a sign of national unity among the Mexican people which unites popular faith and nationalism in a unique blend of culture. Our hope to heal a strained relationship between church and state and to restore the right balance between civil rights and religious liberty was buoyed by this historical memory.

Likewise, our hearing before Judge Panner began on August 4th, the feast of St. John Vianney, a popular French Catholic priest, who served among his people for more than forty years in the mid-eighteenth century. His holiness was undeniable but the many hours he would spend in the confessional offering forgiveness to countless pilgrims has become his trademark as the "Cure' of Ars." His dedication to the sacrament we were so vigorously defending did not go unnoticed.

Since I did not look upon these dates as mere coincidence, I took hope in these spiritual patrons as a positive sign that we might eventually prevail in our search to bring unity in the midst of a struggle for justice between the two strained relationships of religion and state. Yet, I harbored some apprehension since there was no guarantee of anything at this point.

As our team began its brisk walk through the bustling streets of Seattle, the memory of our failed hopes before Judge Panner remained fresh in my mind. Our hopes were renewed for what could be our ultimate appeal.

Archbishop George, Fr. Mike, and I were dressed in our clerical suits, and our attorney Tom Dulcich wore his customary suit and tie. The day was overcast but relatively dry with a cold, stiff breeze as we moved swiftly toward the courthouse just a few blocks away. Store windows were abundant with holiday wreaths and lighted Christmas trees, a reminder of the person who was the central plaintiff in this case for us—Christ himself embodied in his Church.

As we strode past Seattle's imposing stone office buildings and across busy city intersections, the aroma of freshly roasted coffee and baked scones would permeate the early morning air as we walked past those familiar cafes. The city pulsated with a hurried population: a man waited impatiently at the bus stop, looking up every now and then from his morning newspaper; an elderly woman clung to the warmth of her disheveled red coat, mumbling incoherently; agile spiked-haired youths with nose rings moved swiftly against the traffic lights; the more mainstream population of men and women in conservative attire with briefcases strode on with purpose; and all seemed perfectly in synch. We rounded the corner of this colorful panorama and found the massive federal courthouse, far from the familiar Portland courthouse where we'd spent so much of our time four months before. My efforts to juggle church life with this obstacle course I hoped were coming to an end. I was grateful for such patient parishioners.

How would the now recognizable arguments be framed in this new venue? Would there be a repetition of our Portland Federal Court experience in August, or would a new tactic be employed? The hearing before a panel of three judges in Seattle, Washington would last sixty minutes. We were first on the docket. Attorneys and representatives for each side would be present, and attorneys would be timed and allowed twenty minutes for each oral argument. During the course of each argument, any one of the judges could break in to ask questions or to gain clarification. No press awaited us on the front steps of the court house as we passed routinely through security inside.

The courtroom in Seattle was austere; the room was sparsely furnished. Tables and chairs for defense and plaintiff faced the bench with little space behind us for observers of which there were none. Before us on a raised platform was a long bench designed to accommodate our three judges. They would be: John T. Noonan, David Thompson, and Andrew Kleinfeld. Judge Noonan was well-known as a Catholic scholar, a name I had hoped would be on this list, but the other two were unfamiliar to us.

Across the room at another table parallel to us, sat the legal team representing District Attorney Harcleroad, Judge Billings, and Judge Leonard. Judges Billings and Leonard were the trial judges chosen to oversee the future trial of Conan Wayne Hale. His alleged accomplice was to be tried separately and was not involved with the church in any way. Though the two accused men would be tried separately, our greatest resistance was from those who were faced with the investigation of Conan Hale.

Three judges would soon appear, and then the digital clock with its large red numerals would begin the countdown for the mere sixty minutes allotted to hear this case. The room was quiet; we waited on the edge of anticipation. I was grateful throughout this litigation that Fr. Mike had kept the Papal Nuncio in Washington, D.C., informed with monthly updates. I knew many would be praying for us today, which was of great comfort. But in moments I would learn there were millions.

Seated at the table awaiting the judges, I reviewed again the briefs I'd brought with me then noticed an unfamiliar folder on the table—a brief with a light green cover had been added to the stack. We still had nearly twenty minutes before our 9 a.m. hearing would begin, so I scanned the pages of this thirty-six-page document while Archbishop George and our attorney conversed quietly.

This "Brief Amicus Curiae," a friend of the court intervention, came from a mix of sympathetic religious observers. Its presentation was a surprise to me and I would imagine the same for Fr. Mike and Archbishop George since they had made no mention of it, nor had Tom our attorney. Among our friends were the American Jewish Congress, the Church of Jesus Christ of Latter Day Saints, the Baptist Joint Committee of Public Affairs, the Evangelical Lutheran Church in America, the Commission on Social Action of Reform Judaism, the General Assembly of the Presbyterian Church (USA), the Council of Churches of Christ in the USA, and the Christian Legal Society. On this issue of privacy and privilege, they wrote in solidarity with the Catholic Church and the U.S. Catholic Conference of Bishops.

Words of this document were familiar; a repetition of our explicit concerns, but its value lay in the unity expressed by these religious bodies. Long before, we realized this was not solely a Catholic issue but one of concern for all Americans. So the unified voices of these friends became for me a most welcome reassurance.

This gallery of brothers and sisters represented millions of people of faith across this nation; they stood "in support of Plaintiffs-Appellants." As I thumbed through the document, I imagined this great company of witnesses physically present, standing around us, all voicing their apprehension. Momentarily lost in the words of our friends, they began to speak one by one. With no need to parse their words, they spoke with force.

First was the *US Catholic Conference*, representing the American Catholic Bishops in the United States, a group which no doubt heartened Archbishop George, who addressed their flock: "To the Catholic Church and its people throughout the United States." The Bishops then stated, " . . . We are outraged that this personal and private forum of Confession has been compromised . . . We pray that the courts will recognize the violation that has occurred as a legal wrong that demands to be made right." The tone was set for our brethren of the covenant.

The *American Jewish Congress*, an organization of American Jews founded in 1918 to protect the civil, political, economic and religious rights of American Jews and all Americans spoke of their concerns. Of all populations on the face of this earth, the Jews are among those who have suffered the most due to their religious and political history. We are tied to them in history, tradition, and faith, and their viewpoint expressed here was tenacious. "We have filed numerous briefs in support of the right of religious institutions to freely worship God as their beliefs dictate. Rarely in recent years has there been as blatant an interference with that right as occurred here."

To this chorus came the *Commission on Social Action of Reform Judaism*, the Union of American Hebrew Congregations and American Rabbis, a representation of 1,700 Rabbis and more than 1.5 million Jews nationwide. They spoke with passion. " . . . The holding below threatens the sacredness of communication between a rabbi and his or her congregants; endangering a fundamental precept of Judaism . . . the ruling diminishes the traditional and vitally important weight given to implementing the First Amendment's free exercise guarantees when resolving a conflict between those guarantees and other governmental policies."

The *Church of Jesus Christ of Latter Day Saints* with a worldwide membership of over 9.5 million stated: "Firmly embedded in the tradition and teachings of the LDS Church are the concepts of religious freedom and toleration. We claim the privilege of worshiping almighty God according to the dictates of our own conscience and allow all men the same privilege to let them worship how, where, or what they may." (Article of Faith, No. 11).

From the broader Christian world, we heard from the *Baptist Joint Committee on Public Affairs*: "We deal exclusively with issues pertaining to religious liberty and church-state separation . . . We represent the Alliance of Baptists, the American Baptist Churches in the USA, the Baptist General Conference, the Cooperative Baptist Fellowship, the National Baptist Convention of America, the National Missionary Baptist Convention, and others related to liberty and the faith of millions among our congregations."

Then, Clifton Kirkpatrick, a Stated Clerk of the General Assembly of the highest governing body of the *Presbyterian Church*, asked that the Assembly's opinion be considered worthy of respect and prayerful consideration. He represented the largest Presbyterian denomination in the United States, with approximately 2,750,000 active members in 11,500 congregations. " . . . being called to testify in a court of law does not negate the sacred obligation . . . an intrusion by the state such as has been manifested in this case represents a danger to all religious bodies . . ."

The *Evangelical Lutheran Church in America (ECLA)*, the fifth largest Protestant body in the United States, eagerly joined the host of supporters. With more than 5.2 million individual members nationwide and more than 49,000 members in the State of Oregon alone, this was an added force to confront the opposition. Then came the *National Council of Churches of Christ*, a membership of 33 Protestant, Anglican and Orthodox communities of 53 million people, and in particular, its 270 members General Assembly. They aligned themselves in this brief as a "presence of concern."

Finally, the *Christian Legal Society*, a network of more than 4,500 Christian lawyers, law students and law professors offered its opinion. "CLS has defended the autonomy of religious institutions from excessive government interference in state and federal courts for over two decades. CLS has a particular concern over the state's action in the underlying prosecution, an unprecedented breach of an inviolable religious communication and exercise."

As the brief passed beyond individual concerns, these Amici spoke as one. "These actions of the state are not simply 'wrong' but, we will argue, clearly violated the First and Fourth Amendments to the Constitution. Furthermore, by conducting this surreptitious taping, the district attorney potentially violated the Fifth Amendment by creating a situation in which a suspect may virtually have been forced to incriminate himself in order to participate in one of the church's sacraments. The preservation of this ill-gotten gain compounds the wrong and perpetuates the violation. The only appropriate remedy is to restore the status quo and destroy the tape and transcript so that no further violations can occur.

"In spite of the fact that Appellants are defending principles of religious liberty that are fundamental to our legal system, their arguments and interests in this matter have been regularly met with absolute indifference, if not overt derision . . .

"In our legal system, the confidentiality of exchanges between priest and penitent is properly entitled to extraordinary weight, and is privileged for reasons arising out of both the Constitution itself and our common-law heritage. Amici act here to protect all people of faith and their clergy in the exercise of their religious beliefs. We suggest that it is only by overturning the District Court's blatantly erroneous interpretation of abstention doctrine, and remanding for the District Court to consider the vital principles at stake here and direct the destruction of the tape and transcript, that those interests can be protected.

" . . . the common understanding between religious groups that in order to freely exercise their religious beliefs, penitential communications with clergy must be privileged, and that the demands of the civil legal system, if they are in conflict with that obligation, must yield . . ." (Amicus Brief)

The strength of these religious traditions and their united commentary in support of the Church, and even more the fundamental issue of religious liberty, I found inspiring. It emphasized all the more how broad based the issues of this violation had become. In this crucial moment, the theological or historical issues that may yet divide us were put on the back burner. We were unified as brothers and sisters, as American citizens, and as people of faith.

And then, these friends of ours summarized the very core of our united argument making their position crystal clear: "*It is difficult to imagine any more blatant and bold-faced affront to the basic tenets of a religion, short of intentionally committing acts of sacrilege as a matter of state policy.*" (amicus brief)

Such words cut to the point like a razor's edge. Although my read at first was merely an overview, it lifted my hopes tremendously. I wondered what effect these voices had on those who represented the side that had brought us to this level in our legal system. While this brief was not used directly by the attorneys in their arguments, it remained for me, and I am sure for all of us as plaintiffs, an impressive sign of solidarity.

Suddenly my imaginings were interrupted, "All rise, this court is in session." I closed the brief, we pushed back our chairs and stood.

*   *   *

Three judges in black robes processed single file, and then settled in their seats. Before him, each had a nameplate: Judge Noonan sat in the middle, Judge Thompson to his left, and Judge Kleinfeld to his right. They offered polite smiles to all of us as the clock was about to begin its countdown.

I could not help be relieved when I remembered this hearing was almost delayed. It was touch and go for a time as the original desire of the defendants was to postpone this hearing until the U.S. Supreme Court could first determine the constitutionality of the Religious Freedom Restoration Act, known as RFRA.

Under RFRA, the government may not substantially burden a person's exercise of religion unless the government can demonstrate the burden is, "in furtherance of a compelling government interest; or "is the least restrictive means of furthering that compelling government interest." This was a controversial extension of First Amendment rights, one that some felt was unnecessary, but the opinion on RFRA was that it did extend to protection of prisoner's rights. It was a matter up for review by the United Supreme Court so the request to delay this hearing until after that Supreme Court decision would have delayed us indefinitely.

As an alternative, the United States would seek a representation at the hearing to present an additional five minutes of oral argument. The strict sixty minute period of time we were allotted for both defendants and plaintiffs was essentially not negotiable so one of the parties would need to cede those five minutes to the U.S. Government representative or the Judges would need to increase the time to sixty five minutes.

The state objected to any intervention and sought the delayed hearing but the Circuit Court agreed to add the additional five minutes of oral argument so that a representative from the Department of Justice in Washington, D.C. could explain the constitutionality of RFRA and allow the Judges to consider this in their final opinion. Although the resistance of the state was consistent in this convoluted process, it was reassuring that our move forward would continue without further delays since it felt as if we finally reached a point where some success was possible.

So, it was a relief when the judges were seated but one judge surprised us with an unexpected comment as we began. A white haired man with an open, approachable face, Judge John Noonan took the lead and addressed Archbishop George directly: "Good morning, Your Excellency, we want you to know that seated up here is a Catholic, a Protestant, and a Jew." The Archbishop nodded his head in appreciation and responded, "Thank you very much" to this unconventional beginning. No further comment from the judges was offered to the side representing the state nor did they look their way. Yet, to me it seemed they lingered in a momentary expression of assurance and empathy after Judge Noonan addressed the Archbishop.

The lead judge's signal was obvious: These men of law knew this case was not solely a Catholic issue, as our amici had so eloquently expressed, but one of importance to people of religion, Christian and non-Christian alike.

Was it more than coincidental that these particular judges of three distinct religious persuasions were present for this hearing? To that I could only wonder since the choice of judges takes place long before a case is brought to court and since the judges are assigned to cases in a way that would guarantee a proper rotation among more than twenty judges on this particular circuit. Still, I wondered again for a moment if some other spiritual intervention had taken place as the judges were chosen. What were the chances in this tense case of sacred vs. secular that three judges of three distinct religious traditions would decide the fate of this exceptional violation? The parallel with our amicus brief was remarkable, and this combination seemed a point Judge Noonan felt worth making. With that, the clock began its countdown.

Up first was the five-minute presentation made by Matthew Collette, a representative from the Department of Justice in Washington, D.C In a brief summary, Mr. Collette stood before the Judges and explained the government's position in straightforward language: "We disagree with the state who has taken the position in this case that it (RFRA) is unconstitutional."

Judge Noonan asked, "Well, if for instance we determine the Fourth Amendment Claim and get the relief they sought, there would be no need to address whether RFRA is constitutional."

The U.S. attorney nodded then assured them they could go ahead and assume its constitutionality despite the pending Supreme Court consideration of RFRA, and it could still be used as a defense.

Representation from the Department of Justice provided a strong symbolic presence of how far this case had gone. Mr. Collette concluded his brief presentation, the Judges wished him well on his weekend visit with a sister who lived in the Northwest, and thanked him for his clarification. I wondered about the time and expense taken to fly this man out from Washington, D.C., put him up in a hotel, offer a meal or two, and then allow him only five minutes to speak. In the world of law, however, it was of greater value to have a representative physically present rather than simply send a letter or legal brief. In the exercise of our democracy, it was impressive to see that the U.S. Government considered this matter serious enough to extend this reassurance.

So, it appeared that RFRA could be referenced with confidence and the U.S. government would not challenge that. Beyond that, violations of the First and Fourth Amendments could stand on their own. It felt as a coup in our favor.

*   *   *

As the clock ticked down, Tom Dulcich rose from his chair to begin his oral arguments. The arguments were similar to those presented before Judge Panner months before but now with more passion and weight due to the implications of this high court's ultimate ruling.

Tom spoke with conviction: "The facts of this case demonstrate that the taping was planned in advance by the governmental authorities, it was not done in the ordinary course of business, it was authorized by Mr. Harcleroad, yet, they label Fr. Mockaitis as foolish. Further, they cite a case in their brief submitted for this hearing, *United States v. Harrelson,* which was a prosecution for the murder of a federal judge. Defendants fail to note that Harrelson was evaluating the privacy expectations of a career criminal who had personal knowledge of electronic eavesdropping in prison and had actually helped prison authorities record conversations he had with another inmate during a prior stay.

"Defendant's appalling comparison of Fr. Mockaitis to the cold-blooded killers and hardened criminals who assassinated a United States District Judge demonstrates defendants' lack of appreciation for the religious and privacy interest involved in this case. Mr. Harcleroad seeks to shift to Fr. Mockaitis the blame for the creation of the illegal record which now exists, rather than accept the responsibility for his own misconduct. The record in this case establishes violations of the federal Anti-Wiretap Act, of RFRA, and the First and Fourth Amendments."

Tom's voice began to rise with more emphasis: "Defendants' argument that Fr. Mockaitis is presumed to have known his communication with Hale might be monitored fails for four reasons, Your Honor." Then, he raised his wrist just above his shoulder and pointed four fingers upward.

"First, only a tortured construction of the statute gives it the meaning defendants ascribe to it. The Oregon statute cited by defendants does not say that tape recording a confidential priest-penitent communication in an attempt to gather evidence cannot give rise to civil liability.

"Second, The provisions of Oregon's priest-penitent privilege provides specific notice that monitoring should *not* be expected.

"Third, to the extent the Oregon statute allows monitoring without a warrant or consent, it is preempted by the federal Anti-Wiretap Act.

"Fourth, the statute does not purport to suspend the operation of the Oregon Constitution or the First, Fourth and Fourteenth Amendments to the United States Constitution.

"Plaintiffs are entitled to a remedy for these violations. At the heart of Harcleroad's argument is an unstated premise that nothing should be done which might have any collateral effect upon Harcleroad's prosecution of the high profile murder case. This court should not ignore the rights of Fr. Mockaitis and deprive plaintiffs of the relief to which they are entitled, simply because the party responsible for the blatant misuse of official power may suffer negative consequences." (Plaintiffs reply brief to Ninth Circuit Court).

As Tom spoke, the judges proved they were well acquainted with this case. Their understanding was clear to me as they allowed Tom to speak with little interruption and they nodded, as if, it seemed to me, in agreement with Tom's arguments. The core issues remained the existence of the tape and the call for its destruction, the covert procedure of the violation, a ruling on the illegal nature of this action based upon Constitutional violations, and the request for a formal injunction against Lane County jail authorities that this never takes place again.

My thoughts again returned to the voices of our amici, who summarized their arguments by saying the confidentiality of clergy-penitent communications has been properly accorded the highest degree of protection by our legal system. These values are very much at issue in this case because that investigator saw a chance to obtain evidence by knowingly violating the secrecy of the confessional.

"The threat to maintain and use the tape—the ill-gotten gain of this deliberate breach of respect for a constitutional guarantee—must be plainly rejected." (Amici Brief, p. 34).

I sat fascinated by this process of unity, rarely seen among diverse opinions. There was no significant conversation between myself, Archbishop George, or Fr. Mike since we all listened to the careful details. Any sense of victimhood on my part, and its self-centered focus, was being jolted away by this incredible sense of solidarity. I began to realize that I had come a long way towards healing and with a renewed energy could begin to reach out to those who are truly victimized and have no defenders or defense. I don't believe that I ever stopped filtering this event through the eyes of my priesthood but I could not deny the ordinary human emotions that reminded me again that I too stood on clay feet. But, the empathy of the judges, the power of our justice system, and what seemed tangible hope for a final resolution, offered comfort that had yet to be decided. More would come.

Tom remarked on the unprecedented media coverage of our case as he walked to the far side of the Judges bench to also face the participants:

"This case attracted incredible media attention and I think that's what happens when this kind of event occurs. There is, I am sorry to say, a market created for this type of thing and that's one of the reasons we want the structure. The district attorney is the one who violated those rights and in fact his prosecution of these two criminals suffers because of it. As unfortunate as that is, we believe the principles are such that they transcend the prosecution and they're so important that the court should issue not only the perspective injunctive relief and the declaratory relief but also do what we ask in the destruction of the tape."

Judge Noonan glanced at Tom and raised his eyebrows, resting his hand over his mouth and chin. Then Tom said, "For some reason, and we don't know why, the defendants decided to go to a local magistrate or a local state court or a district judge and seek a search warrant to listen to the tape. They sought a search warrant only for this particular encounter between Hale and this visitor, a Catholic priest. If this taping was in the normal course of their procedures, as they claim, then a search warrant would not be necessary."

Judge Noonan broke in: "I have a little trouble telling from the records whether the jail taped 80 or 90 percent of all Hale's visits or 80 or 90 percent of all inmate's visits or whether they were particularly looking out for the priest."

Tom responded, "I think it was Detective Carley who testified that perhaps 80 percent of Mr. Hale's communications were monitored. It was very, very clear from Detective Carley's affidavit that this interception was far from the normal course of business. The taping was not done as part of the routine and there were no security concerns about his visit with Mr. Hale.

"He always wore his roman collar, he wore it on the day he came to visit Mr. Hale. Yet, they're saying he had no reasonable expectation of privacy despite the fact that they didn't tell him. They secretly deputized him as a law enforcement agent from Lane County and now they're saying he is foolish and naïve."

Judge Noonan shook his head in agreement and sat back for a moment while the other Judges gave a slight smile at Tom's words, "There were no security concerns."

Judge Kleinfeld asked: "What if Hale had left the confession, in the confession room, and had written out his confession as a diary entry, he memorialized it, and then he decided to go public. He could certainly do that."

Tom answered quickly: "He could Your Honor. But what we have here is deciding what remedy is appropriate."

Judge Noonan added: "He'll initiate an appeal in case and he'll say the tape was evidence and it has a necessary right to exist but it was destroyed and we'll have to deal with that."

Tom said: "It's true we'll have to deal with those issues but there's no evidence that the Oregon courts will not decide that case directly. What is the worst that will happen if this tape or transcript gets destroyed? First there is no evidence in the record that the Oregon courts will not fully protect the constitutional right to a fair trial of Conan Hale. Our focus here is not on what Mr. Hale did or didn't say it's what the state did.

"I'm inclined to think you're correct," said Judge Noonan. "It seems the government eavesdropped on the confession. Let's suppose that's so. I've never seen a remedy for an unlawful search and seizure that involved destruction of evidence. I'm particularly concerned about it because this is a triple murder case if Hale winds up with the death penalty."

Tom said: "Granted, this is unusual, Your Honor."

Judge Noonan agreed: "It sure is," then again sat back in his chair.

Tom continued: "But suppose we have an attorney whose conversation with a client was secretly recorded. The attorney would say, well, "That's privileged" and that tape would be excluded as evidence in a trial. But the problem here is that the state is claiming that this conversation is evidence seized and we believe that in this particular circumstance the only way to make sure there is an appropriate remedy is the immediate destruction of the tape. If this action was legal, ethical and right, as the state claimed, why was it done in secret? The bottom line, Your Honor, is that there is no other appropriate remedy to restore the balance between church and state that my client seeks.

"The tape was illegal at its inception and continues to be so today. The continuing existence of the tape violates plaintiffs' constitutional rights to privacy and free exercise of religion and statutory rights under the Anti-Wiretap Law and RFRA. Destruction of the tape will accomplish two goals. First, it will alleviate to the extent possible the past and continuing violations of plaintiffs' First and Fourth Amendment and statutory rights. Second, it will establish that the misuse of state power to trample indiscriminately on those rights will not be tolerated.

"The only rights proven to have been violated and which continue to be violated are plaintiffs' rights. The violation of those rights has nothing to do with the criminal case pending in Lane County other than that the existence of that case is being asserted as a reason for disregarding the past and continuing violations of plaintiffs' constitutional interests. This court can and should remedy that violation immediately by ordering the tape destroyed and issuing the other injunctive and declaratory relief requested." (Court brief).

The three Judges had been listening carefully and though I was hard pressed to interpret the scene, my gut sensed agreement and supportive understanding on the part of all three judges.

Judge Thompson then wondered: "One of the obvious questions that I can see is where would they use this tape? This is an issue that has never before come to a court of law. Any information related to similar private conversations has in the past not been admissible. I don't see how this is different other than a request filed to preserve it."

Tom said: "The promise of a sealed tape was made by Mr. Harcleroad six months before this hearing. A promise that was modified two months later when Judge Billings allowed Hale's attorney to listen to the tape and copy it in late July." There was no doubt that Tom was confident in his explanation.

Tom paced back and forth slowly as he continued his argument, "In another effort to sidestep the early question of sacrament or not, the state insisted that the church offered no evidence to establish the allegation in their complaint that Fr. Mockaitis ever administered the sacrament to Hale. This, in spite of the fact that Detective Carley had stated clearly in his affidavit the so called conversation is a sacrament of the Catholic Church."

It wasn't long before Tom finished and then the state was invited to present its case. I knew that I was anxious to hear if the state would present a new approach or new perspective.

Attorney for the state and Mr. Harcleroad, Greg Chaimov, stood up and addressed the three Judges. "Greg Chaimov, attorney for defendants, Your Honor," and then pleaded their position as he referred to the Amicus Brief, "Religious groups from around the nation have offered support to plaintiffs. Plaintiffs and *amici* place their religious values above all other considerations. Our constitution and criminal laws embody other important values the most important of which are ensuring that justice is served and that criminal defendants receive fair trials."

Mr. Chaimov referred once again to the potential destruction of the tape as having a "devastating" effect on the State's ability to prosecute.

Judge Noonan responded: "I'm not sure I would use the word 'devastating.'"

The judge continued the lead. He peppered the defendants' lawyers with questions and clarifications, challenging them to justify their reasoning and behavior.

As Mr. Chaimov stood before the black robed and somber looking panel. Judge Noonan asked, "One of the core issues here is the claim that the state is making on the legality of this taping. Tell me, Mr. Chaimov, why the state claims this to have been a legal interception?"

Chaimov answered, his voice sounded self-assured: "First, Your Honor, Lane County officials—not any of the defendants in this case—intercepted the conversation between Fr. Mockaitis and Hale. Plaintiffs may claim that Mr. Harcleroad obtained it illegally. However, no facts are in this record from which the court can find that Lane County acted illegally or that defendants knew that Lane County acted illegally when it intercepted this conversation. Although plaintiffs have shown that Fr. Mockaitis subjectively believed his conversation would be confidential, plaintiffs failed to establish either that the audio taping was illegal or that his belief was justified under the circumstances.

"The law allows for the interception of conversations in jails and in this case Fr. Mockaitis is charged with knowing that the Oregon statute authorized the monitoring of any jailhouse conversation by an inmate with anyone other than his lawyer."

Judge Noonan leaned forward and queried: "It seems to me, Mr. Chaimov, that the state took advantage of this situation."

"Your Honor," Mr. Chaimov responded, "The audiotape is still in existence because Mr. Harcleroad has an affirmative obligation under Oregon Law to disclose to a criminal defendant all of his recorded statement and prevent the destruction of physical evidence. The priest's federal lawsuit is in direct interference with the state criminal proceeding. However, our position throughout this is that what we did was inherently wrong but we believe it was legal."

Judge Noonan, with a firm voice asked: "Why was it wrong?

Mr. Chaimov looked directly at Judge Noonan: "Well it was wrong for political reasons and for general reasons.

Judge Noonan pushed: "Was it ethically wrong?

Chaimov said: "Well it depends on the situation but this is not a basis for it to be legally wrong.

Judge Noonan with emphasis stated: "Is it your proposition that you can get a search warrant to get to a sacrament of confession? That's your proposition?

Chaimov glanced down for a moment and then looked up: "No, that is not our proposition."

Judge Noonan added: "Well, tell us what it is."

"Our position," Chaimov explained, "is that in the context of the jail, state law expressly allows jail officials to monitor conversation between inmate and someone who is visiting."

Judge Noonan said: "Now tell us why, as stated in Carley's affidavit, the recording of a sacramental confession is constitutional. Is that allowed?"

"Well, it is constitutional in this circumstance as state law allowed the recording of this conversation." Chaimov responded. "So under those circumstances neither Hale nor Father Mockaitis made any effort to arrange for a private conversation."

Judge Noonan, moved in his chair and spoke more strongly with an increased pace: "Well let me give you a hypothetical situation. They bug a confession in an ordinary church."

"Well, that would be a violation," Chaimov answered quickly.

Judge Noonan threw back: "What's the difference?" (Court transcripts)

The judges frustration with the state's position was strikingly different from that of the church's interests. At one point, Judge Noonan peered slightly over the bench to Mr. Chaimov, the state's attorney, and questioned the validity of their legal arguments. His tone was direct: "What were you thinking?" he asked.

The judge continued his line of thought and noted that inmates, if they so desire this sacrament, cannot "go down to St. Mary's if he's charged with murder. He's in jail!" The Judge then broke in with some important history.

"Counsel, as I understand the history of the priest-penitent privilege, during a time of hostility to Catholics in England, they dropped the priest-penitent privilege for awhile. But it remained pretty universal in the States and I would think that because of the universality of that, one form or another of that privilege exists in Oregon. Because of that a priest might have a reasonable expectation of privacy when you hear his confession."

Mr. Chaimov said: "Neither Fr. Mockaitis nor Hale ever asked the jail authorities for a confidential conversation or private room. Nothing in the record suggests that the authorities likely would have denied such a request had it been made."

"I understand that Fr. Mockaitis," Judge Thompson asked of Mr. Chaimov, "was told by someone that he was not allowed to visit anywhere other than in the visitors' area. Is this true?"

Mr. Chaimov responded: "It may have been a misunderstanding if that was said. The statute we reference, Your Honor, does not prevent any member of the clergy from administering religious sacraments at the Lane County Jail. The claim of the plaintiffs that this has had a 'chilling' effect on their willingness to do so is not enough to establish a First Amendment violation."

Far from my experience in ordinary parish life and elsewhere, to imagine the "illusion" had been created that complete privacy would exist and I would be respected there, though by now familiar, still sounded bizarre. I struggled to separate my thoughts of being used from my feelings of resentment so I could reason my way through the facts. Though my sense of vindication was growing, I hoped I would never loose sight of the bigger picture both for the imprisoned and for American society in general. So, this journey of litigation became a kind of healing experience.

Judge Noonan then changed the focus and added: "Let's talk about First Amendment violations. The plaintiffs are claiming that this action violated that fundamental amendment of our Constitution."

"Your Honor," Chaimov became livelier, "The continued existence of the audiotape does not violate the Free Exercise Clause. This case demonstrates excessive entanglement, given that plaintiffs are seeking to have a federal court force a state court to implement canon law. Preserving the audiotape temporarily for possible use in the pending capital-murder prosecution does not pressure Fr. Mockaitis to do anything that is forbidden by his religion, nor does it prevent him engaging in any of his religious practices. The claim that it makes him uncomfortable and reluctant to hear confessions at Lane County jail, would not of itself establish a free-exercise violation."

Judge Noonan said: "Well, Mr. Chaimov, I would imagine that this has had some effect on the perception of Fr. Mockaitis as to his level of trust within the jail surroundings or perhaps within any penal institution. It may have seemed that out of nowhere this happened.

"On page seven of your brief you recite these stipulations as to what Harcleroad has agreed to and its hard for me to understand how he could object to an injunction of this court requiring him to do the very thing he should have refrained from.

"Let's assume there was a Fourth Amendment violation. Then we would get to the remedy that Fr. Mockaitis wants the tape destroyed, you want the tape preserved. Mr. Harcleroad promises that the tape will eventually be destroyed. It seems to suggest that you would certainly not be opposed to an injunction from this court or from any court requiring you to do just that. Is that correct?"

"Mr. Harcleroad has stipulated that he will not use the evidence in the state's case and that he will destroy the evidence when the case is complete," answered Mr. Chaimov. "Off the top of my head I cannot see a problem with an injunction.

"Your Honor, many of the considerations that have kept federal courts from interfering in state court proceedings are present in this case. Even if this court does not fit this case within a rigid pigeonhole, it should conclude that the district court properly abstained from deciding plaintiffs' claims, given the extraordinary nature of the relief sought and the detrimental impact such relief would have on the related state criminal proceeding."

Judge Noonan followed further: "It seems to me the only way Fr. Mockaitis could be at risk of violation of church law would be if he exposed it. But it's perfectly clear this was recorded without his knowledge and that he has done everything possible to prevent disclosure. If somebody else discloses it and plays it on the radio he is not violating the sanctity of his promise. I don't see where Fr. Mockaitis is doing anything wrong. Is that correct Mr. Dulcich?"

"Fr. Mockaitis has done nothing wrong," said Tom as he stood up, "but the Catholic Church, Your Honor, seeks its immediate destruction."

Judge Noonan asked: "Why?"

Tom answered: "Because it's a privileged moment of reconciliation. You look at some of these stipulated facts about how ingrained the confidentiality of the sacrament is and how it hurts him each time that's reviewed and each time its referenced. This case attracted incredible media attention. They transcend the prosecution and they're so important that the court should issue not only the injunctive relief and the declaratory relief but also do what we ask in the destruction of the tape." (Court transcripts)

The rapid-fire volley between attorney and judges forced one to listen carefully. The opinion that the issue was either excessive entanglement or the violation of religious liberty stuck me as nearly a stalemate. As we approached the end of the permitted sixty-five minute hearing, I took a moment to reflect on my notes.

I could not help but wonder about the meaning of *when* exactly the state would follow through on their promise to destroy the tape. It had been mentioned more than once that it would be after the trial of Conan Hale. While an intriguing study in American jurisprudence, the appropriate remedy was to reestablish a balance between church and state. However, I feared it might not include the destruction of the tape.

Further mentions by the judges were made of Constitutional violations about eavesdropping, the search and seizure principle of the Fourth Amendment, and a reference to civil rights damages.

In the end, the defendants' persistent justification of their behavior was in obvious contrast to that of the church's insistence for destruction of the tape and the declaration of Constitutional violations. The moral and ethical exercise of power was at stake in this complicated and extraordinary collection of interests and it struck me that this was a kind of revolution; a small but symbolic war over the power of words and their application. Both the genius and the inherent tension that was created in our Constitutional separation between secular and religious was clear.

How I and so many of us have taken much for granted in the movement of our daily lives. As priest, I knew well the history of religious persecution. I heard often the challenge well meaning parishioners confront to live and speak openly about their faith in both the work place or even within their own families. Persecution does not always come in direct ways; it can often be the faith of one person met with indifference, ridicule, or apathy from another. But here, in this court of law, the discussion between judges and lawyers reflected a much broader perception of religion today. To many it is more of a hobby, an occasional exercise when nothing better is available, or a kind of insurance policy that is used only when a crisis arises. In some cases religion is seen as an inconvenience to the rhythm of daily life; unnecessary since life is going along well. But the religious participation or lack thereof, of any one individual does not negate or lesson its value.

At the time of the state's challenge to the interests of the church before the Ninth Circuit Court, one of the nation's most forthright supporters of religious freedom, Mr. William A. Donohue, President of *Catholic League for Religious and Civil Rights* had spoken before the Subcommittee on the Constitution, a committee of the U.S. House of Representatives in 1996 about the matter of religious freedom. Not only did the *Catholic League* strongly urge the apology of the district attorney but takes the approach of meeting opposition with a firm, clear, and rationale response. Mr. Donohue spoke:

"The *Catholic League for Religious and Civil Rights* endorses the Religious Freedom Amendment . . . James Madison, who authored the First Amendment, made it quite clear what he meant when he wrote the so-called establishment clause . . . The idea that this clause would be used to insulate religion from government would have struck Madison, and the other Framers, as bizarre and downright disrespectful of their original intent . . .

" . . . It needs to be noted that District Attorney Harcleroad maintained to the end that what he did was legal, even if it wasn't 'right.' That suggests that the way the First Amendment is interpreted today gives a green light to overly-zealous prosecutors. (*Catholic League for Religious and Civil Rights*. Copyright, 1997).

Such words reinforced our arguments. It may be worse, even, if an action that is immoral can be sanctioned if it doesn't violate the law.

*   *   *

The twenty minutes allotted for oral arguments on each side, plus the five minutes given to the United States Government intervention, passed by quickly. I was heartened to find our judges had done their homework in preparation for this case. They were well acquainted with the issues and it seemed at times had already worked through to some initial conclusion. It appeared the Constitutional violations of the First and Fourth Amendments rose to the surface, but the most problematic issue remained that of the tape and its admissibility as evidence in a trial. Everyone wrestled with this topic throughout these arguments. The defendants' attorneys remained fixed in their position and we continued our plea for its destruction.

These three judges left us with no definite opinion as to how they would rule. However, reading between the lines for me was not as difficult with them as it had been with Judge Panner. I was feeling much more hopeful.

Once our time was up, the panel of judges was cordial and complementary to the legal teams on both sides. "You've argued the case extremely well," stated Judge Noonan.

Then, with the familiar gavel in hand, Judge Noonan proclaimed, "This court is in recess," as he brought it down solidly.

There would be no second opportunity to develop our points beyond this sixty-minute hearing. This was the end of the line. Yet, I still had questions. Such questions did not change the despicable nature of the violation of privacy in this sacrament and I never stopped caring about Hale's rights in this process. Ultimately, how would the decision of the judges, whatever way it goes, be received by the state or accepted by the church? Would these judges grab the same courageous chance that was offered to Judge Panner or would they too pass it by?

Yet, other factors combined to provide me greater reason for a positive verdict: the speed at which this case was accepted; the more deferential treatment of the judges toward Archbishop George and the interests of the church as a whole; the shared positions of the amicus brief; and the judges' numerous questions directed toward defendants' attorneys. It all served to raise our confidence.

*   *   *

Our day before the Circuit Court judges of three major religions was over, so we began our four-hour trek south to Portland later that morning At least on my part, I also had nothing more to do in this case except wait for the opinion of these men.

Christmas was just two weeks away and the spirit of the season energized me. I knew information hungry parishioners would be waiting to hear any glimmer of hope. The liturgical season of Advent was upon us—a time of waiting for the coming of the Lord at Christmas time. The prophets Isaiah and Jeremiah are often quoted during our Church celebrations. Hundreds of years before the coming of Christ, these prophets had encouraged the ancient Israelites to have hope and to know that God was with them, especially in times of despondency and disillusionment.

To believe that at some moment salvation would come, and a Messiah would bring freedom from oppression was the promise of the Biblical prophets. This promise gave me hope that the church and I would be free of our disillusionment and find right justice. In this sense, the prayer of Isaiah was my prayer as well, "Oh that you would rend the heavens and come down . . ." (Is 63:19). This cry of an oppressed people longing for God to intervene in their lives and rebuild their nation; to fix the unfixable; to clean up the mess that we ourselves created, was the hope of ancient Judaism. It became my Advent prayer as we approached the celebration of the birth of Christ. How long the wait for the decision of the Circuit would be, we did not know, but it was a hope nonetheless. It was now time to anticipate only one thing—the coming of a savior.

Chapter 13

Annus Horribilis

* * *

"Because wrong actions result where free wills operate, the possibility of suffering is inevitable. God does not violate the aggressive person's will to strike the innocent . . . We humans have deliberately abused our free-will, one of God's best gifts to us." (C.S. Lewis—*The Problem of Pain*)

* * *

In the midst of our anticipation some distressing news was revealed. An ethics complaint had been filed with the Oregon State Bar Association against the District Attorney of Lane County. The complaint charged the D.A. with "professionally unethical behavior" as a result of the secret taping at the Lane County Jail. Despite that complaint, the week before Christmas, the final decision came down from the Bar's disciplinary counsel concluding that Mr. Harcleroad had acted with "understandable assertiveness" in trying to solve a serious crime. The State Bar recognized the District Attorney was charged with authorizing the investigation of a heinous crime. It was determined those charged with investigating the case had every right and responsibility to doggedly go after sources of evidence they could find. The State Bar acknowledged this investigative method outweighed the covert nature of the taping.

The Bar concluded the taping was legal under Oregon law, in spite of the fact that the conversation may be construed as a Sacrament of Reconciliation which the Catholic Church requires be held in complete confidence and be immune from intrusion due to its religious nature.

It was judged the district attorney had done nothing unethical and that no action would be taken against him, which implied his behavior was not, "dishonest, fraudulent, or deceitful." But one piece was missing—an appalling lack of understanding for the religious rights of those in jail and the religious sensitivities of the larger population.

To say this finding was hard to take was an understatement. As one who lives a profession which is filled with high moral and ethical expectations, I found this judgment on the behavior of civil officials to be astounding. Human weakness and misjudgment aside, this taping was done with forethought. We priests know well the damage that has been done by a few of our brothers who, for whatever reason, chose to behave in a scandalous manner. By association, all priests were considered suspect, which in itself painted a broad unfair perception of the Catholic priesthood.

The finding of the Bar was a sad association for many in the legal profession who follow a strict code of ethics. Despite all the negative publicity this case had stirred up from a diverse national and international population, the State Bar, representing those in the legal profession throughout the state, discharged the complaint. Was this merely a local aberration or an indication of a more frightening shift in attitude against religious organizations in general?

To bug a church or a jail for this purpose was both unethical and illegal. The battle lines between secular and sacred could not be more distinct. I recalled Judge Noonan's words when he compared confession in a church to the same sacred moment in a jail and stated, "What's the difference?" I was stunned.

In response to this ruling Mr. Harcleroad, as he did in his official apology months before, admitted the taping was, "wrong, but still legal and ethical." I found this continued mantra a fearful twist of rationalization.

I personally sought no harm on the district attorney or to anyone else, but the very principles of justice demanded resolution. The court of public opinion had cried out with force over the course of this litigation, yet a narrow interpretation to the letter of the law was a shield behind which defendants stood and an indication of moral relativism. Mr. Chaimov's answer to Judge Noonan's question during the hearing in Seattle about the legality of this taping was telling: "It depends on the situation." The district attorney was absolved of his behavior so I turned away from this troubling development—an unwelcome Christmas gift.

Then, on a very different note, on Christmas Eve morning, my parishioner Judge Thomas Coffin handed me a letter. Judge Coffin and his " . . . consistently created the illusion of confidentiality . . . ." remark had become a troubling anchor for me to hold. He asked me to read his letter and considered he might send it to *The Register-Guard.*

As a committed Catholic and dedicated family man, with a perceptive legal mind, Judge Coffin spelled out his commentary on the odd developments in this case. His words were a piercing summary of our entire affair and for me a kind of reassurance that despite my mixed emotions, I and the Church were clearly on the right path. His words were passionate and articulate.

Judge Coffin wrote in part:

"In the aftermath of the unprecedented bugging . . . we are left to ponder the following developments and news items:

"The District Attorney has defended the secret taping as legal and ethical, and the State Bar agrees . . . The perplexing dilemma is that the state considers it ethical and lawful to engage in conduct that is 'wrong and inappropriate.'" (Harcleroad's own admission)

"The District Attorney and Bar firmly deny that any deception was practiced . . . This despite the fact that the District Attorney initially defended the eavesdropping as necessary for security purposes, as 'after all, priests have been known to commit criminal acts.' Later, the District Attorney backed off this false justification, and admitted the taping was for the purpose of gathering evidence against Conan Hale. The security angle was rubbish.

"Read the affidavit of the Deputy Sheriff Carley . . . It reveals more than a passing familiarity with the Catholic Church and the sacrament of reconciliation . . . The state thus knew full well that no priest would have administered the sacrament knowing of the plan to secretly tape the encounter. Fr. Mockaitis was recruited to minister as a volunteer chaplain to inmates' spiritual needs. He went through a background security check. No representative of the state ever told him that his ministry was subject to eavesdropping. No signs at the jail warned him of the state's intentions. The state knew that Hale had requested Fr. Mockaitis to visit for the purpose of administering the sacrament, and bugged the encounter in an attempt to use a sacred sacrament of the church as a tool of the state. No deception? The entire setting was a deception, from beginning to end. The state deceived by allowing Fr. Mockaitis to believe his ministry as a priest was being respected by the State, and by singling out inmates of certain religious beliefs for a most perverse investigative method.

"The posturing of the State's lawyers since this indecent assault on religious liberties has only magnified the horror of it . . . What about the District Attorney's concession that the taping was wrong and inappropriate? Are priests and other ministers at the jail somehow at fault and even 'foolish,' for failing to foresee the District Attorney would indulge in wrong and inappropriate behavior to gather evidence? The attack by the state on Fr. Mockaitis in its legal argument only demonstrates the insincerity of its damage-control PR job in the wake of international outrage at this scandal. No deception?

"Even more arrogantly, the state in its briefs has challenged the church's declaration that this was a sacramental encounter. The Attorney General takes it upon himself to school the Archbishop on matters of church theology. The absurdity of the church-state role-reversal escapes the Attorney General.

"The surface articles that have appeared in the media about this incident do not begin to tell the whole story. The manner in which the state has defended the bugging in the lawsuit filed by the church in federal court reveals the seriousness of the danger this action presents to religious freedom. In a nutshell, the state is insisting that it has the right and the ability to abuse even the most sacred rituals of the church for a state objective. Put it this way—if secretly bugging the confessional is lawful and ethical, then there is nothing unlawful or unethical with the state dressing up the police in priestly garb and sending them in to administer fake sacraments of reconciliation to inmates in order to gather evidence against them.

"If anything, the former tactic is even more egregious, because it involves an intrusion into a true sacramental encounter. If this is not an impermissible impediment to religious freedom, the First Amendment is a glass shield." (End letter)

Although, he never did send this out for publication he likely sent a copy to our law team. I speculated that with the well-known position he held in the county and state, perhaps he did not want to influence the outcome or appear to take sides by making such a public statement in criticism of those in his own profession. I respected him for whatever reasons he had for not taking the letter to the public.

Judge Coffin's words spoke volumes which embodied the thoughts that ran through my head and heart, and no doubt through the hearts of Archbishop George and our legal counsel. It offered a harmonious parallel to the interests of our amici group presented during the Ninth Circuit Court hearing. His term "eavesdropping" was perhaps a signal about his agreement that this violated the Fourth Amendment protection against search and seizure. I was grateful for his insight. It would be needed before long so I approvingly added Judge Coffin's letter to my growing personal file.

*   *   *

As in 2009, in early 1997 this Nation prepared for the Presidential inauguration. President Bill Clinton had won a second term and geared up for its launch in January. That second term would become a source of personal scandal to those who elected him. However, many of the issues of today were the same concerns in the late 1990's: mixed opinions swirled around the economy, continuing tensions overseas, the trustworthiness of the President himself, the place of religion in public life, and the usual host of priorities for a new administration, were unresolved as we awaited the outcome of our contentious stand-off between church and state.

For my family, in particular for my mother, Christmas would be bittersweet—the first Christmas in fifty years that she and my father would not be together. In past years, the family would come together to decorate the tree with my parents but my mother decided this was "not the year" to have a Christmas tree and she admitted it would be hardest on her if there were one. It was tough, at least for this first year after my father's death. Still, the remembrance of Christ's birth was not a time to mourn.

In addition to grieving the death of my father and my involvement in the ongoing litigation, a massive forest fire that year and had almost consumed the home of my younger brother Jim, his wife Nancy, and their son Alex. Within a day of the first lighting strike, the fire raged through the dry forested wilderness near the central Oregon town of Bend. Forceful winds blew the flames and flying embers north and eastward consuming acres of dry brush and juniper pines in its path. As the flames came into sight, Jim's family was forced to evacuate. But, due to careful prevention their home was saved, yet many more were not. This year of 1996 would go down as an "annus horribilis."

My brother claimed the survival of his home as a miracle and I never disputed his assessment. I prayed a similar claim would be made in our case, which had become a firestorm but now appeared to be reaching a final verdict. I could only hope.

Chapter 14

Opinions In:
Confession Makes the Top Ten List

* * *

"The practical problem of Christian politics is not that of drawing up schemes for a Christian society, but that of living as innocently as we can with unbelieving fellow-subjects under unbelieving rulers who will never be perfectly wise or good and who will sometimes be very foolish . . . Christianity . . . antithetical to omnicompetent government, must always in face, be treated as an enemy [by the state]." (C.S. Lewis—*Mere Christianity*)

* * *

Like today's recurrent news on the war in Iraq and the measure of the precarious stock market, local newspaper headlines on this story had become common place. Eugene's *Register-Guard* brought the year to a close with a front page headline—*The Year in Review '96* and then the words: *Floods, Crime and Confession*. The "jailhouse tape recording" had come in second as the newspaper's top ten most important stories of 1996, only preceded by reportage of record rains, rising rivers and extreme flooding that had plagued the major northwest cities of Seattle and Portland and the surrounding areas with heavy mountain snows. I clipped the front page story and added it to my burgeoning archive of files and boxes.

The new year, just on the horizon, held its usual promise of a fresh start. I'd not heard from Conan Hale, the inmate since he had apologized for "all the trouble" in the sketch he had sent shortly after the "jailhouse taping" media blitz began. I had no doubt his attorney was keeping him informed of further developments, but to what extent I didn't know. I could have contacted him by mail or made another visit to the jail, but the ongoing litigation complicated this. At the time, there were too many unknowns to deal with, and it seemed best to maintain some distance for the foreseeable future until greater clarity could be achieved to make the right decision for all concerned.

While the church never considered itself to be an enemy of the state, we knew well how the state still considered the church to be a thorn in the flesh of its legal proceedings concerning Hale. I reflected with further distress on the State Bar finding that the district attorney had done nothing unethical when he authorized the secret taping. Yet, parish life moved on for me and the new year brought fresh hope for a positive outcome. All seemed as normal but underneath I carried that unsettled, incomplete feeling as we waited for the opinion of the Circuit Court.

The original event, eight months previous, had become far more than a personal war I wanted to win. The time and expense spent on litigation, discussion, courtroom sessions before judge and judges, and the reams of legal briefs had become a passion that had gone well beyond the point of no return. It was time to move forward with determination into what would surely bring this issue of the priest-penitent privilege and specifically the seal of confession to nearly the highest Federal level of recognition when the Circuit Court Judges would offer their opinion.

More than 200 years ago, Thomas Jefferson stated, "In questions of power then, let no more be heard of confidence in man, but bind him down from mischief by the chains of the Constitution . . ." (*Thomas Jefferson: Draft Kentucky Resolutions, 1798*). Would the opinion we awaited from our panel of judges put an end to this conflict and use the binding force of the Constitution to return the balance between church and state? Would it end this mischief? News would come sooner than I'd expected.

*   *   *

On the morning of January 27, 1997, just six weeks after our Seattle hearing, I received an upbeat phone call from Tom Dulcich: "I'm calling to let you know the Ninth Circuit has just issued their opinion and I'd like you to see it before it's made public. I'll fax you a copy this morning. Look it over and give me a call if you have any questions. I'm sure Archbishop George and Fr. Maslowsky will offer their opinion on the ruling soon. I don't know what Mr. Harcleroad will say." The renewed sense of peace in my life was suddenly jarred by this unexpected but welcome phone call.

"Thanks Tom, I'll be ready for the fax." My adrenalin was pumping and I was filled with mixed emotions of elation and apprehension for I was surprised at how quickly the opinion was issued.

I hurried down the hall to the fax machine in the main parish office and stood ready for the results. I shared with our cheerful secretary Barbara, busy at her desk, that I had gotten the call from our attorney. "Great," she said as she turned from her work, "be sure to let us know what it says. Maybe this will finally be the end of it."

"It sounds like there's some hope, but we'll see," my tone somewhat guarded. Pages began to slide off the fax machine—fifteen pages in all. I forced myself to wait until I'd collated them before even glancing at the print. After the last page rolled onto the tray, I methodically gathered the pages, stapled the upper left-hand corner, and then quickly walked to my office to read in private. But I was not alone in my desire to hear the latest. Barbara followed close behind as she sought her second cup of coffee. "So, what's the verdict?" she asked, as she filled her cup, her smile eager for good news.

I turned and teased her, "I get the first read."

She waved her hand in agreement and promised not to interrupt me. I closed the office door and sat down on the high-backed desk chair to begin my study:

Appeal from the United States District Court for the District of Oregon, Owen M. Panner, District Judge Presiding. Argued and submitted, December 12, 1996— Seattle, Washington. Filed Jaunary 27, 1997. Before: John T. Noonan, David R. Thompson and Andrew J. Kleinfeld, Circuit Judges. Opinion by Judge Noonan.

I felt a certain respect merely reading this opening line. While this was a conventional legal document from a significant court of this land, it would be for me and for many others, an unprecedented ruling and either a very personal vindication or a disappointment. As I first skimmed the opinion, words were brought to light for their familiarity.

I turned the cover page, immediately noting now familiar facts— recognizable enough to recite in my sleep—which traced our frustrated efforts to have the tape destroyed. The document recounted the persistent efforts by the state to thwart the requests of the church. Certain words jumped out, " . . . alleging civil rights claims, violations of the Religious Freedom Restoration Act (RFRA), the Wiretapping Act, and the Oregon Constitution."

The opinion cited the decision of Judge Panner who, " . . . denied the plaintiffs' claims and held that Hale's " . . . rights to a fair trial outweighed the First Amendment rights of Mockaitis and George and dismissed the action. Mockaitis and George appealed . . ."

As it listed the demands the Church requested, in the mind of Judge Noonan, they were appropriate: "Much of the relief they sought would not interfere with the ongoing state prosecution. The complaint sought an injunction against future interception and recording of sacramental confessions in the jail and a declaratory judgment that any such activity was unconstitutional . . . In the RFRA, Congress prescribed that government shall not substantially burden a person's exercise of religion . . ."

It appeared Judge Noonan had relied on the force of Religious Freedom Restoration Act as the basis for his decision. Noonan continued, "Taping a sacramental confession was an easy way to secure evidence, but the ordinary means of proving a case by good police work were the least restrictive means of furthering the prosecutor's desirable goal . . .

"The taping of the confession was a violation of the RFRA, and so should not have been a part of the ordinary course of duty of any law-enforcement officer . . . the rite was focused on and preserved for exploitation as state's evidence." However, he claimed, " . . . That the taping was done in the ordinary course negated the willfulness required by the Wiretap Act . . . Harcleroad's retention of it was not a felony."

I was rattled by what sounded as if taping confessions was done in the "ordinary course" of their duties. It was willful in the sense that they had intentionally targeted the particular sacramental encounter, but the nuance of legal language was at play here.

The Judge supported the claim I had a reasonable expectation of privacy under two bases: "The Oregon Evidence Code and the history of the nation, which has shown a uniform respect for the character of sacramental confession as inviolable by government agents interested in securing evidence of crime. All fifty states have enacted statues granting some form of testimonial privilege to clergy-communicant communications. It would be strange that a privilege so universally recognized could be readily subverted by governmental recording of the communication and its introduction in to evidence."

More specific violations were spelled out: " . . . Harcleroad violated the civil rights of the plaintiffs secured by the RFRA and the Fourth Amendment . . . with the exception of the case for destruction of the tape . . ."

If it was not to be destroyed, I wondered what would become of the tape, the living desecration still in existence.

I read Judge Noonan's words offered some relief: "On remand, the district court was to grant the plaintiffs's request for declaratory relief, and issue an injunction in favor of Mockaitis and George restraining Harcleroad and his agents and employees from further violations of the RFRA and the Fourth Amendment by assisting, participating in, or using a recording of confidential communications from Lane County Jail inmates to any member of the clergy in the member's professional character . . . In addition, much of the relief they seek would not interfere with the ongoing state prosecution . . ."

I sat up straight, my hope reenergized that our demand for restraint on jail authorities might be granted. This order would prevent and bind the district attorney or any officials at the county jail from *future* secret or open plotting to record or monitor conversations between clergy and inmates. As our friends from the amicus brief had implied, this would be good news for them as well. However, it still said nothing about the use of the *present* tape already in their possession.

Therefore, it appeared that church officials would prevail on two out of three things requested:

1. An injunction against future interception and recording of sacramental confessions in the jail and a declaratory judgment that any such interception and taping was unconstitutional.
2. The effort to have this declared both illegal and unconstitutional. The Constitutional violations were stated: RFRA [First Amendment] and the eavesdropping charge against the Fourth Amendment.

It was the final request, however, that was yet to be ordered by this Court. That request was direct: Issue an order to destroy the tape and transcript(s) immediately. Pages of legal posturing and opinions relating to violations, hearings, dismissals, appeals, confrontations, challenges, questions, doubts, deceptions, and disappointments, made for a slow walk through this legal forest.

There was further condemnation of the district attorney's challenge to the First Amendment and to RFRA: " . . . Harcleroad has an additional challenge to the constitutionality of RFRA, a challenge deadly in its implications for religious liberty. It is that RFRA, because it advances the exercise of religion, is an establishment of religion and therefore offensive to that portion of the First Amendment."

Judge Noonan referenced the intervention by the United States during the hearing in Seattle, and then continued with a strong disagreement with the district attorney: " . . . We reject Harcleroad's challenge to RFRA for three reasons. The first two reasons explain why Harcleroad's facial attack on the constitutionality of the statute fails. The third reason responds to his challenge to the statute as applied . . .

"First, Congress under Section 5 of the Fourteenth Amendment has the power to enforce the provisions of the Bill of Rights that the Fourteenth Amendment incorporates and makes binding on the states . . .

"Second, Harcleroad's Establishment theory is that whenever Congress exempts religion from generally applicable law it unconstitutionally advances and therefore unconstitutionally establishes a religion . . ."

The legal jargon puzzled me so I paused for a slower second reading of the paragraphs not yet absorbed in my non-legal mind.

Judge Noonan then ticked off several examples of what society would resemble if the district attorney's reasoning were applied: " . . . The exemptions and deductions of the Internal Revenue Code . . . . must be bad. The deferments of the Selective Service Act must be invalid. The creation of chaplaincies in Congress and in the armed forces—particularly striking promotions of religion—must be suspect. The narrow logic of this attack is refuted by the experience of the nation. Of course the statutory protection of the free exercise of religion is good for religion. Neither the benefit nor the means are contrary to the first liberty assured by the First Amendment and made concrete by RFRA . . . We join the other courts of appeal that have considered this challenge and rejected it . . ."

"Third, the acts of the prosecutor here did not amount to the neutral application of any Oregon statute but were an attempt to use the statutory authorization to monitor inmate conversations in order to gain access to a confession expected to be given in accordance with a religious rite. As Carley [the detective] put it in his affidavit to the judge, he expected the confession to contain 'a full and complete acknowledgment' by Hale as a condition of his receiving absolution . . . Deliberately, the religious rite was focused upon and preserved for exploitation as state's evidence . . .'"

After Judge Noonan identified the state's *modus operandi*, the ominous nature of this attack was unquestionable. Descriptions of familiar events reignited disturbing memories and mixed feelings of intimidation and anger but I pressed on.

The Judge then spelled out his position on Harcleroad's claim that this clandestine taping had no real effect on my ministry. This section of the Circuit Court's opinion became a blend of legal defense and Catholic theology.

Judge Noonan wrote:

" . . . No question exists that Harcleroad has substantially burdened Fr. Mockaitis's exercise of religion as understood in the First Amendment. Fr. Mockaitis was exercising his religion in a priestly function. He was seeking to participate in the Sacrament of Penance understood by the Catholic Church to be a means by which God forgives the sins of a repentant sinner and restores the sinner to life in God's grace. It is a sacrament that from experience the Catholic Church has surrounded with extraordinary safeguards so that the content of the penitent's confession will not be revealed unless the penitent himself chooses to reveal it; and these safeguards have the evident reason that the knowledge, belief, or suspicion that freely-confessed sins would become public would operate as a serious deterrent to participation in the sacrament.

"When the prosecutor asserts the right to tape the sacrament he not only intrudes upon the confession taped but threatens the security of any participation in the sacrament by penitents in the jail; he invades their free exercise of religion and doing so makes it impossible to minister the sacrament to those who seek it in the jail."

These were precise words that gave me hope for complete vindication. I placed the papers on the desk before me, and then stretched my arms high and reached for the ceiling, to release the tension in my body, for the long read was an effort in concentration with somewhat unfamiliar concepts. Yet, I wanted to get through it in one sitting. Then I noticed Judge Noonan's agreement with our stand that Judge Panner should not have abstained in deciding the fate of this case.

"Focusing on the requested destruction of the tape, the district court in effect overlooked what the plaintiffs asked . . . it makes an error to abstain from deciding this case where serious violations of the laws and Constitution of the United States are alleged and substantial relief can be afforded without disruption of a state criminal trial."

However, in the next paragraph I found words about the future of the tape:

"A question does exist as to the preservation of the tape until the termination of the proceedings against Hale; or rather, there may be two questions: Does preservation substantially burden Mockaitis's exercise of religion? Does Harcleroad have a defense under RFRA? As to the first, Mockaitis has stated that the continued existence of the tape gives him discomfort and that every new public reference to it is hurtful to him. His reaction is understandable. Out of nowhere, as it must have seemed to him, the performance of a rite that he believed was enshrined in secrecy became a matter for the media, for the courts, for the public at large. His sense of betrayal is reinforced by each reference to the confession's existence on the tape. But it is hard to see that these unpleasant reminders substantially burden his free exercise of religion any more than memory of the first intrusion must rankle . . .

" . . . The reasoning as to the burden imposed on Father Mockaitis applies analogously to the burden imposed on Archbishop George . . . A substantial burden is imposed on his free exercise of religion as the responsible head of the Archdiocese of Portland by the intrusion into the Sacrament of Penance by officials of the state, an intrusion defended in this case by an assistant attorney-general of the state as not contrary to any law. Archbishop George has justifiable grounds for fearing that without a declaratory judgment and an injunction in this case the administration of the Sacrament of Penance for which he is responsible in his archdiocese will be made odious in jails by the intrusion of law enforcement officers . . . We take note of the stipulation that Lane County Jail has 'agreed not to intercept or tape conversation between Catholic clergy and inmates . . .' The stipulation is far from satisfactory. It does not state to whom the jail made this promise, or who at the jail made it, or how long the promise is good; and it appears to accord a blanket immunity to conversations with Catholic clergy not extended to clergy of other faiths . . ."

I then noted Judge Noonan did support an additional charge then made an historical point of comparison which placed this event in line with past historical challenges before the courts to this sacred confessional seal.

"The violation of the Fourth Amendment . . . First, ORS Evidence Code S 40.260, Rule 506, 'Member of Clergy-penitent privilege,' provides that (a) member of the Clergy shall not, without the consent of the person making the communication, be examined as to any confidential communication, made to the member of the clergy in the member's professional character.' As Mockaitis could not be examined directly in court on a confession, it was reasonable for him to suppose that the prohibition of Rule 506 could not be easily circumvented by the prosecutor taping a confession made to him.

" . . . The history of the nation has shown a uniform respect for the character of sacramental confession as inviolable by government agents interested in securing evidence of crime from the lips of criminals . . . DeWitt Clinton, later Governor of New York and at the time Mayor of New York City, a noted statesman and astute analyst of the spirit of the new republic, speaking for the Court of General Session, declared:

"A provision conceived in a spirit of the most profound wisdom, and the most exalted charity, ought to receive the most liberal construction . . . In this country there is not alliance between church and state; no established religion; no tolerated religion—for toleration results from establishment—but religious freedom guaranteed by the constitution, and consecrated by the social compact.

" . . . suppose that a decision of this court, or a law of the state should prevent the administration of one or both of these sacraments, would not the constitution be violated, and the freedom of religion be infringed? Every man who hears me will answer in the affirmative. Will not the same result follow, if we deprive the Roman Catholic of one of his ordinances? Secrecy is of the essence of penance. The sinner will not confess, nor will the priest receive his confession, if the veil of secrecy is removed . . . and this important branch of the Roman Catholic religion would be thus annihilated." (People v. Phillips, N.Y. Cr. Gen Sess. (1813), as reported by a lawyer who participated in the case as amicus curiae)

Judge Noonan continued: " . . . If the inviolability of religious confession to the clergy were not the law of the land, the expectation of every repentant sinner, and the assured confidence of every minister of God's grace, a prosecutor would have a cheap and sometimes helpful way of uncovering evidence of crime . . . to wire a church known to be frequented, say, by criminal organization. Such a fear does not exist because no one expects any prosecutor to engage in such a strategy."

The Judge determined: " . . . it must be concluded that no evidence has been offered that would have led a priest in Father Mockaitis's shoes to expect that his participation in the Sacrament of Penance would be bugged . . . He was reasonable in relying on the nation's history of respect for religion in general and respect for the sanctity of the secrets of confession in particular, and so had a reasonable expectation of privacy . . . There is reason to protect Father Mockaitis's expectation of privacy in hearing confessions. Archbishop George's expectation is, analogously, equally reasonable . . ."

Judge Noonan supported our claim that my civil rights of privacy were violated and perhaps those of the inmate as well. " . . . As our analysis under RFRA and the Fourth Amendment indicates, Harcleroad has violated the civil rights of the plaintiffs secured by RFRA and by the Fourth Amendment . . ."

And then, the Church and I found some vindication.

"We remand for a grant of the plaintiff's request for declaratory relief, holding that the taping of Father Mockaitis's encounter with Hale and its subsequent seizure by Harcleroad violated RFRA and the Fourth Amendment. We remand to the district court for the issuance of an injunction . . . The injunction should restrain Harcleroad and his agents and employees from further violation of RFRA and the Fourth Amendment by assisting, participating in or using any recording of a confidential communications from inmates of the Lane County Jail to any member of the clergy in the member's professional character.

"We also remand to the district court to take evidence as to the attorney's fees to which the plaintiffs are entitled under the Civil Rights Act for both the litigation in the district court and on this appeal. They have prevailed, not as to all the relief sought but nevertheless substantially, on the one claim on which attorney fees may be awarded. The judgment of the district court is REVERSED and the case is REMANDED for proceedings in accordance with this opinion." (Ninth Circuit Court of Appeals: *Mockaitis v. Harcleroad,* 1/27/97)

*   *   *

I leaned back in my chair, closed my eyes, and absorbed this moment of victory but wondered, while my expectation of privacy was undeniable, what of Conan Hale's? That answer was never clear; although I had taken him on his word months before that he had no knowledge of the taping. What had begun in silence then suddenly burst on the public scene, thrusting both priest and prisoner on center stage, now seemed ended with the clear, definitive voice of a noted Judge of great integrity. In my wildest dreams as a member of the clergy, I could not have imagined such a scenario.

Nonetheless, this opinion was a sign, not only for me, but by direct association, for Archbishop George, every priest, every member of the clergy, and for all parishioners in this country. This Circuit Court had rendered a strong reaffirmation in support of the sacred seal of the Sacrament of Reconciliation and by association to those who lead all people of faith—our amici. This was a decisive condemnation of the entire procedure undertaken by jail authorities under the auspices of the district attorney. It was the first time a violation of the seal of confession was alleged in a capital case in the United States, and the first time an attempt was made in court to define a violation of the seal of the confessional as a First Amendment violation. The Judge's words added a new force to the law.

Judge John T. Noonan, a scholar of both law and religion long before he was appointed to the Ninth Circuit Court, had used his full expertise to bring down this ruling. As a matter of process, it would be up to Judge Panner to see that the remedies were enforced, with the exception of one denied request. The tape would live on.

Although the Circuit Court judges did not authorize the tape's use, they did not order the tape destroyed so the best we could hope for is that the tape would never be used. Respecting the procedures of the upcoming trial of Conan Hale and his right, as all Americans, to a fair trial, was always a value. After Hale's trial, would it then be destroyed as was promised by the district attorney and repeated by lawyer Chaimov in our court hearing months earlier as we sat before Judge Panner?

The near iconic status of the tape would remain unresolved because its future status was yet to be determined by Judge Billings. How would he react to this ruling since it seemed to place the church and its interests squarely in his courtroom where he felt we had no right to be? The door was left open to threatening possibilities that could create even more entanglement since the admissibility of the tape was not spelled out. The tape was tainted by the method that had been used to seize it in defiance of the law, both the American Constitution and Canon Law of the Catholic Church. Even though it seemed the defendants' implication of the tape as admissible "evidence" had been nullified by the Circuit Court, the impending trial of Hale presaged more complexities.

So, the tape, the enduring record which had sparked so much verbiage and hostility, was left for what purpose? Only that it be declared inadmissible and then destroyed? The fight would somehow go on once Hale got to trial. Is it legally impossible to order the tape destroyed? Did Judge Noonan effectively order it forever sealed and therefore render it inadmissible? Round and round I went with my own circular reasoning. The situation called for much pondering as I carried this concern with me on a daily basis.

Though my daily life was relatively stable and my position as pastor carried on with the variety of needs in a busy Christian community between meetings, time with the sick and shut-in, planning for various children and adult education programs, and celebrating Sunday and daily worship with the good people of the parish, I had reached a point by now that I was long ready to have this over with. Yet, ahead of us the question of the tape's ultimate use or non-use at Hale's upcoming trial weighed heavy. Would there still be a way for County officials to "legally and ethically" judge the tape admissible?

Perhaps there was still enough of a flame burning for right justice to keep this process going. I flipped back to review some sections of the opinion for better understanding. There I underlined phrases, sections, and words for emphasis. I was fairly sure neither the Archdiocese nor the state wished to go a further step—an appeal to the United States Supreme Court to have that tape destroyed.

Since the event began in April of 1996, the cumulative stress of the litigation and all the "tape talk" had worn me out, but the church had achieved some significant victory. The overall affect on Hale was unknown to me but I never wanted to forget that he too was victimized in the state's attempt to investigate a crime. Was this really the end of a nine-month battle? For the church, it was a time of victory though an incomplete solution. Part of me, along with a penitent, remained locked in a drawer where some future ill purpose could play itself out.

*   *   *

Public reaction to this opinion, however, would be measured with words carefully chosen to exhibit fairness to both sides of the concerns, in particular the public response of Archbishop George. No one in the church, including myself, wanted to make this the cause of an irreparable rift between church and state.

Archbishop George's comments were necessary for all clergy of the Archdiocese. In a brief letter he wrote, " . . . the Ninth Circuit Court of Appeals has ruled that the taping of a Sacramental Confession in the Lane County jail was unconstitutional and illegal, and that the rights of Father Mockaitis were violated . . . we are very grateful for this decision.

"I want to express my appreciation to you and your parishioners for your prayers and support during this long ordeal . . . . The ruling is vindication for the Catholic Church and recognizes the religious freedom of all Oregonians."

Of course, the opinion of the Ninth Circuit Court hit the airwaves rapidly and became front-page headlines in the major Oregon newspapers as well as a subject for further analysis. Of particular interest was the district attorney's reaction. Many eagerly awaited his public response to the ruling. Some would find Harcleroad's comments less than expansive.

The Register-Guard, reported: " . . . Harcleroad said he hasn't yet had time to analyze the appeal court's ruling that the taping violated the priest's Fourth Amendment protection from unreasonable search and seizure . . . . 'It's too soon to give you an opinion on that. We haven't made a decision about what our next step will be . . .'"

The Oregonian reported the comments of principal players in a front-page article entitled, **Court Rules Jail Taping Unlawful**, on January 28, 1997:

"The Ninth U.S. Circuit Court of Appeals did not agree to destroy the tape, as the Roman Catholic Church had requested. Nevertheless, church officials embraced the decision, saying an important precedent has been set.

"Judge John T. Noonan said that 'when the prosecutor asserts the right to tape the sacrament, he . . . threatens the security of any participation in the sacrament by penitents in the jail; doing so makes it impossible to minister the sacrament to those who seek it in the jail . . .'

At a later date, Judge Noonan wrote that he considered this case a bellwether for the clergy-penitent privilege. Reflecting on the lack of public protest in the manner which William F. Buckley had suggested, he said, "It was a surprising change in the climate that it should come up—there should have been an attack on it."

Fr. Mike, the archdiocese spokesman said the church will fight to keep the confession out of the trial. He commented that for the first time we have a court that has said categorically that this tape recording is illegal, unconstitutional and cannot happen again. The hope of the church was to work with Lane County officials to resolve the question of the tape itself in a manner that would not prejudice the criminal proceedings nor violate the confidentiality of the sacramental forum. " . . . Citizens can now feel confident of the privacy and inviolability of that encounter . . . The appeals court did not say this tape has to be preserved; in fact, the court said the tape is illegal evidence . . ."

In a more pointed manner, a former Lane County district attorney, Pat Horton, blasted the way his counterpart had handled this case and was unashamed in his criticism. "First, he committed an act that is absolutely something that should never be tolerated in a civilized society. He then compounded this ethical and moral breach by attempting to justify it." Horton then added his further critique toward other Oregon prosecutors for not criticizing Harcleroad for authorizing this jail eavesdropping.

General public reaction continued from varied corners but was almost universally in favor of the Ninth Circuit opinion. I took heart that however battered the seal of confession had been up to this point, this ruling was a significant victory, almost complete.

Meanwhile, those responsible for the secret taping maintained a public "no comment" in response to the ruling of Judge Noonan. The district attorney remained out of the public eye. His silence and that of other state officials on the ruling of the Circuit Court was not a surprise but it was unsettling. But as Fr. Mike stated earlier, and Archbishop George agreed: "An appeal to the U.S. Supreme Court is possible, but any such decision will hinge on consultation with the state attorney general's office."

Rev. David Deibel, a lawyer from the Diocese of Sacramento, California, with a licentiate in canon law, further summarized our mixed success this way:

" . . . The bad news is that the tape and transcript still exist and will until the conclusion of the criminal prosecution, as had originally been decided by the district attorney for Lane County . . . The writer cannot help but think that the specter of sacramental communications being subverted by unscrupulous individuals, or by the state in its search for justice, would in the end erode the very values the law seeks to protect. After all, our greatest myth as a people is that we exist under the reign of law." (*The Priest*, Our Sunday Visitor Publishing, August, 1998.) I found all this commentary, as consistent in its theme as it was, to be at times overwhelming in its universal force.

No further developments were proposed from Mr. Harcleroad with the exception of his continued challenge to the constitutionality of the RFRA clause in the First Amendment. It would not be until July 1997 that the U.S. Supreme Court would find RFRA to be unconstitutional in an unrelated Catholic Church land use case from San Antonio, Texas.

Though, the Religious Freedom Restoration Act may have been found unconstitutional at that time later variations on this protection have been introduced over the subsequent years. In the end the issue remains the same: the government does not interfere in the religious practices of American citizens unless there is a justifiable and compelling reason to do so; and those reasons would be problematic to justify. We felt secured under the First Amendment.

*   *   *

Throughout all of this I too continued to maintain a public silence, which was frustrating at times, but I was never mute to those who came to me in a more private way. Once the opinion was reached by Judge Noonan, however, I did agree on two local television interviews. Yet, I felt much more needed to be said to those in private settings, and to them I made my thoughts and feelings crystal clear.

The support and prayers of so many had brought me more to a point of gratitude than remorse but the circle was not yet closed. To most this had been a fascinating journey of legal maneuvering but to me this was a personal cause I wanted to win and total victory was not yet in sight.

At one point, alternatives to the tape's destruction were proposed. Fr. Mike suggested a remarkable scenario, "If we could excise the voice of the priest from the tape so that all that is left are the inmate's statements, that might perhaps be a satisfactory solution . . ." In that unique proposal, who would listen to the tape in order to "excise" my voice? Wouldn't this solution of compromise leave the penitent in an even more vulnerable spot and place the church in a most awkward position? The delicate process of how to handle the tape became more complicated in its weirdness and it seemed a somewhat desperate scenario.

Fr. Mike's well-intentioned alternative to outright destruction of the tape, however, suggested a person would be listening to a confession under the sacramental seal. Therefore, they too would breach the seal of inviolability. Under church discipline, they would be obligated to maintain absolute confidentiality themselves. But, at least six people had already listened to the recording and we were never sure whether this included the district attorney himself. Maybe *I* would be offered the chance to remove my voice by listening to it privately while splicing and re-recording. It was a tangled notion to me.

I did not favor this proposal, nor did I feel that anyone should touch that tape except to eliminate it. Inherent conflicts created more complexity. In the end, this option was never undertaken. The likelihood that the tape would be used in some public form was very real. However, in spite of revealing more of my opinions privately, I felt the events I'd endured continued to penetrate my thoughts and they were evolving. While I would have preferred further action, an appeal to the U.S. Supreme Court, I also felt compelled to hold on to my memories and experiences for I never stopped believing this was a story that needed to be told.

The Church would continue its effort to keep the taped confession forever sealed and ultimately destroyed. But could we rely on the verbal promise of the district attorney that the tape would be destroyed after Conan Hale's trial?

*   *   *

Although I'd been urged by friends and many parishioners to initiate a personal law suit, I was frankly afraid to do so. I was concerned about public reaction—of people assuming I only wanted some sort of retribution, "my day in court," or a major financial settlement. One attorney told me he would have gone for 1.5 million dollars in punitive damages if I had contacted him earlier. That offer I honestly considered but never accepted. This was not about money.

Yet, by early February 1997, I seriously considered doing whatever I could personally to send an additional message to state officials anywhere who might yet again take it upon themselves to tape-record or monitor an encounter, sacramental or not, between a member of the clergy and their penitent or parishioner. I contacted Portland attorney Mike Kelly to explore initiating a civil law suit against the State and Lane County for violation of my civil rights in the jailhouse taping. Mike jumped on the issue from our first meeting but wondered if it would be possible, at the eleventh hour, to take any action.

What I really desired was the kind of justice that would deter anyone from breaking the sacramental seal again; I wanted other priests to feel at ease with inmate penitents, knowing their prison ministries and sacramental encounters were free of eavesdropping; I myself wanted to feel safe hearing the confession of inmates anywhere; and yes, I expected a settlement, a dollar figure, no matter how modest, that would publicly and concretely indicate that consequences attended First Amendment violations. I felt this would put a very large exclamation point at the end of this long sentence.

But if I were going to proceed, I only had one year left to file a civil suit, and I knew the process of negotiation, setting dates with legal mediators on both sides, could easily take months to decide. In addition, Conan Hale's trial was postponed, and then rescheduled for one year later, due to the sudden death of Joe Kosydar, the state's lead prosecutor. With no new trial date set for Hale, and no further litigation by the church on the tape issue underway, I decided this would be the easiest time to take on the challenge. I placed my trust in attorney Mike Kelly who worked tirelessly for me so we moved ahead with the civil suit which indeed took months to negotiate. State officials were shocked that I would initiate such an action and felt the case was a waste of time. That it had "no merit."

CHAPTER 15

Issues Dark and Ugly

*　*　*

"Evil can be undone but it cannot 'develop' into good. Time does not heal it. The spell must be unwound, bit by bit, with backward mutters of disserving power . . ." (C.S. Lewis—*The Great Divorce*)

*　*　*

It appeared the tape, a symbol of much more than a mismanaged investigation, that no one wanted to touch but everyone could not avoid was still fair game as the legal groundwork for Hale's pretrial was underway.

The delicate issue of dialogue with the state over the status of the tape lay before us, and full implementation of the Ninth Circuit Court ruling remained uncertain. Nonetheless, the Archdiocese proceeded cautiously. Tom Dulcich, on behalf of the church, requested an extension for time to file a petition for rehearing. Much of this was done quietly, behind the scenes, with little involvement of myself and no more public reporting at this time. Time to reconnect with a more agreeable ministry was given to me but I was never far from the ongoing legal side-show. The lives of parishioners had of course moved on with the many other concerns of work and family life so some sense of normalcy was returning, yet I knew this was the potential eye of a new storm.

A few weeks after the Court's opinion was published there was some movement on the disposition of the tape. In February 1997, Tom informed us that Hardy Myers, the new Attorney General, had agreed to that request. In a letter to Archbishop George, Tom wrote:

" . . . I was able to get the agreement of Hardy Myers, the new Oregon Attorney General, for a joint extension of time so that we can discuss what may be done with the tape short of destruction. This will be a sensitive process of negotiation. If it fails, we may have to revisit the idea of going back to Lane County Circuit Court to attempt to convince that court or some other state court to assist us in our goal.

"Mr. Myers indicated that his office would probably not seek an appeal to the U.S. Supreme Court . . ."

The long delay of our case, as the Supreme Court considered our situation, if at all, and the probable delay of Hale's trial as a consequence, would have worsened already strained relationships between church and state. The trial of Conan Hale was yet to happen but the date was growing closer and Lane County was eager to move forward with it.

Both the state and church preferred to work this out at home rather than engage in a long and costly process of application to the Supreme Court. However, I feel we missed a chance—at least at that time. A Supreme Court scenario would have made a definitive statement about the relationship between American citizens, their religious leaders, and the far reaching protection of the First Amendment. As a member of the clergy I knew that whether we realized it or not the outcome of that decision would have made significant legal history far beyond this case.

Since that was not to be it was time to focus further efforts as Hale's trial was planned more extensively. The green light of "no destruction of the tape" urged forward movement so the controversies repositioned themselves where I feared most—back where it began; in the hands of the district attorney and the investigators of Hale's trial.

*   *   *

Unknown to me at the time, an earlier pre-trial discussion about the tape created an ominous possibility that if granted would have pushed the incident farther. Judge Billings, Terri Wood, counsel for Hale, and the assistant district attorney, Joe Kosydar, had wrestled with the question of disposition of the tape's admissibility in court. That discussion was made several months earlier but by this time the Ninth Circuit opinion was well known. The question of whether it should be destroyed was never broached. But, their hope to use the tape in some manner was clear.

Judge Billings spoke to Terri Wood and Joe Kosydar saying, " . . . We have one last thing to take care of, the tape seized at the time the defendant requested that the Catholic priest come over to the jail.

"Ms. Wood," the Judge addressed her as he reviewed her request, "I'm looking at your motion, and I see that you've asked the Court to consider modification or lifting of what you refer to as a gag order . . . so as, 'to allow persons with knowledge of the contents of this tape recording to disclose the contents in the course of judicial proceedings in the above—entitled cause . . .'" The Judge looked up from his papers and added:

"But, as I said in Item 3: Counsel for the defendant shall not discuss the contents of the tape with the news media or others unnecessary for the preparation of defense."

Ms. Wood responded with a tone of deference: "Of course, whenever counsel is under an order, she doesn't want to risk contempt of court, so what I am trying to say here is that I want the opportunity to be able to talk about that tape in the course of judicial proceedings in this case, . . . if questions come of that, in terms of being able to cross-examine witnesses for the state . . . you might get into a situation with myself or a witness on the stand, where you might feel it was risking contempt of court by answering the question."

The judge answered politely: "Well, then, what I don't want, by entry of an order, is in some way to limit or bind what needs to be decided in the future with respect to admissibility . . . I would not want that to be taken as some kind of statement that the Court agrees that the *thing* (italics added) is admissible or the conversation in the courtroom about it is appropriate."

Judge Billings turned to Mr. Kosydar and asked: "What's the state's position with respect to the second part of the defendant's motion?"

Mr. Kosydar stood to acknowledge the obvious: "It goes without saying that this is something that's generated, from all corners of the earth, some publicity. If, during the time of trial an issue comes up where someone feels that there needs to be some type of full-blown disclosure of the contents of the tape, seems to me that we can do that at that point. I would ask the Court to keep it the way it is."

With a decisive tone, Judge Billings spoke with clarity and a hint of frustration: "I'll leave to objections, as they may be raised; the question of to what extent may either side use that tape.

"The Court would observe that this thing first came to the Court in what I think all would agree is a highly unusual fashion. The Court has kept this tape in a safe downstairs. I don't want to keep it anymore! I see no purpose in why the Court should have it. We've been through all this federal decision regarding it. It's an item of potential evidence. It's not a shrine that needs to be encamped in our safe. I don't think there should be constraints on a particular item which originally was seized by the state as evidence in this case. This Court is not under any type of restraint by virtue of the federal court decisions.

"The Civil proceedings instituted by the Catholic Church against the District Attorney and other public officials have been concluded, and no federal court order precludes the admission of this tape by the State of Oregon as evidence for the prosecution in the above-styled cause . . ."

"I'm going to ask Mr. Vactor, who is our court administrator—if he is kind enough to get that thing out of the safe to hand it over to Mr. Kosydar."

With an eager voice, Mr. Kosydar responded: "I'll take it." (Court Transcripts).

I was grateful I was not aware how close the tape was coming to be ruled admissible.

*   *   *

That *thing*, as the Judge referred to the tape, four months after the Ninth Circuit opinion was issued, was again in a precarious position. Though the Circuit Court's ruling was significant, I wondered if any on our side felt the recipients of that ruling were particularly moved. While Judge Billings was not involved in the eavesdropping at the jail, he made room for the tape as admissible evidence in spite of the Ninth Circuit Court ruling. Both the state and Ms. Wood could have access to the tape, refer to it in jury selection if they so wished, and possibly make reference to it in the trial of Conan Wayne Hale as "evidence." Tom's initial comment, "They just don't get it" rang true in my ears.

If this was to be the end result, the seal of confession was about to take on a new historical meaning. How would I or any member of the clergy explain to our parishioners that the seal of the sacrament was now conditional? This would challenge the entire integrity of the sacrament and, as the Church had consistently said, would potentially open the door to further intrusion by the state. I thought about the interests of our amici standing in solidarity for what they too recognized would be a ruling on them.

From this point forward, the picture changed. Conversations with attorneys, the court briefs, and arguments were infrequently reported in the public domain. No moves to a higher court or hearings before judges were undertaken. In terms of my personal civil suit against the State of Oregon and Lane County, a settlement was reached on December 27, 1997. Newspapers reported the settlement, and it was now a matter of public record that I'd accepted a total of $45,000, to be paid by both State and County, with a thirty-three percent contingency due my attorney.

Yet, the state and Lane County viewed my efforts [the civil suit] as ludicrous, meaning it "had no merit," particularly since the suit was filed so long after the fact. Still, Mike Kelly negotiated with determination with the State and Lane County until they agreed on a settlement. Eventually, they did so with "no admission of wrongdoing" on their part, just to put an end to it. When my parishioners got wind of the settlement, they quickly came to my support. More than one felt I should have held out for more but that was not a battle worth fighting and would have skewed the initial intent.

*   *   *

As Hale's trial approached in the early spring of 1998, new actions were taken by the church and public interest in that impending trial sped things up as the county began its search for jury members. Tom Dulcich called Mr. Harcleroad to inquire about the status of the tape. After speaking with the district attorney, Tom wrote back to us: "The tape is currently being held by the sheriff's office in a secure evidence locker. Harcleroad said that his office does not intend to offer the tape in evidence . . ."

He further stated that Mr. Harcleroad expected the existence of the tape to be a very big issue, particularly in the process of jury selection. Tom wrote, "We do not have any certain way of knowing where the tape might be used other than to monitor the course of the trial . . .

"We still have the potential remedy of seeking a writ of mandamus or attempting to intervene in the criminal case for purposes of objecting to use of the tape, but our chance of any success in such a proceeding is small . . ."

Tom's assessment was bothersome. The comment of the district attorney, which implied jury selection may be influenced by the tape's status, was not good news for too many other doors were still left open due to Judge Billings' feelings on the tape and its possible admissibility.

As we pondered what options were still available, several persuasive insights came to the surface:

The position of the State which implied that the case against Hale may have to be dismissed if the tape is destroyed was considered a red herring. If relevant to any issue, Hale can always elect to testify regarding what he told the priest. The "evidence" isn't destroyed, it simply assumes another form.

Without Hale testifying, the tape is hearsay. Yet, the State keeps pointing to the fact that this is a death penalty case as a reason to preserve the tape in case something on it might persuade a jury to spare the defendants life. At the most, the destruction of the tape might take the death penalty off the table.

Judge Coffin stated: "In the end, what the State really wants to do is impose the death penalty and it is concerned that the eavesdropping caper might frustrate that goal."

These points, the product of discussion and reflection, with the assistance of Judge Coffin, cut to the core reasoning of what I felt was the real truth.

*   *   *

Jury selection for the trial of Conan Wayne Hale began in March of 1998 so we stood poised for this historical challenge to the seal of confession and the privilege of our First Amendment protection. The Archdiocese carefully watched the developing process leading to Hale's trial. Nearly 600 potential jurors had been summoned to begin appearing in Lane County Circuit Court for possible service in Hale's trial. But final jury selection and opening statements in the case were not expected to happen before March 30, nearly two years after the secret tape was made.

What sort of questions might potential jurors or those in the selection process have? How much of an issue were attorneys planning to make of this illegal evidence?

It seemed logical to assume the ruling of the Ninth Circuit on the nature of the state's action as unconstitutional, illegal, and a violation of privacy overshadowed any further question as to the use or existence of the tape. However, the *moral* force of the Circuit opinion held no weight in this.

The state pushed the idea that the right to a fair trial for Hale hung in the balance. But, this "spell" of the tape had to be unwound. We knew that both the state and Ms. Wood were tenaciously determined to preserve the tape and they appeared headed to find a way to either reveal its contents or play it in court. I resisted what might yet come into play if a finger neared the play button. This mix of light and darkness, of secular and sacred, simmered within me.

I measured the question of attending Hale's trial, but I did not feel comfortable or welcome considering Judge Billings' response to the church, nor did I know what sort of attention would come my way from the media. I decided to keep the separation between the church's interest and this trial distinct so I sought the assistance of a reliable parishioner, Ed Krupka, who offered to attend a part of the trial if I wanted him to. Ed stayed in touch so I would know how the trial was progressing, if they were going to play the tape, or if either side intended to make any use of it. The eyes of the church also watched the proceedings carefully as I knew that church officials were additionally concerned.

For more than two years this issue shadowed me wherever I went. Buy now I had let go of most resentment as time offered me perspective and distance healed frayed emotions. Yet this new challenge was perhaps the toughest wall to penetrate since the dispute was now transformed to a new venue.

*   *   *

Things were tense for the community at large in the first days of Hale's trial. This was a very big local story. The issues relating to the triple-homicide were dark and ugly and had touched the Eugene community. The courtroom was packed and seating was available on a first come, first served basis only. Expressions changed and heads turned as Hale was brought into the courtroom wearing a blue shirt and khaki pants with a locking knee brace that prevents defendants from escaping. He sat quietly and seemed to take no notice the murder victims' relatives who filled two rows in the back of the packed courtroom. As opening presentation began, Terri Wood presented her case for the jury as she stood inches away from the jury box. Judge Billings sat back in his high backed leather chair and watched intently. Terri Wood spoke with strength:

"Certainly, there's no evidence before the Court that it can conclude that Mr. Hale consented, and in a knowing or voluntary manner, to the electronic recording of his conversations. He simply had no choice. If he wanted to communicate face to face with his mother, his stepfather, friends, family, this is the only opportunity that he has to do so . . .

"So, clearly, there's been no consent by Mr. Hale to the process that's being used by the state to gather evidence against him . . . what the State has done is engage in continual warrantless collecting of evidence against Mr. Hale for use in a criminal prosecution . . ." Then she referred to the "so-called confession to the priest" as one violation of Hale's privacy. Ms. Wood returned to her chair with a serious expression as an attorney for the state took the opposite position:

"This inmate presents substantial jail security issues . . . and the potential does exist that this type of monitoring of the defendant could garner information which could aid them in the investigation."

Judge Billings patiently listened, as did the jury, and then the judge commented on the recorded statements, also making reference to the infamous tape: "We now know, apparently by the benefit of the 9th Circuit, that conversations between a defendant and a priest, and, I presume, others of similar occupation might have to be likewise protected as a matter of privilege and not as a matter of constitutional law . . ."

It was a tense moment but this argument, coupled with the state's position that, " . . . unless there becomes some real need to actually go into disclosing the content of that conversation (with the priest) . . . keep it the way it is . . ." Privilege or not, this uncertain sense of possibility was unsettled. I had no way to observe Conan Hale so I simply kept the proceedings in prayer.

Over the last two years, I wondered how often I had hounded heaven with this issue. The Lord was kept very much informed on all the developments both sacred and secular.

As the trial unfolded, the Archdiocese again contacted Judge Billings about its continued concern that the tape would be used.

Tom Dulcich wrote to the Judge:

"My clients have seen newspaper reports about the trial of Conan Hale taking place in your courtroom. References have been made in the newspaper articles to the tape recording . . . in April 1996.

"I write to make a request on behalf of my clients. I ask the court to provide my clients notice, through me, if any party seeks permission to play the tape recording . . . my clients believe this would be inappropriate, given the ruling of the federal court . . ." Tom included a copy of the Circuit Court decision. The Judge's response was sadly not surprising, at least in its tone:

" . . . Whether or not the tape to which you make reference will be offered as an exhibit," wrote Judge Billings, "and whether there will be an objection to its receipt, will be the decisions of the parities. It is not appropriate nor does the Court have interest in seeking to advise non-parties about the possibility that evidence may be offered at some stage in a trial.

"I fail to see your purpose in submitting to the Court a copy of the Ninth Circuit Opinion. This response is not intended to encourage further argument or dialogue."

With this curt response from the judge, I flashed back to his first statement two years before and his reminder that we had no "justifiable" cause in seeking destruction of the tape. From a strict legal perspective, it is true we were not parties to Hale's case but I found it offensive to be minimized as a side interest. Hale's trial continued uninterrupted.

As evidence was presented, photographs shown, and a visit made to the scene of the murders in the back logging roads surrounding Eugene, the days of the trial became a wrenching process for the jury who listened to forty-one days of testimony from both sides. The entire process from jury selection to end of trial was a disturbing ninety day experience. In the end, the tape was never requested by the jury or played in court. But, that was hardly the end of the matter.

*   *   *

As the trial neared its verdict and sentencing phase, Ms. Wood pled for the mercy of the court. She spoke in an unusually tender and pleading tone as she described Hale's early childhood as painful and disturbing.

She connected that early life, over which she said Hale had no control, to his present state. Standing close to the jury, she looked at them and continued:

"We have asked much of you in this trial. Almost three months ago we began this process. We brought you to a courtroom, and we . . . asked questions and questions and questions. And what we determined from that was that all of you could start with an open mind, an open heart, that you could start by being fair and impartial, that you would take no side immediately, that you would make no decisions quickly, that you would use reason, you would use considered judgment, that you would use your life experiences to make very serious decisions.

"You have done that. You have been extremely attentive. You have been focused. And most of you have taken notes at length. And we appreciate that.

"We're at a different stage . . . You have the choice of life or you have the choice of death. It'll come as no surprise to you that at the very end of my statement I'm going to ask you to rely upon all of your life experiences, to search your life experiences, your values, your ethics and your morals, your philosophies, your religious beliefs, your spiritual beliefs, and to spare my client's life, [Wayne] Conan Hale's life . . . a human being is more than just one act, more than multiple acts. They're still a human being.

"I indicated to you that the death penalty sentencing is uniquely a process of moral assessment. This is it. You make that decision. You make that decision individually. It's clear that deciding whether someone deserves to die is surely the most profound moral assessment anyone could make. In that process, each of you individually will search for and find your personal belief." (Court transcripts)

She asked the jury to be compassionate and to spare her client's life. She paused for a brief, silent moment as she gazed at the seated members, then returned to her place. It was a desperate attempt.

After nine hours of deliberation, on May 27, 1998, Hale stood stoically as Judge Billings read the verdict. Jury members found Conan Wayne Hale guilty of aggravated murder. The courtroom was silent, except for Hale's mother who gasped as she heard the decision of the jurors finding her son guilty of the most shocking of crimes. The Judge then addressed the jury, "It is a tremendous and highly difficult service for this community that no one else can understand. You have done what you believe is right, and what I believe is right."

Then, Judge Billings with a somber voice said: "Mr. Hale, do you have anything to say?" Hale stood face to face with more than two dozen of the victims' relatives and addressed the court: "When I stand before God and

He is reading my sins, the thing God will see is the blood of Jesus Christ covering over those sins . . ."

With a look of disdain, Judge Billings then said to Hale, "You would have been far more of a man if you had just said, 'I've got nothing to say . . .'"

According to many, justice had been found. Conan Wayne Hale was handed the death penalty in the sentencing phase and would be sent to Salem, Oregon, to stand on death row at the Oregon State Penitentiary Maximum Security facility. There to endure full days of isolation and the endless round of appeals. Jury foreman Brad Finley described the deliberations as, "the most emotionally draining thing any of us has ever had to do."

*   *   *

For me, the presence of darkness was heavy as I heard about the verdict. In my life and years as priest I had never faced the force of evil as much as I had over these last two unforgettable years. The daily temptations and inconveniences of life pale in the face of this. At a news conference that evening, jurors and victims' families were the focus. The scene was distressing. Victims' families hugged the jury foreman, shook his hand, and thanked him for his service. Mr. Brad Finley responded simply, "It's only our civic duty."

My attendant parishioner later reported his personal observations of that day in court. "There was a lot of anger in the courtroom from the families whose teens had been killed," he said. "It was pretty ugly. Many of them were grieving."

To me, the anger and outrage Ed had witnessed was inevitable. I felt great sadness for the loss victims' families were experiencing over this tragedy. Their excruciating pain and the depth of their grief was understandable, and their calls for revenge both foreseeable and troubling. All our talk about forgiveness and love in the Christian faith was overshadowed by the vindictive tone of the reports from that courtroom.

My reporter Ed stated that more than a dozen of the victims' relatives spoke during the afternoon sentencing. Most expressed the shock, grief and loss they and their families have suffered.

Some of the victims' relatives questioned Hale's sincerity about his jailhouse conversion, and then wished him a haunted, painful life before he died in the execution room. Another blasted Hale, "You have no heart and you have no soul and you have shown none of us any remorse. None." Another rejected the attempt by Hale's lawyers to grant mercy based on the troubled childhood he'd had. Yet another, filled with pain and contempt said: "I would like to be there to see your face when they strap you on that gurney to put you to sleep." (*The Register Guard:* 5/28/98). As Ed had confirmed, it was indeed an ugly scene.

Sadly, justice and mercy rarely co-exist in the courtroom, and the next morning's reportage reflected the community's outrage with an out-of-the-ordinary, large front page headline nearly one-inch tall: **Killer Hale Gets Death Penalty.** As I read newspaper reports and listened to the tone of local television anchors, I found myself saturated with revulsion in the spitefulness of it all. It struck me as a vindictive, desperate solution to a tragic event.

*   *   *

With Hale facing an uncertain future on death row and the final disposition of the tape still unresolved, I was left with some doors open and others slammed shut. While the church remained as distant as possible from the proceedings in regard to Hale, we were inextricably entwined through my involvement with him long before Hale faced the jury to hear their "guilty" verdict. With the exception of expressing concerns about the disposition of the tape, no intervention was made by the church in his trial. And whether it was right of me or not, I had no contact with him but I had not forgotten him. It had been a long, personally exhausting experience from the discovery of the tape recording to the end of Hale's trial that I found myself wanting to put the matter behind me for a period of time and move forward. Yet, I often thought of Conan Hale and prayed for him over those years for this event was indelibly marked in my mind. The families of the three young victims had seemingly gone back to their lives but the trauma of the event, I would surmise, became an open wound that would slowly heal. I wondered if real justice or healing would ever be achieved by this.

No execution is immediate so Conan Hale would enter the long run of automatic appeals as the question of his innocence or guilt would ultimately be examined, reviewed, and re-examined for some time. The seal of confession, battered and bruised, had survived as a protected privilege. I was grateful our friends of the court, who had so eloquently expressed their concerns to the Ninth Circuit Court, were also vindicated. Whatever crossed Conan Hale's mind on the day of his sentencing would not be beyond reassessment during his time on death row. If there is a glimmer of hope in this story, that would be it. By being allowed to live for whatever time he had, he could come to a self-reflective moment, to examine his life. I believe he was owed the grace of that time. This man would no longer be allowed to mingle with the general population and he would have to face daily interaction with darkness in the most unnatural of secured confinements. Yet, there are some who would say, "He deserves it."

*   *   *

Nearly a year after his conviction, I received a second letter from Hale, the first being the sketch with the note of apology he had sent to me shortly after the taping three years before. This new communication was not what I'd expected. He even referred to my civil suit and was expressive with mixed messages.

On February 23, 1999, Hale wrote:

"Father Mockaitis,

"Hello Father, how are you? The thing I don't understand is why did you turn your back on me? I have written you before asking you to please forgive me. I had not known they were tape recording. I then got no response.

"Even now you won't call me brother. Why? Have I not confessed my sins to you and to God in Heaven? For if a friend, brother, or someone you know comes at night and asks for food, give to him freely. Does that ring any bells?

"As you can see by my writing, I am upset with you. You did everything but protect the innocent. I do not blame you for where I am. Because of my pain and heartache, you have gotten money.

"Now don't get me wrong. I am not asking for money. That money you have gotten is my blood money. Ever since that taping no one from any church will talk with me. You are the first in three years. The church and the people of the church have turned their backs on me.

"See, you have all these people to protect you. All I had was God. I believe I will return home again someday. King David, St. Paul, and many others had to spend time in prison for things before going home. If they can do it, so can I.

"I pray you are never put into a spot to be held in contempt of court, or excommunicated. Well my brother in Christ, I must close for now. May God bless you and peace be with you always.

"Love in Christ,"
Wayne Hale (end letter)

I was taken aback by his mixed words which implied he had been in contact with me regularly but "got no response." His words nagged at my subconscious. I had wondered about the loss he must have felt by my absence following the surreptitious taping and the letter made his feelings plain. But, my assignment had changed and I found myself caught up in a new move and new focus for my ministry.

I filed his letter away but over the years my determination to put pen to paper had not faded. My memory of the events surrounding the taped confession gave rebirth to living memories I later found were much closer to the surface than I cared to admit. The violation of the taped confession was far from a closed issue and we heard nothing more about whether the tape had been destroyed as the district attorney promised it would be after the trial of Conan Hale.

Still, the need to tell this story continued to evolve within me and eventually would have me writing to Hale on death row. It was only right that I tell him about my research and the hope to write not about the confession but about the violation and its implications. Meanwhile, the sentence given Hale, though not the central focus of this story, disturbed me nonetheless.

*   *   *

The death penalty remains a divisive and controversial issue and has been a cause for debate in the U.S. Supreme Court. Whether capital punishment is justice or revenge is still a matter for passionate discussion. As a citizen and a Catholic priest, I stand opposed to the death penalty based on both religious and moral principles on the dignity of life and the inconsistency of its enforcement. It is neither just nor necessary. This "legal homicide" is more than carrying out justice or being tough on crime. The clash of values between what is best for the safety of society and what is the moral and spiritual base for the dignity of the human person is the foundation of the opportunity for individual reform and to make restitution. Yet, that reform does not take away responsibility.

However, groups such as *Amnesty International*, watchdogs of right justice and in particular the reporting of cruel and inhuman punishment throughout the world, report that the United States is among only a handful of nations which has not abolished the death penalty. China, Iran, and the U.S. account for over 81% of the executions recorded by *Amnesty International.* Since the year 2000 only four countries—the U.S., the Democratic republic of the Congo, Pakistan, and Iran—are known to have executed juvenile offenders.

On the seventh of December, 2000, the Presidents of the European Parliament, the Council and the Commission at the European council meeting in Nice, France, signed the *European Union Charter of Fundamental Rights*. That charter sets out, for the first time, the whole range of civil, political, economic and social rights of European citizens and all persons resident in the EU.

In the Preamble of that Charter it states: *Conscious of its spiritual and moral heritage, the Union is founded on the indivisible, universal values of human dignity, freedom, equality and solidarity; it is based on the principles of democracy and the rule of law.*

And, in Chapter 1, Article 2, it states in simple but dramatic language: *No one shall be condemned to the death penalty, or executed.* Such a direct commitment is worthy of praise and gives pause to think why this Nation, with all of its religious and civil liberty, its flourishing churches, religiously based health care institutions, first-rate institutions of higher learning, and faith based charitable organizations served by compassionate and caring human beings, continues to tolerate the option of such a primitive form of punishment which is undeserving of this more enlightened time in which we live. Scientific studies have consistently failed to find convincing evidence that executions deter crime.

Helen Prejean, well-known advocate to abolish the death penalty, author of *Dead Man Walking*, and her more recent work on two death row inmates, *The Death of Innocents*, published in 2004, has been a moral compass on this issue for many years. She reflects, "Is God vengeful, demanding a death for a death? Or is God compassionate, luring souls into love so great that no one can be considered "enemy." (*The Death of Innocents*)

Sister Helen, a Catholic Nun, began her prison ministry in 1981 when she dedicated her life to the poor of New Orleans. She became pen pals with Patrick Sonnier, the convicted killer of two teenagers, sentenced to die in the electric chair of Louisiana's Angola State Prison. Her eyes were opened to the Louisiana execution process and she turned her experiences into a book, *Dead Man Walking*, which was eventually nominated for a Pulitzer Prize in 1993. Yet, she makes clear that her position is motivated not only by her faith but also by social conditions. She asserts that Hollywood movie stars, famous sports figures, the rich, famous and beautiful, would never be put to death for a crime. Could you imagine the social outcry if a popular Olympic athlete or movie star, found guilty of a capital offense, was executed? We came close to it in 1996.

In her recent work, *The Death of Innocents*, Sr. Helen reflects:

"The stories are going to break your heart. Then there are the appeals courts which deny constitutional rights and rubber stamp death sentences without ever allowing a fresh hearing of the evidence . . . In the end, we all lose our innocence."

In her compelling arguments, Sr. Helen refers to people she has known who have worked in organizations to abolish the death penalty such as, *Murder Victims for Reconciliation*, or the father of a murdered victim and other such parents who have been through great personal anguish and were still able to forgive. As the founder of *Survive*, she advocates for victims and continues to counsel inmates on death row and the families of murder victims as well.

While we should always have the deepest compassion for the victims of violent crime, and in particular for their family members, the death penalty only serves to create more victims.

The official position of the Catholic Church in opposition to capital punishment is well-known. A document from the American Catholic Bishops spells this out in a 2005 text entitled, *The Culture of Life*, in which the Bishops explain what the Church professes:

"We share a justified anger and revulsion at terrible and deadly crimes. In calling for an end to the use of the death penalty, we do not seek to diminish in any way the evil and harm caused by people who commit horrible murders . . . our family of faith must care for sisters and brothers who have been wounded by violence . . . . For many left behind, a death sentence offers the illusion of closure and vindication. No act, even an execution, can bring back a loved one or heal terrible wounds.

"The sanction of death, when it is not necessary to protect society, violates respect for human life and dignity.

"—Its application is deeply flawed and can be irreversibly wrong, is prone to errors, and is biased by factors such as race, the quality of legal representation, and where the crime was committed.

"—We have other ways to punish criminals and protect society." (*Culture of life and the Death penalty*. United States Conference of Catholic Bishops. 2005, Washington, D.C.)

Over the years my self-study on this issue has convinced me the profound truth of these words. If a person is guilty, *humane* justice remains the *correct* justice.

Of course, neither the Church nor I had any opportunity to apply these principles in Hale's sentencing phase.

*   *   *

Death penalty aside, protected, privileged relationships remain essential for our society since they are based not in covering up essential information which may pose a threat to the safety of citizens or produce so-called evidence for investigators but because respect for the sanctity of the human conscience and the genuine search for personal conversion is an option and an invitation for all. Yet, today's culture continues to bring this into question.

In a February 16, 2002 article, *The New York Times* headlined, **Secrets Confided to Clergy Are Getting Harder to Keep.** The *Times* cited several scenarios such as O.J. Simpson and his heart-to-heart chat with Rosie Grier in which Mr. Grier allegedly overheard Simpson's admission of guilt, Robert Hanssen, the F.B.I. agent arrested on charges of spying for the Russians, and the rise in sexual abuse scandals at that time, they wrote:

" . . . clergy/penitent privilege is no longer considered inviolable. New statutes for reporting information suggest a troubling erosion of religious freedom. "It's a very disturbing trend,'" said Edward Mc Glynn Gaffney Jr, a professor of law at Valparaiso University School of Law. 'These most recent developments are a sad departure from the age-old tradition of respecting secrecy around confession.'"

They noted, "The legal climate began to shift in 1996 . . ." Then went on to cite the case of the taped confession in Oregon. Judge John Noonan predicted, " . . . the Supreme Court may soon be compelled to weigh in on the clergy privilege. Mr. Gaffney added, 'The more crimes that are exempted from normal respect for priest-penitent privilege, the sooner we'll have a critical mass of lower courts in disagreement with each other." (*New York Times*).

Early in January, 2008, the Supreme Court reviewed a case in which two condemned inmates pleaded for mercy. They petitioned the Court to consider the method of execution by lethal injection in Kentucky as a violation of the Constitution's 8th Amendment ban on "cruel and unusual punishments." The petitioners in *Baze v. Rees* state that a particular combination of drugs used in the execution process has a high likelihood of producing severe and unnecessary pain in the prisoner. However, it does not concern the constitutionality of the death penalty itself. This collective information brings one to ponder this issue on many levels. As one who has served in parish ministry nearly my entire priestly career, I would be hard put to tell parishioners that the seal of confession is conditional. I cannot imagine any priest or minister who would feel otherwise.

*   *   *

One positive outcome of the taped confession case was the yet unresolved issue to re-visit the clergy-penitent privilege in the State of Oregon. The delicate balance between religious freedom and governmental interest was at issue. The Constitution of the State of Oregon, Article I, Sections 2 and

3, guarantee freedom of worship and freedom of religious expression. Such protections are not unique to Oregon by any means so the broad scope of this effort was seen as aligned with other such protected liberties.

Under Oregon law, until 1999, the clergy-penitent privilege was held by the penitent—not by the member of the clergy. The possibility of a priest being subject to subpoena by the attorney of a client accused of a serious crime was real, placing the priest in an untenable and inequitable position. The solution was amending the statute in which a member of the clergy would hold the clergy-penitent privilege independent of the penitent.

In February of 1999, this is exactly what the Oregon Catholic Conference brought to the floor of the Oregon legislature. The proposed HB 2329 was "the product of a work group created by the House Interim Judiciary Committee as a result of the April 22, 1996 taped confession . . ." The request was straightforward, to amend the clergy-penitent privilege to read: "Even though the person who made the communication has given consent to the disclosure, a member of the clergy may not be examined as to any confidential communication made to the member in the member's professional character if, under the discipline or tenets of the member's church, denomination or organization, the member has an absolute duty to keep the communication confidential."

The speedy adoption of this amendment, with little question, was a victory for more than 300,000 Catholics in the State of Oregon and for all those who value a sacred privacy sought for the purpose of healing the wounds that bind us, regardless of religious affiliation or not. Oregon is not alone in permitting a member of the clergy to hold the clergy-penitent privilege. Twelve other states extend the privilege to a member of the clergy: Alabama, California, Colorado, Georgia, Illinois, Indiana, Michigan, New Jersey, Ohio, Vermont, Virginia, and Wyoming. This action was a significant victory of the taped-confession case.

As the Ninth Circuit Court stated in its opinion: "If the inviolability of religious confession to the clergy were not the law of the land, the expectation of every repentant sinner, the assured confidence of every minister of God's grace, a prosecutor would have a cheap and sometimes helpful way of uncovering evidence of crime by obtaining a court order under &2516 of the Wiretap Act to wire a church known to be frequented, say, by families or other persons believed to be associated with a criminal organization." (*Mockaitis.* 104 F.3d at 1533).

Still, there was more that I needed to do.

CHAPTER 16

Death Row: Conan Hale On Appeal

* * *

"Revenge loses sight of the end in the means . . . at such a moment we really do know that our character, as revealed in this action, is, and ought to be, hateful to all good men and, if there are powers above man, to them." (C.S. Lewis—*The Problem of Pain*)

* * *

As of the writing of this book, Conan Wayne Hale has not been executed and no date is pending for his execution. He has resided on death row since 1998 at the Oregon State Penitentiary with more than twenty other condemned men. In such cases we are tempted to focus on the heinous charges and essentially forget these men exist, at least until the execution (*legal homicide*) is carried out. After my visit in 2006, described in the Prologue of this work, I'd sent Hale a letter as an opportunity to renew our contact but also to pay a long overdue pastoral visit. I invited him to write back, which he did:

> "Dear Father Mockaitis,
> "Hello and greeting for God our heavenly Father. I want to take this time to thank you for writing. I also hope that you will write more often. We can talk about anything you'd like? It has taken me 10 years to really see what happened about 11 years ago. I want you to know that I hold no ill will toward you or the Holy Church.

"For many a years, I was angry, hurt, and felt rejected. But one day I saw a priest here at the prison and he helped me in a lot of ways. I too have always kept you in my thoughts. Though I must say, they were not always good!

"I must now ask you for forgiveness of my sin toward my evil thoughts of you at times. I am setting my life straight. I have faced many evil men over the last 10 years. I just hope you will take a chance and continue to write.

"I pray that you and I can become friends. Know that I will keep you in my prayers always. May you never lose faith or heart for the good fight between good and evil.

"May God bless you Father Mockaitis and may peace fill you always.

"Respectfully and Sincerely,
Conan Wayne Hale"
Oregon State Prison: Death row

It was obvious that Hale had resented me, yet now it seemed the change I noticed in him two years before had taken root—compassion and respect had produced growth in him; new green shoots rose on what had been hostile, barren ground. His anger toward me was based on a combination of three things: he felt abandoned, his mother had not visited him for some time, and that I hadn't contacted him after his final conviction. I had a sense of this in 2006 but now I began to realize its full impact.

Yet, I continued my occasional contact with Hale beyond that 2006 visit. In late January, 2008 we corresponded again and he shared more of his hopes as I wrote back to him when he informed me that he was up for another hearing on his case; one of many appeals in the life of death penalty prisoners.

"Dear Fr. Mockaitis,
Hello and greetings in Christ our Lord. How are you? I thank you for responding to my letter so quickly . . . I have asked the Dominicans if they will take me as an honorary monk. I know I can help people; I just need a little time with God to find out what is my way. I will keep you in my prayers. I am sorry you had to stop working in Eugene. I take full responsibility for that. I had a good legal visit yesterday. I just might make it out of prison some day. Please keep my mother Katie in your prayers. She has had a hard time with all this, as of late.

"I am hoping to hear from her again soon. I really miss visiting with her. The last time I had an actual visit was three years ago . . . I love my Rosary prayers. I just got done saying one, right before I started writing you. I hope you can come over for a visit. May God bless you, May Jesus comfort you, May Mother Mary keep you, May peace be with you always.

Sincerely in Christ,
Conan Wayne"

I wanted to follow up, so I arranged to see him again.

*   *   *

It was late February, 2008 and this second visit to the prison was less anxious than the one a year and a half before but my thoughts about him were still strong. His sincere, though simple faith, was a life-line for him. Once I arrived at the main desk, I learned that our contact would take place in the general visitor's area, not on death row. My mind flashed immediately to our initial visit in April, 1996—glass between us as we spoke over the intercom system.

The security procedure was more efficient this time and before long, I was taken by police escort down the stark corridors. To my right was a large room marked "privileged visits," where inmates sat with family and friends devoid of physical separation but under the watchful eyes of several officers. It was a Friday afternoon, so the room was full of family members in loud conversations, animated with smiles and laughter. Blue dressed inmates appeared grateful for this less restrictive environment. Some appeared to be playing cards, while others were just relaxed in small groups around low tables and seated in chairs. But, such open privilege remained forbidden for Hale and other inmates. I was escorted to a booth and waited for his arrival. But, I was not alone in this contained surrounding as other family members on both sides of me were busy in conversation with jailed inmates.

Before long, Conan Hale arrived, looking clean, neat, and every bit unassuming. He waved, smiled and sat down as he picked up the black handset on his wall. His shaved head, full beard, and round face presented an ordinary person. Two tattoos were prominent on each arm, something I missed at the last visit. However, I noticed weariness in both his posture and tone of voice as he leaned forward with his head a bit lowered. I was about to hear of new information concerning his mental health, his hearing voices, that caught me by surprise.

We began with the "how are things" reporting then he commented:
"I think the first time we talked like this . . ."

I then interrupted, "Yes, I remember it well, Conan." There was no need to say anything more but then I asked about his most recent appeal just two weeks before and learned more about his background. I asked if he would mind I share this information as part of research for my book. He shook his head and said, "Whatever you think would be helpful is fine. Maybe someone will read the story and I could help them in some way." He spoke easily at first but his speech became more rapid as he shared information about his appeal before the judge.

"It went well," he said, "I've been diagnosed as schizophrenic since I was fifteen. This new medication I'm on is pretty powerful. Most normal people couldn't take it. But, the voices are xznot as loud and it keeps me stable. I'm hoping the judge will reconsider the evidence and accept an insanity plea due to the schizophrenia. I can't be tried on aggravated murder charges again so maybe the best that would happen is I'd move to the state mental hospital for treatment. I could be there as long as thirty years I was told."

As Hale spoke, I found myself taken back by this new information on his mental health. I never heard about his schizophrenia nor about its use as a possible defense in his past trial. In addition he admitted his diabetes and told me he was on insulin. I asked about his mother, Katie—if he had any recent contact with her.

"No, I've written but she's never written back. I haven't seen her in a couple years. My step brother early on was in contact but I haven't heard from him in a long time either. I remember writing to the Archdiocese not long after I arrived here—I wrote many times but never heard back from anyone." I'm not sure why he had written to the Archdiocese, or perhaps the Archbishop himself. I assumed he was seeking some sort of further help, but he never explained his reason. Yet, his sense of rejection was palpable.

I began to put the pieces of the puzzle together and felt sad for his isolation. This lack of contact from the church authorities, something I was unaware of, was the real source of his anger at me. While I'm not sure what the letters contained, I was also kept in the dark about their arrival. I wondered about how he was coping with this and said, "I'm concerned, Conan, about your spirit."

He offered, "I pray the Rosary a couple times a day and listen to the Catholic radio station after I get up about four a.m. It's very tough in here to keep any kind of spiritual life. But, Deacon Allen brings Jeff and me communion each week and Bishop Steiner is coming for Mass in March. I've learned about the Divine Mercy Chaplet and I pray that as often as I can."

I found myself moved by this young man's commendable attempt to rise above the darkness on death row, his daily hours of isolation, and his desire to be of help to others in some way. He had come to a level of awareness for his past life, he admitted that he had done harm when he was younger but we left the issue of the tape alone. Then he offered a surprising assessment.

"I looked at the options I had," he said, "and I thought I'd try again. My new lawyer has been a help so we took a look at the insanity defense. But, I'm tired of this. It's been a long time and a lot of effort and I don't know whether the judge will consider this case again or not. I don't think I'll hear anything for more than a year. I'm not afraid of death. If the state wants to kill me, what can I do?"

As he spoke those near final words, my heart was struck with the weight of it all. The heavy burden of years of appeals and dashed hopes for reconsideration seemed to wear him down. While his spirit was positive I could also sense defeat. Our legal system, much of which we should be proud of, is not perfect. The guilty have been found innocent and the innocent have been convicted as guilty. Never did Hale feel he should be released from the penal system but only given another chance. Earlier, in his previous letter, he expressed the hope for an entirely new trial. Now, I came to see how his prayer life, the many rosaries, the relationship with his friend Jeff on death row, the energy of new faith and some people who did care about him as a human being and not a "killer" was all he had.

He then told me about a new discovery from the scriptures that had given him some comfort. It was the scene of Jesus, dying on the cross with the two thieves on either side. As Jesus turned to the repentant thief and offered him the promise of "this day you will be with me in Paradise," I sensed Conan found an empathy which offered him some hope. I could not have agreed with him more. Then, I looked at the time and realized its urgency.

I offered to pray with him, which we did. His devotion had not lessened since I last saw him a year and a half before. We agreed to stay in touch and I knew that he would be here for some time. I stood up to leave, we smiled and waved to each other, as I turned to the exit door and awaited the officer to lead me back to the reception area. The privileged visiting area seemed even more alive by contrast with the stark confinement of Hale. Yet, something inside me remained unanswered.

As I walked back to my car, I recognized this visit taught me an indelible lesson about the power of grace, love, and compassion. In one sense, the story of this inmate, his very sad life, and the tragic outcome for all those concerned, preached an effective sermon. While civil law needs to be clear and definitive for the protection of law abiding citizens and punishment for offenses is a necessary deterrent to crime, the more we can recognize that another, greater power is at work in the human spirit for those who genuinely seek it, the more we can avoid harsh and extreme solutions. The legal road is not easy and it weighs heavy. Conan Hale, as well as others such as him, has discovered this truth. Is it worth the expense, time, and effort to make a change and seriously reconsider whether the death penalty is just and humane treatment? For Hale, the last chapter is yet to be written.

*   *   *

While I could not resist the memory of the sight at the court house where those grieving families let their feelings be known after Hale's trial, I do understand some may feel great resentment that this man still sits on death row while three teenagers are dead and families have experienced an irreplaceable loss. Therefore, one might question whether Hale's conversion is genuine, or just some sort of escapist ploy. I was never sure Hale understood the seriousness of the taped confession but he did understand the value of the sacrament.

During this visit we barely mentioned what happened on that dark, nighttime mountain road in December of 1995. After all, the jury and a judge already tagged Hale as a killer and a sad excuse for a human being, something I never found.

However, Conan Hale is one who I believe has found Christ. Such inmates are wounded and toughened human beings who have done horrendous damage with their lives. They are disturbed, frightened, and hardened by misfortune in life. But our society is least sympathetic and unforgiving to the point of revenge toward those who have done such wrong. Although these people, if indeed they are truly guilty, are responsible for their behavior and restitution of some kind is necessary. But, if we profess to be Christians, or any people of good will, then we must reach out as Christ himself did to both victims and the guilty.

For whatever sin Hale needs to repent, as for any of us, faith alone does not take that responsibility away. Yet, before me sat a young man enthused about the Lord, and in his young faith he faced sin in his life. What purpose would it serve for him to pretend any of this on death row? Would this change his sentence? Conan Wayne Hale had exhausted his first round of appeals but he could still undergo a round of federal appeals, which may take several more years. His death penalty has not been lifted. In spite of all that, a new life had begun for him behind these bars as I noticed in 2006 and it was neither lessened nor any less convincing a year and a half later. His faith is all he has.

I recalled the day when I received a small card from Hale. On the cover was drawn a green cross. The arms of the cross were surrounded by a gold circle indicating the Trinity—the Father, Son, and the Holy Spirit. A gold and brown border enhanced the artwork. He wrote that he'd created it freehand, and I was impressed by how well balanced he had drawn the figure of the cross, and how beautifully encircled he had designed the Trinity. Such things may appear simple in the freedom of daily society but they show a profound connection with the spiritual even as one spends the vast majority of his day sitting in isolation.

*   *   *

My belief is that the power of grace is embodied in this man. What the future of his new understanding will bring to him remains a question. As painful as it is, the only road to true peace is to forgive ourselves.

Now, there is a final yet unresolved statement to be made.

EPILOGUE

Whatever became of the tape itself—the illegal record of the first confession Hale and I had shared as priest and penitent? A reader concerned with individual rights—both those of privacy and religion—will likely find the answer quite disturbing.

During the 1996 hearing in Federal Court, the district attorney had promised that the tape would be destroyed after the trial of Conan Wayne Hale; that trial concluded in the spring of 1998. While Vatican officials asked to be kept in the loop as the legal proceedings played out, the matter was handled entirely by the local Archdiocese with no Vatican intervention. Public outrage and commentaries had been expressed around the globe by Christian and non-Christian groups alike, the Ninth Circuit Court of Appeals had offered a definitive ruling, and the demands of the Holy See had been straightforward: the tape must be immediately destroyed. Yet, state officials still claim the tape as "evidence." The tape was never destroyed, nor has the state's demand to preserve the tape been retracted.

In 2008, after serving consecutively in the sixth of his four year terms, Mr. Harcleroad announced he would not seek re-election as district attorney. No one else had filled that position for twenty-four years. Of all the good and bad that the district attorney was cited for, this incident was likely the most far reaching in its implications. There was no mention of this case in the long history of his accomplishments or failures. The new candidate, Alex Gardner, stated: "I will continue to support crime prevention, and aggressively investigate and prosecute crime . . ." (*Register-Guard*). While the safety of the public is essential and the local district attorney has an obligation to enforce the law, I could only hope and pray that there would never be such a difference of opinion again on the definition of "aggressively investigate."

Judge Jack Billings, the trial judge in the Hale case, as I interviewed for this book, confirmed to me that the tape had never been played in his courtroom. He looked me squarely in the eye and said, "The only reason was because it was not considered to be of evidentiary value." He then firmly added, "If they [the state] had thought otherwise, I would not have hesitated to play that tape in court." I found his statement shocking and wondered what sort of Pandora's Box such an action would have opened had the tape been found to be *of* evidentiary value to either the prosecution or defense of Hale's case.

To this day, the tape lies stored in a drawer marked as *Property Evidence* in the Lane County Sheriff's office in Eugene, Oregon. There it remains a living violation—a red flag of warning to all American citizens who hold dear the Constitution, their religious freedom, and their First Amendment Rights.

(End)